MODERN-DAY
MIRACLES

MODERN-DAY
MIRACLES

How Ordinary People
Experience Supernatural
Acts of God

By Paul Prather

Andrews and McMeel
A Universal Press Syndicate Company
Kansas City

Library of Congress Cataloging-in-Publication Data

Prather, Paul
Modern-day miracles : how ordinary people
experience supernatural acts of God / Paul Prather.
p.   cm.
Includes bibliographical references.
ISBN 0-8362-2174-5 (hd)
1. Miracles—Case studies. I. Title.
BT97.2.P73   1996
231.7'3—dc20   96-17939
CIP

Attention: Schools and Businesses
Andrews and McMeel books are available at quantity discounts
with bulk purchase for educational, business, or sales
promotional use. For information, please write to
Special Sales Department,
Andrews and McMeel,
4520 Main Street, Kansas City, Missouri 64111.

This book is dedicated to my parents,
L. Paul and Alice Prather,
and to my wife, Renee,
who through their steadfast
faith in God—and in me—
have taught me much about miracles.

CONTENTS

Acknowledgments   *xi*

ONE
What Is a Miracle?   1

TWO
Miracles Throughout History   19

THREE
Twentieth-Century Miracles   30

FOUR
Arguments Against Miracles   42

FIVE
Arguments in Favor of Miracles   57

SIX
Miraculous Conversions   70

SEVEN
Healings   88

EIGHT
Miracles of Deliverance   104

CONTENTS

NINE

Appearances   119

TEN

Prophecy   137

ELEVEN

Speaking in Tongues   155

TWELVE

Miraculous Faith   172

THIRTEEN

Why Now?   190

FOURTEEN

What These Accounts Have in Common   199

FIFTEEN

How You Can Receive a Miracle   213

Selected Bibliography   223

"For it is written, I will destroy the wisdom of the wise, and will bring to nothing the understanding of the prudent. Where is the wise? Where is the scribe? Where is the disputer of this world? Hath not God made foolish the wisdom of this world? . . . Because the foolishness of God is wiser than men; and the weakness of God is stronger than men. . . . God hath chosen the foolish things of the world to confound the wise; and God hath chosen the weak things of the world to confound the things which are mighty."

—St. Paul,
The First Epistle to the Corinthians

ACKNOWLEDGMENTS

I OWE A DEBT OF GRATITUDE to each of the fifty or so people who allowed me to interview them on the subject of miracles, as well as the dozens of others who provided me support or revelation through their published accounts.

There are a number of people I need to thank by name. I'm grateful to Jake Morrissey, my editor at Andrews and McMeel, for the opportunity to write this book and the freedom to do it my own way.

Several college, university, and seminary scholars offered me their time and the benefits of their research. Especially helpful were Eunice Irwin, Darrell Whiteman, and Steve Seamands at Asbury Theological Seminary, Robert Miller at Midway College, and Charles H. Kraft at Fuller Theological Seminary.

At the *Lexington Herald-Leader,* researchers Linda Minch and Linda Smith-Niemi voluntarily dug up arcane bits of knowledge for me from their mysterious computer databases. Last but not least I'd like to thank Tim Kelly, exalted grand Pooh-Bah of the *Herald-Leader* newsroom and all-around good guy, who twice now has allowed me generous leaves of absence to write books, just because he knows I like to do it; now *that's* a fine boss.

CHAPTER ONE

WHAT IS A MIRACLE?

THE BEST-SELLING BOOK of all time opens with a miracle. Genesis tells us that the world once was dark and without form. Then God said, "Let there be light," and instantly, divinely, a great light broke forth and shattered the darkness. That initial miracle, so the Bible says, illuminated the earth before the earliest humans existed.

Miracles have enlightened the earth, and revealed glimpses of its Creator, ever since. The Bible's miracles don't end with Genesis, as anyone who attended Sunday school as a child knows. That holy book is full of accounts of the miraculous, as are most holy books. When the God of the scriptures seeks to deliver his people from Egyptian slavery, he parts a sea and dries its bed so they can walk across. When Daniel is tossed into a den of hungry lions, God sends an angel who shuts the lions' mouths. When Jesus must establish himself as the Son of God, his heavenly father bears witness by feeding five thousand people with five barley loaves and two fishes, opening blind eyes, straightening crippled legs, and even raising the dead. When God decides to redirect the life of an ambitious religious official named Saul of Tarsus, he knocks Saul to the ground with a blinding light—a replay of that original miracle of creation—and re-creates Saul's understanding of God's identity and of his own.

For many of us who live in the Western Hemisphere late in the twentieth century, those biblical stories are quaint or even inspiring. Yet ours is an age in which miracles would on first glance seem to have waned. Sometimes, at least, supernatural intervention appears less common, less dramatic, and far more vulnerable to the scientific arguments of skeptics than it did thousands of years ago in the Middle East.

But is it really true that God has forsaken miracles today? Do remarkable recoveries from cancer result only from chemotherapies and never from prayers? Is true enlightenment achieved only through university educations and never through divine revelations?

I used to assume that the age of divine miracles was past, but I don't think so anymore. Over the years I've encountered a good many other people who don't think so, either. The private lives of citizens great and small are touched by divine acts, some of them virtually equal to any recorded in the Bible or the Quran. God still breaks into human time in poignant and even stupefying ways. Consider these examples:

A Politician Survives an Awful Crash

Governor Brereton Jones flew at 1,600 feet above Kentucky's rolling hills, aboard his state's expensive Sikorsky S-76 helicopter. It was August 7, 1992, a routine flight for the busy chief executive, the three aides accompanying him, and the helicopter's two pilots. Jones and his entourage were traveling from the state capital, Frankfort, to Fort Knox to dedicate a road and meet with local officials in the small town, which is dominated by an army base.

The blue sky was clear when the chopper hit a bump and wrenched the governor from his thoughts about the day's activities. "What was that?" he asked. An aide replied that they'd run into an air pocket.

Then, whump! The helicopter's occupants felt another hard jolt. Jones smelled smoke. The Sikorsky suddenly lurched—and fell like a sledgehammer dropped from a skyscraper. Jones's stomach leapt up as if to smother his heart. This was no mere air pocket.

Reflexively, state trooper Danny Reed, Jones's bodyguard, jumped from his seat next to the governor and yelled for the pilots to take control of the craft. But the Sikorsky started spinning. Reed quickly saw there was nothing anyone could do. They were going to crash. The hard hills hundreds of feet below them whipped toward the six men.

Death lay only instants away. Reed, a Baptist layman, struggled against the pull of the gyroscoping craft back into his seat and clasped hands with the governor, the wealthy owner of a thoroughbred horse farm. Reed prayed aloud, but the craft's whine was so great Jones couldn't hear him. Reed begged God not to let the helicopter catch fire when it hit the earth and not to let anyone die. Inexplicably he became calm. At the same time, Jones was praying silently but just as fervently. He made more promises in the next few seconds than he'd made during his whole campaign for governor.

The helicopter smashed into the earth amid a ear-rending roar and disintegrated into a tangle of ripped, ricocheting shards of metal. As the Sikorsky tore apart, highly flammable aviation fuel sprayed from ruptured lines across Jones, Reed, and the others, soaking them. Jones and his entourage were about to become human torches.

But the Sikorsky didn't erupt into flames.

"The impact was hard," Jones said later. "I thought I had broken my back." Momentarily blinded by the fuel in his eyes, he groped his way to a hole in the side of the wrecked helicopter. He crawled through it, still believing the helicopter would explode any second. Once he'd cleared the chopper's jagged wreckage, he rose unsteadily to his feet and walked up a nearby hill. "Adrenaline is a wonderful thing," he said. Then he stumbled, fell, and couldn't gain his footing again because his back hurt too badly.

In fact, everyone aboard survived. They more than survived. Like Jones, all five of the other battered, rattled men escaped the wreckage with what were comparatively minor injuries given the speed and violence of the crash. Jones's back was jammed, but not broken. He recovered fully.

Jones—whose term as governor has since expired—frequently attends Presbyterian and Episcopal churches, but isn't given much to public declarations of piety. He's not one of those politicians who wields his religion like a political cattle prod. So it came as a surprise, and raised eyebrows around the state, when he told reporters immediately after the crash that he was certain he and his companions had been delivered by a divine miracle—and declared that he knew why God had spared him, at least. God wanted him to help pass a health-care reform package that would benefit the state's citizens, Jones insisted. Indeed, he spent much of the rest of his term in office working tirelessly for better health-care benefits, with notable success.

Today, he remains adamant that God rescued him. "There's no way we could have survived that without divine intervention," he said.

Reed, the bodyguard, isn't a politician. Still, long after the accident, he, too, remained convinced the men had been saved by divine intervention. More than a year later he told me, "I feel that was a miracle."

A Struggling Singer Lands a Contract

Nothing much had ever worked out for Billy Ray "Bo" Cyrus, a polite, handsome kid whom others said was nice but possessed limited prospects. When he was a boy his parents split up after thirteen years of marriage. This was in a time when people in Flatwoods, Kentucky— a blue-collar village along the Tri-State border where Kentucky, West Virginia, and Ohio meet—just didn't get divorced. Added to the pain any child of divorce would feel under such circumstances was that Billy Ray's grandfather was the pastor of an ultraconservative church nearby that condemned divorce, too. The boy thought of himself as stigmatized.

He had a quiet religious streak himself. During his teen years he attended a local Christian church and often read the Bible at home. Later Billy Ray excelled in high school sports, particularly baseball, but his obsession with sports didn't interfere with his religious devotion. His mother, Ruth Ann Adkins, not a regular churchgoer, remembers more than once driving to meet Cyrus's bus as it rumbled into town in the wee hours of a Sunday morning after a baseball or football game. Billy Ray would climb wearily into her car and warn her not to let him sleep late. He wanted to go to church. "It was a natural thing for him," she once said.

After graduating from high school, Cyrus briefly played college baseball, but he wasn't much of a student. He really lusted for a career in professional sports. He even landed a pro tryout or two, but couldn't make a team.

After that failure, an "inner voice" told Billy Ray to buy a guitar and learn to play it instead of baseball, even though by now he was a little old to take up music. Billy Ray taught himself to strum a few chords and eventually formed a band called Sly Dog that landed a gig at the Sand Bar nightclub in Ironton, Ohio. There, he discovered a harsh new set of realities: the music business is cruel. Sly Dog fell apart in 1984 after a club fire destroyed its equipment. Cyrus took off for California for two years, to make it in the music business out there. He ended up selling cars instead.

He returned home and hooked up with a band called the Players, which started a four-year stint at a Huntington, West Virginia, honky-tonk called the Ragtime Lounge. Before that, the Players had knocked around the Holiday Inn and Hyatt circuits. Cyrus—by now a gyrating, prancing singer who also wrote songs—furnished the well-toned muscles and original music the Players needed, even though other musicians around the Tri-State bar scene joked behind his back that he was only a mediocre talent at best. Still, Billy Ray and the Players built a regional following that packed the Ragtime past its fire-code capacity. The group's biggest fans were working-class women attracted to Cyrus's sweaty moves, hard biceps, and satiny long hair as much as to his voice. It was a far cry from the religious devotion of his boyhood.

It also was a far cry from the big-time world of show business that Billy Ray had begun to dream about. Cyrus's Ragtime Lounge dressing room was a tiny mop closet stacked with cardboard boxes. Sometimes a bucket rested in one corner, an ice-maker in another. To keep his spirits up and his mind focused on the better days that he hoped would come, Cyrus scribbled positive-thinking mottoes on the dressing room's Sheetrock walls, quotes from inspirational writer Napoleon Hill and others.

Cyrus soon decided to make it big in Nashville, the country music mecca. He and his band played the Ragtime five nights a week. Many weeks, Billy Ray used his two days off to drive six hours one-way to Nashville, where he would knock on the doors of agents, managers, and producers. He made dozens of trips, often with his mother. "Every single time," he told me later, "I would go down to Nashville with my guns loaded and be ready to go down there and attack. And every time

I'd leave, I'd feel like a whipped pup." Several times Cyrus's dad, Ron Cyrus—a Kentucky state representative and head of the state's AFL-CIO—tried to convince him to seek a real career, one with regular hours and a future. Billy Ray wouldn't listen.

Years clicked by as he followed this grueling routine and finally, slowly, he began to make headway. In 1988, he signed a management contract with Grand Ole Opry performer Del Reeves, only to have the relationship fall apart. Eventually Reeves would sue Cyrus.

Then, in 1989, Billy Ray was signed by Jack McFadden, one of Nashville's best-known country-music managers. McFadden tried to interest a record company in Billy Ray. A year later, however, he still didn't have a recording contract. He'd finally come so close to success, close enough almost to grasp it, only to fail yet again. "I was at the point in my life where I was just completely beat up," he said.

One Sunday night he was driving south from his small house in Ironton, Ohio, to play at the Ragtime in Huntington. As he drove, an odd thing happened to him. That inner voice of his, the same one that once had told him to learn to play the guitar, spoke again. This time it told him to stop at the Flatwoods, Kentucky, church where his grandfather, now dead, had been pastor.

Flatwoods was on the way to Huntington. Cyrus hadn't attended the church for fifteen years, but he obeyed the voice. He detoured off the main highway and pulled into the church's parking lot. When he entered the sanctuary, the evening service was well underway. "I heard the preacher saying, 'God loves a desperate man. God loves a desperate man,'" Cyrus said.

He knew that he'd been led there by God. Sitting in church that night, he prayed a desperate prayer for help. "I began praying every morning and every night, on my knees," he said. "About a week later, that same inner voice told me what to do, as far as who to call in Nashville, who to go see."

Cyrus visited Mercury Records executive Harold Shedd. "Harold Shedd looked up and said, 'I'm going to structure you a little deal,'" Cyrus said.

It was that easy. Grateful and humbled, Cyrus reconsecrated his life to God and began attending his grandfather's old church regularly.

On Sunday nights, he'd leave services early to play at the Ragtime. The pastor, the Reverend Donald Adkins, would pray for him before he went.

That "little deal" he signed with Harold Shedd quickly blossomed into one of the biggest deals around, and Billy Ray Cyrus became an overnight phenomenon in country music, the likes of which the industry has rarely seen. Critics continued to grouse about what they saw as his lack of talent, but his first single, "Achy Breaky Heart," turned into a worldwide mega-hit and his multiplatinum first album, Some Gave All, debuted at No. 1 on the country charts and also topped the pop charts for an incredible seventeen weeks—unprecedented feats for a new country artist. Cyrus found himself nominated for five Grammys and topping Billboard magazine's list of top country concert draws. He hit the list of America's highest-paid entertainers and became a multimillionaire. He's since cut several more successful records.

As a newspaper reporter, I interviewed him for a biographical 1993 article that appeared in the Lexington Herald-Leader. That's when he told me the story of his desperate prayers. Cyrus said, without hesitation, that God had placed him on center stage so he could spread a message of hope to struggling children in steel-mill towns like the one in which he'd grown up. The message: Cyrus was just an ordinary kid with mediocre grades and few noticeable abilities; whatever he achieved, others can achieve. "I'm Billy Ray Cyrus from Flatwoods, Kentucky, a man who had a dream," is the way Billy Ray liked to say it to journalists. A dream that, with positive thinking, perseverance—and a great deal of what Cyrus saw as divine intervention—became real.

Do We Live in an Age of Miracles?

I grew up in small towns and rural communities around Kentucky, where the miracle stories contained in the Bible became as much a part of my early lore as my mother's reminiscences of sitting before an old, upright radio on cold evenings while listening to broadcasts of "The Shadow," or my father's tale about his college friend who in youthful exuberance grabbed the base of a telephone pole, swung around it, caught his class ring on a protruding nail, and sliced off a finger ("Now the girls won't love me anymore!" the friend cried). Which is to say that I assumed the biblical stories to be true, more or less, and that I found them by turns humorous, or intriguing, or frightening. But like my parents' tales of their own bygone days, the Bible's miracles seemed to belong to an ancient past—somebody else's past. They had nothing directly to do with me. I knew I would never listen to "The Shadow" on an upright radio in an unheated farmhouse, and equally assumed I would never see God restore the sight of a blind man.

My father was then a Southern Baptist preacher, as well as a school-teacher, and, for several years, an administrator at a Baptist college. My mom, a housewife, was an equally staunch Baptist. In those days some Southern Baptists, including my parents, held the theological view that the age of miracles had ended in the first century with the deaths of the original apostles. They looked askance at other Christians who still acted as if God was very much in the miracle business today, such as the ragged Pentecostals who met in a small, white frame building on the poorer end of one town where we lived.

Our understanding of miracles changed in 1976, while I was a ne'er-do-well student at the University of Kentucky. By the time the cancer was discovered it had invaded my father's entire body: his head, a kidney, his bones. First, doctors operated on a tumor on his skull. They opened him up and stitched him shut after removing only enough tissue for a biopsy. Surgery wouldn't do the job, they'd known as soon as they saw the tumor. Dad's neurosurgeon told me a few minutes afterward that the cancer had spread so far that they could draw marrow from any bone in his body and it would be malignant.

In the days that followed, the physicians—Dad had a team of doctors working on him—tried to decide how to prolong his life. The matter was complicated because he was a diabetic; some treatments that might slow the spread of his cancer would aggravate his diabetes.

And then something happened that I still find hard to grasp. One day I visited my father in his hospital room. He told me that God had spoken to him as he was praying. The Lord had told him he was going to be healed. I can't remember exactly what I thought, except that I was puzzled and sad. My father didn't normally claim to have received divine revelations regarding faith healings, or anything else.

The physicians continued to run tests and debate a course of treatment. Then, before the doctors could administer a single medicine, my father's cancer vanished. Completely. Samples from the skull biopsy had been confirmed as cancerous. As an amazed pathologist continued to pass slides containing the samples under a microscope, they changed to benign before his eyes. I now realize that earlier, even before the biopsy on the tumor in Dad's head, strange things had started happening. The cancer's probable source, a kidney tumor, had been clearly visible in X rays, but a second set of X rays had showed no sign of a tumor.

Now a bone-marrow test returned negative. Dumbfounded, the team of physicians sent their findings to another hospital for confirmation. They assumed they must have missed something. Either my father hadn't been stricken with cancer to begin with and they'd misdiagnosed his case, or else the cancer still was lurking somewhere undetected. At the second hospital, however, the doctors arrived at the same conclusions as the initial team of physicians had. My dad indeed appeared to have had cancer, they said; now he didn't. They had no explanation either.

As I write this, twenty years have passed since those terrifying, exhilarating weeks in early 1976. My father is sixty-five years old. He's never suffered a recurrence of cancer. Say what you want, but my father told me what was going to take place before it happened: God had said he intended to heal Dad. Then, apparently, God did just that. I bear witness that I saw what I believe to have been a miracle. I'd never seen one before and didn't expect one then. It was one of the defining events of my life. It forced me to confront the possibility that God is *real*— that he continues to involve himself in human affairs.

I assumed, however, that the kind of supernatural intervention I'd witnessed was exceedingly rare. Today, as I've said, I think differently.

We live in a scientific age. When we're sick, we turn to laser surgery rather than to the incantations of holy men and women. Indeed, some secular and seminary scholars alike have argued that the biblical miracles themselves never happened as they're recorded. The stories, they say, are the products of myth-making and wishful thinking, or else they are literary devices designed to hint at less material, spiritual principles. Perhaps there's a measure of truth to that.

On the other hand, I've frequently recounted the story of my father's miracle to friends, co-workers, or acquaintances, some of them religious and some not. Nearly every time I've told my story, another person in the room has volunteered, "Hey, that happened to my aunt." Or to a brother, or a spouse.

We often are deceived by looking at matters only on the surface. Most people don't talk about miracles much in public—after all, we don't want to be taken for dunces. Still, the numbers show that the great majority of us believe firmly, if privately, that supernatural miracles do take place today. A 1990 poll by the Princeton Survey Research Associates found that 82 percent of the three thousand Americans asked agreed with this statement: "Even today, miracles are performed by the power of God." A secular magazine, *Self*, polled its readers—college-educated women of diverse faiths or no religious affiliation at all—and found that 39 percent said they'd personally received or witnessed a miracle.

My father's miracle touched off a considerable controversy in his Southern Baptist congregation between those who believed God had supernaturally healed him and others who believed he was the beneficiary of a happy coincidence that had been blown out of proportion. In the end, Dad left the Southern Baptist denomination and formed a small, independent congregation that was charismatic in theology.

"Charismatics" such as my father—and, eventually, my mother, too—are Christians who embrace the present-day "charisms," or miraculous gifts, of the Holy Spirit that are spoken of in the New Testament. They're similar to Pentecostals, although charismatics tend to hail from mainline Protestant or Roman Catholic backgrounds and to be somewhat more affluent and better-educated. Partly out of family loyalty and partly out of interest, I attended my father's congregation for several years. There I saw a number of remarkable manifestations that I gradually came to believe were supernatural in origin.

Also, I later happened to marry into a family of Pentecostals. Earlier in my life, we more mainstream churchgoers had derided Pentecostals as "Holy Rollers" because their branch of Christianity is based on a belief in modern-day miracles of many types: speaking in tongues, prophecy, healing, and the like. But in the seventeen years of my marriage I've learned a great deal about Pentecostals. I've seen, for one thing, that some of the miraculous "signs and wonders" that take place in their services could be the very human results of emotionalism run amok. A second thing I've learned, through attending hundreds of Pentecostal services, is that many of the phenomena do not appear to be the results of raw emotionalism; they seem beyond rational explanation.

The third thing I've learned is that Pentecostalism, with its insistence upon modern-day miracles, holds broad appeal worldwide. In researching his book *Fire from Heaven*, respected Harvard University religion professor Harvey Cox studied Pentecostalism around the globe—and determined it to be the fastest-growing branch of religion in the world. There now are 400 to 500 million Pentecostals, and their numbers are increasing by 20 million a year, Cox says. He has said that within a few decades Pentecostals will surpass Roman Catholics as the largest subgroup of Christianity. Pentecostals once were denigrated by those of us in the Christian mainstream. Now, outside the United States, at least, they are the mainstream.

But this is not a book about Pentecostals. Since 1990 I have been the full-time religion writer for the *Lexington Herald-Leader*, a Pulitzer Prize–winning metropolitan daily. My job has brought me into regular contact with people of all social classes and religious bents, from governors to gardeners, from Methodists to Muslims, from Catholic scholars to cafeteria cooks. I've found that a belief in miracles is common to many of them.

It's True Across the Various Faiths

Accounts of miraculous help show up everywhere. The Baha'i faith, for example, originated in the 1800s in Persia as an Islamic reform movement. It meshes the teachings of its central prophet, Baha'u'llah, with a respect for Jesus, Muhammad, and Confucius, among others. Like any new religious movement, the Baha'i faith proved enormously controversial in its earliest days and faced fierce persecution. According to Baha'i teaching, one prophet, the Bab, was sentenced to be publicly shot on July 9, 1850, before thousands of witnesses in a public square. The Bab and a disciple were suspended by ropes against the wall of a military barracks. A full regiment of Armenian Christian soldiers under Colonel Sam Khan was marched into the square to act as the firing squad. Khan said he was reluctant to shoot the Bab for fear of incurring God's wrath, but the calm Bab assured him it would be okay.

The hundreds of soldiers took their positions and aimed. At the signal their muzzle-loaded weapons exploded in unison. Gun smoke billowed through the square, blocking the two condemned men from the crowd's sight. When the smoke finally thinned, the Bab's disciple stood unscathed beside the wall. The Bab was gone. The bullets fired at them had severed the ropes that bound both men, yet hadn't scratched the men themselves. Soldiers found the Bab a few minutes later in the cell he'd occupied the night before, giving instructions to his secretary.

The crowd went nearly berserk with fear. The Bab and his friend remained under sentences of death, but the Armenian soldiers flatly refused to participate further in their execution. A Muslim regiment was organized and marched into the square to act as a second firing squad. The Bab and his companion were suspended by ropes again and this time were shot to death.

Miracles happen even to those who don't practice an organized religion. In 1967, José Feola, who since has retired as a medical school research professor, lived in Berkeley, California. He was driving alone to a coin laundry. His car was in the left lane of a two-lane, one-way street. "In the middle of the block I heard this voice that said, 'Change lanes!'" said Feola, a native of Argentina. Startled, Feola cut his car into the right lane. Immediately, another car careened around the corner into the lane he'd just departed, headed the wrong way on the one-way street. Feola barely missed what might have been a fatal collision.

Feola considers himself religious, but not in any traditional way; he's not a believer in the divinity of Jesus Christ or a churchgoer. "A voice saved my life," he said. "I never recognized the voice." He knows it wasn't his own, because it spoke in English and his native language is Spanish. He doesn't know if it was God. "You can call it whatever. It's very difficult to say," he said. "I'm convinced there is something beyond our life. Evidently there is something that protects you—or protects some people."

The Scientific Approach Is Limited

Increasingly, scientists and religious scholars alike are studying these kinds of remarkable events. There's substantial scientific evidence that the supernatural, or at least a belief in the supernatural, can produce dramatic results. Take prayer as an example. It is one of several ingredients often found in the mix when people claim to have experienced a miracle. Jones and Reed prayed as their helicopter fell from the sky. Billy Ray Cyrus has attributed much of his country music success to the desperate prayers he offered. My father was praying when God assured him his cancer would be healed.

I once interviewed a prominent physician named Larry Dossey, who predicts that doctors soon will encourage patients to pray as well as take pills—because prayer leads to startling improvements in patients' health. Dossey doesn't belong to any organized religion, but he's a former panel co-chairman at the National Institutes of Health and the former chief of staff of Humana Medical City-Dallas. "Not to recommend the use of prayer as an integral part of medical care will one day constitute medical malpractice," he writes in his book *Healing Words: The Power of Prayer and the Practice of Medicine.*

Dossey says that many first-rate scientific studies suggest prayer can alter everything from complications after heart surgery to the movements of one-celled algae. He points to a survey by Dr. Daniel J. Benor of 131 controlled, scientific trials of prayer conducted by various researchers writing in the English language. In two thirds of those, Dossey told me, prayer led to statistically significant changes. Prayer had a documentable effect whether those praying were in the same room as the subjects of their prayers or miles away. Prayer appeared to help hospital patients even when neither they nor their doctors knew they were being prayed for. Prayer helped subhuman forms of life such as plants and fungus to grow faster or slower, depending upon the aims of the particular experiment.

"Prayer works," Dossey said. "I don't think there's any doubt about that. . . . It really is one of the best-kept secrets in medical science." It's silly to attribute the historic belief in prayer to mere superstition, he added. There's no way millions of people would have kept praying through the centuries if prayer didn't help: "I don't think people are that gullible."

Researchers don't know yet how prayer works; they know only that it does, and that it appears to be more than simply the power of positive thinking. Another interesting finding is that the particular denomination of those praying doesn't seem to matter much. "The prayers of born-again Christians work," Dossey said. "The prayers of Muslims work. The prayers of Buddhists work—and Buddhism is not even a theistic religion."

I don't mean to suggest that prayer is a miracle in itself. But prayer is one denominator that's often present when miraculous events happen.

Consider, too, the conclusions of John Killinger, a renowned religious scholar in the mainline Protestant tradition, which is not noted for its belief in the miraculous. Despite their religious credentials, most mainline scholars assume there are naturalistic explanations for "supernatural" events, whether the events are recorded in the Bible or in a weekly news tabloid. But Killinger has changed his mind over the years, he told me in a 1993 newspaper interview. "For a long time now, I've believed that the empirical way of looking at the world is very limited," he said.

Killinger said that there are just too many accounts of supernatural intercession to ignore them, from episodes of ESP to tales of spectacular healings. Put the stories all together and it's a vast body of evidence. "These are not isolated, aberrational cases," he said.

I agree. Something's happening that no honest observer can easily dismiss. Somehow, God continues to intervene among ordinary men and women, religious and nonreligious. If anything, this divine activity is growing.

In the following chapters we'll look at this phenomenon of miracles in greater depth. We'll examine the arguments against miracles by investigators who don't believe. We'll listen to tale after tale of miracles past and present. And we'll answer the most important question: What can average people like you and me do to increase our chances of receiving a miracle?

WHAT IS A MIRACLE?

How Do We Identify a Miracle?

Before we go further, a word about definitions. Just what is a miracle?

There are various answers to that. *The New Catholic Encyclopedia* describes a miracle as "an extraordinary event, perceptible to the senses, produced by God in a religious context as a sign of the supernatural." Within that framework, though, scholars and clergy often talk about several categories of miracles. Two broad types are discussed most commonly.

At the top of this brief pecking order are miracles for which there are no known explanation: Jesus is born of a virgin, walks on water, or is raised from the dead. Even in the Bible, these kinds of acts tend to be rare. They are violations of the known laws of nature. When it seeks to canonize a new saint, the Vatican requires scientific proof of miracles that probably could be classified among this first category. *Time* magazine published an article in 1995 about Monsignor Michele Di Ruberto. He's a Vatican official whose job is to verify miraculous acts that supposedly happened after prayers to candidates for sainthood. Currently, Di Ruberto is working his way through 250 red-bound volumes containing accounts of such alleged miracles. Few of the claims will pass the Vatican's test, which is the most stringent in Christendom.

For the Vatican, a miraculous healing, for instance, must involve an illness that is serious and that has received a firm diagnosis by qualified medical personnel. The sick person cannot have been getting better at the time of the healing and cannot have been suffering from an ailment that would be expected to improve over time. The patient cannot have been receiving medical treatment—which in itself could negate most claims of modern-day healing, in that medical care is nearly ubiquitous in the developed world. Additionally, the healing must be instantaneous, complete, and permanent. It must outstrip any professional, empirical ability to explain it. Some cancer remissions aren't even considered until they have lasted at least ten years.

As scientific and psychological research become ever more sophisticated, and as medical treatment becomes more universal, it is becoming almost impossible to prove such a miracle, and some Catholic authorities have criticized the Vatican's standards as too demanding.

However, the vast majority of miracles, past and present, fall into a second category. They are unusual, even spectacular, events that are open to interpretation. There might well be nonsupernatural explanations for these acts, but those who experience them firmly believe, with some reason, that they were instigated by God or some other supernatural force.

Protestant theologian James I. Packer of Regent College argues on behalf of this category of miracles. "They have told us that a miracle is God suspending an overriding natural law," Packer says in a *Christianity Today* interview. "But that is a secular definition, reflecting a deistic world view—a view, that is, that sees God's world as a closed box of forces from which the Creator is ordinarily standing at a distance, uninvolved."

Instead, Packer says, the biblical view is that God remains directly involved in all of life's events, great and small, regular and irregular. Describing miracles as "signs and wonders" is perhaps a better way of thinking of it, he says. Miracles are "signs" of God's power and mercy and they are "wonders" because they make people "stop and blink"; they cause people to think about the Almighty. Many biblical miracles, Packer continues, are, simply, "remarkable coincidences that occur in situations where desperate people have been praying." (Sounds like Billy Ray Cyrus's record contract, doesn't it?)

As an example of this idea, a Catholic priest has pointed to the book of Exodus, where Moses visits Pharaoh repeatedly, asking the Egyptian potentate to release his Hebrew slaves. Each time Pharaoh refuses, and each time the Egyptians are struck with a new plague, from contamination of their water supply to an overabundance of frogs. These plagues all could be accounted for in human terms. It doesn't necessarily require an act of God, say, for water to become contaminated. Yet people who observed the plagues understood them to have been caused by divine intercession, and that belief filled them—temporarily—with the faith necessary to follow God's will.

Similarly, a friend of mine, journalist Linda Piwowarski, reported on the strange help that Margaret Ralph, a Catholic scholar, received when she took the intimidating comprehensive examination for her Ph.D. in literature from a large state university. Ralph, a busy wife and mother, had worked for eighteen years toward her doctorate, taking one course a semester. When it finally came time for her "comps," some of her course work was nearly two decades old. She asked a professor what to expect on the examination and was told, "If it's written in English, it could be on the test." Ralph studied several months and still felt woefully unprepared.

The examination was divided into several parts, to be taken on separate days. The first day of testing fell on the Monday after Easter. As she sat in church on Good Friday, Ralph happened to notice that sermons were a form of medieval literature. On Saturday she read a book on medieval sermons. Sunday, while reviewing old classroom notes, she discovered a set of notes comparing medieval sermons to Chaucer's "The Pardoner's Tale."

The next day, the central essay question on her exam asked her to compare the structure of medieval sermons to Chaucer's "The Pardoner's Tale."

That night, as Ralph prepared for the second day of her comps, she reached near-exhaustion. Her husband suggested she just relax and read a book. "You've done all you can," he said. She agreed, and for pleasure picked up a book on Spenser's *Faerie Queene* that a friend had given her.

Tuesday, she was assigned a ninety-minute essay on Spenser's *Faerie Queene.*

"I knelt down and said a prayer of gratitude before answering the question," Ralph told Piwowarski for an article that appeared in *Catholic Digest* magazine. "I'd done my best and it wasn't enough, so God gave me what I needed. For me, it was a kind of Exodus experience."

Again, what happened to Ralph might have been a series of coincidences. But although she holds a Ph.D. and now is a respected scholar, Ralph remains convinced that God, for whatever reasons, interceded on her behalf.

It's this far more common, popular definition I'll be using when I refer in this book to "miracles." Many of these acts, if not all of them, are open to differing interpretations by skeptics. That's perfectly fine. But the people who experienced the events believe them to have been wrought by God, and that assurance has warmed the recipients' hearts and deepened their faith.

CHAPTER TWO

MIRACLES THROUGHOUT HISTORY

ANTHROPOLOGISTS ESTIMATE that we humans have worshiped various deities for 2 to 3 million years. For all that time, adherents of the countless faiths that have arisen on earth—no matter the century or the continent they called home—have sworn that their gods worked startling miracles. Some of these miracles are said to have been witnessed by scores, and even hundreds, of people.

Such tales of supernatural intervention play a big role in forming any particular system of otherwordly beliefs. "The function of miracles is to provide a proof for the religious claims," said Abdul-Aziz Sachedina, a professor of religious studies at the University of Virginia, who is a Muslim.

When Muslims profess that the Quran was imparted to Muhammad intact, and that it remains in perfect form today, they are, of course, telling us about a wonderful event that took place in Muhammad's life. But they also are establishing that Muhammad was Allah's prophet. When the ancient Jews talked about God's having parted the Red Sea so that a nation of Hebrews could escape their Egyptian pursuers, they were celebrating the escape of those men, women, and children. But they also were establishing that their God was the highest deity and that they were his chosen people.

Not surprisingly, miracle stories particularly are said to abound in the lives of a religion's founder. The Christian New Testament tells us that Jesus Christ was born of a virgin and that his arrival was accompanied by such signs as angelic choruses and the appearance of a portentous star. Later, Jesus is said to have passed on wonder-working powers to his chief disciples.

Likewise, some Buddhists say Buddha was born of a virgin and that his birth also was accompanied by other wonders as well, said Eunice Irwin, an assistant professor of Christian mission and contextual theology at Asbury Theological Seminary in Wilmore, Kentucky. Buddha supposedly gave his disciples miraculous powers, too. "You don't know if those are legends," Irwin said.

Which raises a ticklish point. Christianity is far and away the majority religion among Americans who claim any faith at all. It certainly is my religion. As the church always has confessed, I firmly believe that Jesus Christ is my lord and savior. But if the accounts of miracles in my religion help establish it as the best of faiths, how do I explain the miracles that have occurred in yours? Whatever their own religion, those who believe in miracles must get around this dilemma.

Some people argue that the supernatural acts reported by religions other than their own are superstitions or the results of hysteria or even hoaxes. In other words, our miracles are real, but yours are fakes. Some, such as a Christian author with whom I spoke, believe that supernatural acts do happen among people of other religions, but that those acts are works of Satan, who is bent on deceiving people into avoiding the Christians' God.

Still others hold that God is quite willing to perform miracles for people who happen not to belong to their own organization. Sachedina pointed out that the Quran contains favorable accounts of many miracles that God worked among the traditional prophets of Judaism and Christianity, although these are interpreted through Islamic theology.

Both the Roman Catholic Church and C.S. Lewis, the late Cambridge professor and Anglican who probably ranks as our century's most eloquent defender of Christianity, have admitted that God doesn't necessarily limit his works to Christians, much less to members of their particular denominations. "God could work miracles in connection with another church or another religion for purposes that would not conflict with His approval of the Christian Catholic religion," says the New Catholic Encyclopedia. "He could do so to confirm the faith of adherents of another church or religion in one or more of the particular truths taught by that church or religion. . . ."

Lewis felt much the same way. "I am in no way committed to the assertion that God has never worked miracles through and for Pagans or never permitted created supernatural beings to do so," he writes in *Miracles: A Preliminary Study*. However, Christian miracles as recorded in, say, the New Testament are more meaningful than those recorded among the holy books of other faiths, Lewis says, in that they have a clear theological purpose. He implies that they illustrate the core teachings of Christianity's founder, Jesus, whose divine acts of healing, exorcism, food multiplication, and the like, revealed that God the Creator was active in the world, cared about individuals' needs, and wanted to free them from the bondage of bad living.

My goal here is not to solve this thorny issue, which would take another book in itself. My purpose is merely to record a few of the accounts of miracles that have come down to us throughout history and from across the religious spectrum. Do with them what you will.

Primal Religions

The oldest religions are the animistic and pagan sects, which vary in their details but are polytheistic, don't claim a particular founder such as Jesus or Muhammad, and hold that human destiny is controlled by countless spirits inhabiting trees, rocks, mountains, and clouds. These spirits are believed to interact with people and to sometimes take human or animal forms.

Polytheistic Greeks worshiped a particular god of healing, Asklepios, the "hero physician," a real man whom they believe to have been deified and whose presence was symbolized by a serpent staff. Greek legend says that Zeus killed Asklepios out of jealousy, but that even after his death the physician continued to work innumerable wonders. His cult began at Tricca and eventually included at least two hundred temples throughout the Greco-Roman world, the chief one being at Epidaurus. Seventy ancient case histories still exist detailing miraculous cures performed by Asklepios. The case histories include the patients' names, diagnoses of their sicknesses, and accounts of the dreams

experienced by the sick as they slept in temples. In the cult of Asklepios, dreams generally preceded cures, as did ritual baths, animal sacrifices, and other ministrations.

Asklepios proved so successful a healer that he became the most
popular deity in the Hellenistic world, and his cult flourished for eight
hundred years. In 291 B.C.E., for example, Roman authorities sent a delegation to Epidaurus asking the god's help in stemming a plague rav-
aging Latium. Asklepios agreed, took the form of a snake, and slithered
on board a Roman boat that was drawn up the Tiber River. At Ostia the
snake left the boat for a nearby island. The Romans built a temple there
to Asklepios—and the plague quickly ended.

One current scholar, Robert J. Miller, editor of *The Complete Gospels*
and a member of the controversial Jesus Seminar, which has questioned
much of the material in the Christian New Testament, told me that
early Christian preachers ran headlong into the disciples of Asklepios.
The missionaries touted Jesus' healing miracles as signs that he was the
only son of God. In effect, the Greeks replied, "Big deal. Asklepios does
such miracles all the time."

On this continent, Native Americans have for centuries practiced a
form of primal spirituality that includes shamanism and many accounts of supernatural visions, healings, and prophecies. Vision quests,
particularly, have enabled certain Indians to see directly into the spirit
world. Author Ake Hultkrantz, writing in *Native Religions of North
America*, tells of Spanish missionary Fray Alonso de Benavides, who in
the 1600s ventured into the American Southwest. An Apache chief became intrigued with de Benavides's teachings and attended a Christian
Mass. By the time the service ended, the chief had become crestfallen.
He explained that he couldn't believe in the missionary's religion.
When de Benavides asked why, the Apache replied that he had not once
seen the missionary's God appear on de Benavides's altar and so considered Christianity impotent. By contrast, during his own rituals, he
said, he could see his native religion's spirits quite clearly.

Irwin, the seminary professor, once worked among the remote
Subanen tribe in the southern Philippines. The daughter of one of the
tribe's more powerful leaders told Irwin a story. During what Irwin
later judged to have been the 1920s, the Subanen people suffered a se-

ries of raids by Moros who would hide and snatch members of the tribe, then sell them into slavery. To escape their enemies, the Subanen fled their homes. They soon ran out of their food staples, rice and yams, and nearly starved. One day a woman dressed in white—the Subanen storyteller described her as a "sky woman"—appeared among the tribe. She led the famished people to some palm trees and showed them how to cut through the trees' bark and eat the nourishing marrow inside. She saved their lives. The sky woman then remained among the tribe for many years afterward and even bore children there. Irwin thinks the story was true. "I believe it's possible that the person was an angel," she said.

Early Miracles in the Founded Religions

Historically, miracles have played a significant part in the spreading and the lore of nearly all the world's faiths, including the major, founded religions. After Buddha received enlightenment, he returned to his native city, Kapilavastu. There, tradition says, Buddha levitated and even walked in the air. Flames and currents of water shot from his body. To convince his relatives of his calling and as a sign that might convert them to his beliefs, Buddha rose in the air and hacked his body into many pieces, which fell to the ground. He then reassembled the parts. Buddhist missionaries were said to have performed many powerful works, especially in China. In the 300s, Fo-t'u-teng made it rain and produced water from dry wells.

In Islam, Muhammad was less enamored of the miraculous. He told pagans who taunted him about this unwillingness to perform wonders that the creation itself was full of signs that pointed to Allah. Yet Islam contains its share of reports of the supernatural. One story says that when Muhammad was a child, two angels washed his heart and removed from it a black clot.

An illiterate man, Muhammad received his first divine message in about 610, at age forty, from the archangel Gabriel; his visions continued sporadically for many years. At Mecca, Allah, working through Muhammad, split the moon. Unbelievers witnessed the miracle, but attributed it to sorcery. God warned that they would be punished on the last, great Day of Judgment, when they would be resurrected face down for their lack of faith.

Another story says that a Christian once embraced Islam and began writing down Muhammad's revelations for him. Then the scribe returned to Christianity and bragged that Muhammad possessed no knowledge except what he, the scribe, had given him. Allah struck the man dead. His people buried him. But the next morning they found his body lying atop the ground. Assuming that Muhammad and his friends had uncovered the body, the scribe's companions dug a deeper grave and buried him again, but the following morning the earth had rejected the man a second time. Still the man's friends assumed this to be the result of mischief by Muhammad, so they dug another grave— only to find their friend lying on the dirt a third time. Finally they realized what was happening, and left the body unburied.

Miracles in Ancient Judaism

There's not a great deal of discussion in modern Judaism about supernatural works of power. Still, Judaism was founded on a belief that ancient Israel possessed a unique relationship with the Hebrew God and that God was powerfully involved in preserving that nation. Just look at the story in Genesis of Abraham and his son, Isaac. "It starts there," said Tsion Ben-David, director of the Israeli government's tourism office in Chicago and an authority on Jewish and Christian history.

You probably know the biblical story. God forms a covenant with elderly, childless Abraham that he will bless the old man and give him the son he desires so terribly. The Almighty promises to preserve the son and make Abraham's descendants as numerous as the stars in the sky. Yet after that son, Isaac, is miraculously born and has grown into boyhood, God—as a test of Abraham's faith—commands the old man to take Isaac to a mountain and sacrifice him. Abraham obeys. He ties Isaac to an altar, raises his knife above the boy. Then, before he can plunge the blade into his son's chest, an angel appears, stops Abraham, and points to a ram caught in a nearby thicket. The angel tells Abraham to sacrifice the ram instead. Isaac, along with the future nation of Israel, which has descended from Isaac's loins, is saved.

Throughout the Hebrew Bible, God acts again and again to save the Jews. "Really, it's endless," Ben-David said. Many modern Jewish scholars propose naturalistic explanations for some of those events, he said. But however you explain any individual deed, the sum of them indicates that an unseen hand is indeed working on behalf of Abraham's descendants. Throughout ancient history, nation after nation tried to disperse or destroy the Jews: the Canaanites, the Hittites, the Assyrians, the Greeks, the Romans. Instead, "they all vanished," Ben-David said. His explanation? "We are the chosen people. We are the people who are taking care of the Holy Land."

Miracles in Historic Christianity

No religious system contains more historic stories about miracles than Christianity. Jesus apparently delighted in performing miracles of many types, and particularly divine healings of lepers, paralytics, deaf people, the blind. He exorcised demons. He raised the dead. He calmed storms. And he returned from the dead three days after he'd been executed.

After his resurrection, Jesus' disciples carried on the tradition, the New Testament tells us. In a story found in the Acts of the Apostles, Peter and John are on their way to the temple to offer up their daily prayers. They pass a lame beggar who asks them for money. The two apostles stop. "Silver and gold have I none," Peter replies, "but such as I have, give I thee. In the name of Jesus Christ of Nazareth, rise and walk." The beggar instantly is healed—and goes away "walking and leaping and praising God."

One evening at a church service, Paul preaches so long that a young man, Eutychus, nods off and falls from a third-floor window. The fall kills him, so Paul interrupts his sermon, walks downstairs, and resurrects the youth, then returns to finish his homily. Shipwrecked on an island, Paul is gathering wood for a bonfire when a poisonous snake slithers from the sticks and bites Paul's hand. Paul tosses the snake into the fire and goes on about his business, to the astonishment of the island's pagan residents, who decide that he must be a visiting god.

Tales of miracles never have disappeared altogether from Christianity. A controversial second-century revival movement called Montanism after its founder, Montanus, erupted in Asia Minor beginning in about 156 or 157 and lasted for decades. Montanists prophesied the future routinely and provided words of supernatural insight into the secrets locked in the hearts of individual men and women. Like the first-century Christians at Pentecost, many Montanists spoke in languages they hadn't studied and others divinely interpreted those messages. All of this made them suspect among the staid church hierarchy. Nonetheless, the Montanist revival lasted for a century and gained wide prominence within the Church.

A number of Christian scholars have documented that the supernatural "gifts" attributed to the Holy Spirit didn't cease with Montanism, either. Historian James E. Bradley, writing in the scholarly journal *Pneuma,* notes that the respected church father Origen recorded in about 245 C.E. that he had been an eyewitness to exorcisms and miraculous healings. In 256, Novatian wrote that the Holy Spirit had placed prophets in the Church and continued to give the gifts of speaking in foreign tongues, "wonderful works" of power, the discernment of spirits and healings. Old church documents such the *Didache* and the *Shepherd of Hermas* provide guidelines on the appropriate lifestyles for prophets and miracle workers, implying that such ministries were common.

Bradley observes that tales of healings and exorcisms became even more prominent in the fourth century and thereafter, and appear in the writings of everyone from Athanasius to the Cappadocian Fathers to Ambrose to Jerome and even to the discriminating Augustine, who observes in *The City of God* that in his day miracles continue to occur in Jesus' name and then provides detailed narratives of twenty-five divine healings. Augustine records cases in which blind eyes are opened, cancer vanishes, and kidney stones disappear as well as an episode in which a boy run over by an ox cart recovers.

Such stories have continued through the ages. In *The Hiding Places of God*, prizewinning British journalist John Cornwell recounts the exploits of a Franciscan monk named Joseph of Copertino, who in the 1600s became known as the flying monk because of his unsettling habit of suddenly levitating from floors during his religious ecstasies. Joseph even snatched bystanders into the air with him. Such tales raise eyebrows now, but Cornwell—no apologist for the miraculous—notes that Joseph's seventy flights took place before many witnesses, including educated and sophisticated skeptics.

Protestants split from the Roman Catholic Church during the Reformation of the 1500s. One matter that had irritated the separatists was that Catholic leaders seemed far too uncritical about miracles and accepted every report that happened along. Yet the more influential movements among Protestants would also include outbreaks of supernatural works.

In the late 1700s and early 1800s, many Methodists believed in—and experienced—dramatic conversions, prophetic dreams, visions, and divine healing, writes historian John H. Wigger in a 1994 article in the *Journal of the Early Republic*. Some Methodists swooned to the floor, knocked flat by what they interpreted as God's power; a few remained in trances for days at a time. One man reported having seen a woman raised from the dead. Some Methodists spoke in tongues. "In fact," Wigger writes, "it may not be an exaggeration to say that this quest for the supernatural in everyday life . . . was the key theological characteristic of early American Methodism."

The most dramatic meeting that took place during the Second Great Awakening, a huge revival that swept the South at the beginning of the nineteenth century, was held in August 1801, at Cane Ridge Church in rural Bourbon County, Kentucky. In a time before there were cars for easy transportation and radios, TVs, or telephones for publicity, an amazing crowd of twenty thousand people flocked to the open-air meeting, which lasted for days and was led by several preachers. The crowd included the state's governor, James Garrard, prostitutes, robbers, pious churchgoers, and both blacks and whites. Worshipers were overcome by what they took to be the Spirit of God. They laughed uncontrollably, danced, jerked, screamed, and fell to the ground by the dozens as if dead. Critics of the meeting said that some people barked like dogs "treeing the devil."

Whatever its critics might have said, the Second Great Awakening, characterized by meetings such as the one at Cane Ridge, altered the course of American sociology by helping change the South from a haven for criminals and rowdies into the most evangelical region of the United States.

Miracles in Christian Splinter Groups

Christianity has spawned its share of splinter groups, which traditionalists tend to classify as cults but adherents describe as genuinely Christian. We also find powerful events reported among those sects, such as Christian Science and the Church of Jesus Christ of Latter-day Saints.

Mary Baker Eddy began formulating the principles that became Christian Science about 130 years ago. She long had searched for a cure for her chronic bad health and had tried various mind-over-matter techniques. However, Eddy was a student of the Bible and disliked those approaches because they omitted the power of God. In 1866, she fell on an icy sidewalk in Lynn, Massachusetts, and suffered serious injuries from which her doctor said she couldn't recover. Once again Eddy read her Bible closely, this time focusing on its accounts of miraculous healings performed by Jesus. She received a "profound insight" and was dramatically cured.

To be healed without medicine, Eddy decided, sick people must change their thoughts and tap into the "divine Mind," the Christian Science term for God. In 1875, Eddy published *Science and Health with Key to the Scriptures,* which created a sensation. Subsequent editions of the volume included a one-hundred-page compilation of testimonials from people healed after reading Eddy's book.

Since their religion's inception, members of the Church of Jesus Christ of Latter-day Saints—the Mormons—have indeed attributed much of their good fortune to divine intervention. "There is, in our experience, a kind of steady, regular occurrence of miraculous events," said Paul Hedengren, an assistant professor of philosophy at Brigham Young University in Provost, Utah. Miracles do not form the religion's core, he cautioned. It's just that "miracles follow faith. . . . God wants to help us."

Larry C. Porter, a professor of church history and doctrine at BYU, provided me detailed information from various Mormon documents about a miracle that took place in 1846 before hundreds of eyewitnesses. Following persecution of the sect, many of the Mormon men of Nauvoo, a Saints city in Hancock County, Illinois, already had departed on a trail-blazing mission to the West, leaving behind their women and children. Enemies of the Mormons seized on the men's absence to drive the remaining Saints from the region. Some 640 Mormon women and children, along with a few remaining men, were expelled in September and fled across the Mississippi River to rural Iowa. Their temporary camp since has been known as the "camp of the poor." Some slept in wagons, others in hastily improvised tents, others in horrible shelters of brush. Cold, autumn rains raked them. By early October the refugees nearly were starving.

On October 9, 1846, a huge flock of quails, thousands of birds, flew up the riverbank toward the place where the Mormons were huddled. For some reason, as if from a long flight, the birds became exhausted—and simply fell into the camp, into the tents and lean-tos. Some even landed on the breakfast tables. Too tired to fly away, the fowls became easy prey for the famished Saints, who caught the quails, cooked them, and avoided starvation. The event was witnessed by passengers on a passing steamboat.

That miracle was similar to one recorded in Exodus and Numbers, when God fed the nation of Israel with quails in the wilderness. The parallel was clear to the Mormons; they interpreted the quails as a sign of God's favor.

CHAPTER THREE

TWENTIETH-CENTURY
MIRACLES

A S I'VE POINTED OUT, polls indicate that even most of us who
were raised in the scientifically minded Western Hemisphere believe that divine miracles are possible, and that a large minority of us
say we actually have seen or experienced supernatural acts. Yet at the
same time, many of us have been taught not to expect miracles or to
trust others' accounts of them. If our culture holds a prevailing attitude toward spiritual works of power, it's probably a guarded skepticism. We are, then, paradoxes. We believe and we don't believe. We
witness what appears to be a marvelous manifestation of divine presence, then rationalize it away. "Gee, what a coincidence," we say. Or,
"Man, was I lucky."

I've wrestled with this double-mindedness in my own life for two
decades, since my father's spontaneous recovery from cancer. One fact
that has struck me, however, is that no matter how educated or dubious we moderns have become, reports of miracles haven't decreased.
If anything, in sheer numbers stories of the miraculous have increased,
on a worldwide scale.

Tsion Ben-David, the Israeli tourism official, says that his nation
has experienced help in the twentieth century that might have made
Moses' jaw drop. "The rebirth of Israel in 1948 is one of the major
miraculous events that could happen in the history of Judaism," he
said, "to come back after 2,000 years to our own land."

The facts, available in any public library, truly are astounding. Between late 1947 and 1949 during their war for independence, ill-equipped and poorly trained Jews took on the British Army, the United Nations, and the various Arab countries, and prevailed in one of history's great military upsets. In May 1948, for example, the ragtag Jews were attacked by the Lebanese from the north, the Syrians at the Lake of Galilee, the Iraqis at the Jordan River, the Jordanians in Samaria, and the Egyptians at Gaza, as well as by two guerrilla forces. The Arab troops possessed a huge numerical advantage. They had artillery and air support. The Israeli Defense Forces were armed with small arms, mortars, and a few old French howitzers, and were forced to fight on several fronts. A massacre of the Israelis appeared inevitable. Yet the Israeli Defense Forces time after time whipped the better-armed Arabs. In the village of Kfar Darom, to the south of Gaza, thirty youthful defenders delayed an overwhelming force of Egyptians for a month. By 1949, the Israelis had won the war.

Repeatedly over the past half-century, the Jewish nation has matched that performance with others equally incredible. In 1967, facing economic strangulation and hostile forces mobilized on three fronts, the Israeli Army and Air Force attacked. On June 5, 1967, Israel detached 200 jets against the Egyptian Air Force, the largest in the Middle East with 370 interceptors, fighters, and bombers. On the first day of battle the Israelis destroyed 200 Egyptian jets, plus thirty-two transports and helicopters, while losing only nineteen of its own aircraft to ground fire. Not one Israeli plane was shot down by an Egyptian jet. The same day, June 5, the Israelis wiped out Jordan's Royal Air Force and destroyed two thirds of the Syrian Air Force. In all, they destroyed 300 Arab planes that day while losing 20 of their own. The next day, they took out Iraq's Air Force, too.

On the ground, the Israeli Army then routed the Egyptian Army in four days, killing 15,000 Egyptian soldiers, compared with Israeli losses of 300 men. By June 10 the Six Day War was over. In all the Israelis suffered 3,200 killed and wounded; the Arabs lost 40,500. Israel won 67,000 square miles of land.

The Yom Kippur War broke out in 1973 and, among other things, produced the largest tank battle in world history—some 1,500 tanks fought in one Sinai confrontation. The lead brigade of the Egyptian

21st Armored Division lost 93 tanks; the Israeli brigade that faced it lost 3.

Ben-David said that Israel's military victories are only one aspect of the miraculous there. In a five-year period the little country relocated 600,000 Jews from the former Soviet Union. In thirty-six hours, during the midst of a war in Ethiopia, Israel managed to bring 16,000 Jews from that country to Israel. Within a few years, Israel increased its total population by 17 percent.

It's all the result of God's work on Israel's behalf, Ben-David said.

Miracles Among the Yogis

Paramahansa Yogananda, the Swami ascetic, published his *Autobiography of a Yogi* in 1946. It contains stories of miracles among Yogis during the first half of this century, of which one example will provide a flavor.

While a student pursuing a bachelor's degree at Serampore College, Yogananda and his roommate, Dijen Babu, after classes often visited the ashram of Yogananda's spiritual master, Sri Yukteswar. One day, Yukteswar was summoned to Calcutta on business. The next day Yogananda received a postcard from the guru asking him and Babu to meet Yukteswar at the train station the following Wednesday at 9 A.M.

At 8:30 A.M. Wednesday, Yogananda perceived a telepathic message from the Master saying he had been delayed and not to bother with the nine o'clock train after all. Yogananda passed on the message to Babu, who was irritated by Yogananda's reliance on what struck him as merely a hunch.

Babu insisted they go to the train station anyway, but Yogananda refused. Angry, Babu went on alone, leaving Yogananda sitting in their boardinghouse room. The room was dark, so Yogananda moved closer to a window. The sunlight streaming through the window began to glow intensely and the window's iron bars disappeared. Within the light appeared the complete body of Sri Yukteswar. Yogananda rose from his chair, dropped to the Master's feet, and touched his orange canvas shoes. Yukteswar's swami cloth brushed against the student.

The Master told Yogananda that he would arrive in Serampore on the 10 A.M. train. Then the guru said that what Yogananda was witnessing wasn't an apparition, but his actual, flesh-and-blood form. As a confirmation, Yukteswar said, he would be wearing these same clothes when Yogananda and Babu met him at the station. A little boy would exit the train in front of him, carrying a jug.

The Master blessed Yogananda. A roaring sound filled the room and then the guru's body melted away. Not long afterward, Babu entered, still flustered. Sri Yukteswar hadn't been on the nine o'clock train, Babu said.

Yogananda assured his friend that Yukteswar would arrive at 10 A.M. instead. Together, they departed for the train station. As they entered it, Yogananda recalled, he saw the station filled with the light of the guru's aura. The two roommates waited. Sri Yukteswar exited from the train, dressed exactly as he had been when Yogananda saw him in the window of his room. Before the Master walked a small boy carrying a silver jug. The power of the experience struck Yogananda with fear. His master merely smiled and greeted the two students in a friendly manner. He'd tried to send a message to Babu, too, he said good-naturedly, but Babu couldn't understand it.

An Explosion of Miracles Among Christians

Christianity, more so than any other faith, has seen a multiplication of reported miracles. Taken in its totality worldwide, this current explosion probably surpasses the church's first-century heyday of miracles, which followed the famous anointing of the Holy Spirit's power on the Jewish holiday of Pentecost more than 1,900 years ago.

This century has produced its own, three-pronged Pentecost. The first outpouring began in Southern California in the early 1900s and became the modern Pentecostal movement. The second wave also began in California, during the 1950s, and is known popularly as the charismatic renewal. The charismatic movement introduced Pentecostalism to millions of Episcopalians, Roman Catholics, Baptists, and Methodists, although those who embraced it frequently were asked by non-charismatics to leave their old congregations. Several scholars now have identified a "Third Wave" of the Spirit that they say is imbuing many more people within traditional, mainline churches with wonder-working power, people who would never describe themselves as Pentecostals or charismatics. Whatever name you give this ninety-year-old revival of the miraculous, scholars of all theological bents agree on one thing: it is, as scholar Cecil M. Robeck Jr. has said, "the biggest thing that has hit the church since the Reformation," four hundred years ago.

A One-Eyed Preacher Who Changed Christianity

Half-blinded by boyhood smallpox, one-eyed W. J. Seymour grew up to be a man desperate for God's presence. He longed to be filled with the kind of spiritual power he'd read about in the New Testament, rather than live out his days with the nominal Christianity practiced by most Christians.

While residing in Houston early in this century, Seymour happened to attend a church service where a woman named Lucy Farrow prayed in a language he'd never heard. He took that to be the supernatural gift of speaking in tongues that is mentioned in the Bible in the Acts of the Apostles, I Corinthians 12, and elsewhere, a gift Seymour equated with the powerful biblical experience called being filled with, or baptized in, the Holy Spirit. Soon Farrow introduced the eager Seymour to a preacher named Charles Fox Parham, for whom Farrow had worked as a governess; Parham had led Farrow to her spiritual gift. The renewed presence of supernatural power to which Seymour aspired initially had broken loose during the winter of 1900–1901 at Parham's former Bible school in Topeka, Kansas.

It was an odd mix all around. Seymour was black; Parham not only was white but sympathetic to the Ku Klux Klan. When Seymour asked to attend Parham's new school in Houston, Parham declined to enroll him. Instead, Parham told Seymour he could sit outside the classes, beneath a window or in the doorway, and listen to the lectures if he wished. Seymour agreed.

In this uncomfortable way he learned quite a bit about the Holy Spirit, but couldn't receive what he wanted most—that powerful Spirit-baptism and the gift of speaking supernaturally in tongues he hadn't studied. Soon he met another Christian woman, who told him about a little Holiness group that was meeting in California. It was led by a Sister Julia W. Hutchins; the people of her flock had been thrown out of their Baptist church because they, like Seymour, wanted the baptism in the Holy Spirit.

Seymour borrowed the train fare to Los Angeles and soon began preaching in Hutchins's storefront church. After a dispute, Hutchins locked Seymour out of the building. Persistent, Seymour started his own tiny church. It met in the house of janitor Edward Lee, where Seymour was staying, and then in a house at 216 North Bonnie Brae Street.

On April 9, 1906, as they prepared to attend a Bible study, Lee told Seymour of a vision he'd received. The apostles from the New Testament had come to him and shown him how to reclaim the ancient gift of tongues. That night at the meeting in the house on North Bonnie Brae, Seymour prayed for Lee—and Lee immediately started speaking in a language no one recognized. Soon seven members of the house-church, including Seymour, had been baptized in the Holy Spirit. They all began to shout and to speak in unknown languages, and they drew a crowd.

By the next morning the home was packed. Neighbors walked in the door to see what was happening—and found themselves knocked to the floor by God's power, one participant wrote later. Sick people were healed. Sinners repented. The revival kept going. The group's fervor and the size of the crowd soon were so great that the house's porch collapsed.

No one was hurt, but the meeting had to be moved to 312 Azusa Street, a white, wooden building that previously had been a Methodist chapel and a stable. It was near a tombstone shop. The meetings there lasted three years, day and night. A thousand people often packed inside the modest building, with as many as fifteen hundred standing outside. Between 1906 and 1907 Los Angeles newspapers printed nearly four hundred stories about the revival, many of which made fun of it and labeled Seymour and the other worshipers as fanatics.

It's true that this famous Azusa Street revival was not the first Pentecostal outbreak. Parham's Bible school probably claims that distinction. But the Azusa Street meetings marked a turning point in modern Christianity. At a time when the races rarely mixed and women weren't allowed even to speak in some churches, the Azusa Street revival was led by Seymour, a black man, who soon presided over many whites, including white preachers from the South who traveled to California. Hispanics took an active part, too. Women and even children preached. Rich and poor met under the same roof. Word of the meeting spread. Similar revivals erupted in Canada, England, Scandinavia, Germany, India, China, Africa, and South America.

Sadly, the Azusa Street revival itself died out when racism crept back in. White Christians broke off to form their own churches. Still, Azusa Street served as the beginning of a major revitalization of Christianity. It helped open doors all over the world to the exercise of many kinds of miracles, not just speaking in tongues. For five decades, however, the Pentecostalism that began there largely was confined to working-class and poor congregations. It was disregarded by more "respectable" groups.

Pentecostalism Goes Upscale

A mighty transformation of Pentecostalism began in the 1950s. In 1951, healing evangelist Oral Roberts urged a rich California dairy owner named Demos Shakarian to start a group that might reach other affluent laymen with the Pentecostal message. Shakarian agreed and founded the Full Gospel Business Men's Fellowship International, which grew into a major success. It introduced the miracle-rich revival of the Holy Spirit to thousands of middle-class members of mainstream churches. The FGBMFI, as it is called, soon was holding breakfast and dinner meetings in hotel banquet rooms in virtually every town in America.

The FGBMFI was just one means by which Pentecostalism was

spreading. The renewal made some notable converts through other means during the 1950s. One was a Yale Law School graduate named Pat Robertson. While attending an evangelical seminary in New York City, Robertson, a Baptist, began praying with influential neo-Pentecostals such as Harald Bredesen. Like Seymour fifty years earlier, Robertson started longing for the powerful Holy Spirit baptism.

In his autobiography *Shout It from the Housetops*, Robertson recalls that he searched for this spiritual fulfillment for many months, often to the neglect of his family and the dismay of his wife. One night his young son, Tim, fell ill with a fever that shot up to 105 degrees. The child became unconscious. His muscles contracted spasmodically. Robertson and his wife, Dede, were terrified.

Robertson, feeling a tremendous guilt for having spent so little time with his family, instinctively laid his hands on the child's burning head and prayed. A power surged into Tim, and Robertson himself was overshadowed with an awareness of God's presence and love. Tim opened his eyes and told his father that he needed to use the bathroom. When the child returned, beads of perspiration had popped out on his face; the fever had broken. Robertson, relieved, began to weep and to thank God aloud. Within a moment he found his speech garbled. His words had shifted into a new language. It was, he writes as if some deep, primal part of him had been given its own voice. Robertson, the son of a U.S. senator, had become a Pentecostal—or, as upscale converts preferred to call themselves, a charismatic.

The migration of Pentecostalism into the historic Protestant churches remained mostly underground until 1960, when an Episcopal priest, Dennis J. Bennett, rector of the staid, upscale St. Mark's Episcopal Church in Van Nuys, California, announced that he had been filled with the Holy Spirit and had witnessed miraculous manifestations of God's power. Some among his congregation were pleased and latched onto Pentecostalism, too. Others were outraged. Bennett's public stand touched off a firestorm that drew national coverage from television, newspapers, and news magazines. Soon Bennett left for a smaller congregation in northern California. The publicity from his experience had set a trend, though. In virtually every denomination, small groups of ministers and lay people sought and then experienced this infusion of spiritual power. For instance, a Gallup poll of United Methodists taken in the late 1970s, less than two decades after Bennett's Pentecostal declaration in the Episcopal Church, found that 1.7 million Methodists, or 18 percent of the denomination, described themselves as charismatics.

Everywhere, this outbreak was met by a mix of joy, skepticism, and hostility. The charismatic movement in mainstream congregations touched nearly every local church, but many mainline Christians didn't accept it as legitimate. Charismatics, then, sometimes left to form independent congregations. Others remained in their old churches on Sundays and attended Pentecostal meetings during the week.

In the late 1960s, the renewal hit the nation's largest denomination, the Roman Catholic Church, when a group of Duquesne University students and faculty members received the baptism in the Holy Spirit. A quarter-century later, some 10 million U.S. Catholic—nearly one Catholic in every five—had taken part in the movement, which by then had been blessed by two popes.

This second wave of Pentecostalism also exploded in other countries, where stories of its power outstripped even the manifestations taking place in the United States. One of the most famous revivals started on the tiny Indonesian island of Timor four nights before an unsuccessful Communist coup. A Timorese Presbyterian named Mel Tari became that revival's best-known spokesman through his book *Like a Mighty Wind*. Tari writes that, on September 26, 1965, two hundred Indonesian Christians were gathered in a church praying when a rushing wind roared through the building, just as it had in the biblical book of Acts when the earliest Christians were filled with the Holy Spirit. Tari, who was present, says the village's fire bell rang after a man at the police station saw flames whipping from the church building. But the flames weren't destructive. They were the flames of the Holy Spirit's supernatural presence. A woman standing near Tari, who could speak only Timorese, began to pray fluently in English, a language Tari recognized from his school days.

The revival spread quickly and multiplied church membership on

Timor and then throughout the region. By Tari's account, extraordinary miracles became commonplace. In *Like a Mighty Wind*, he tells of a whole mission team fording a flooded, thirty-foot-deep river—by walking across the water's surface.

He says he helped preside at a funeral in Amfoang, where the dead man had passed away two days earlier. The body had begun to stink terribly in the tropical heat. The assembled Christians sang some hymns, Tari writes. By the time they got to their eighth song, the dead man woke up, looked around, smiled, and announced that Jesus had brought him back to life. As word of the resurrection spread, the Christians made twenty-one thousand converts in the Amfoang area.

After Tari's book and other spectacular tales surfaced, a careful Christian thinker named George W. Peters decided to investigate. In a meticulous little book, *Indonesia Revival: Focus on Timor*, Peters later cast doubts on many of the reports of miracles. When he tried to measure the river that the missionaries supposedly had walked across, for instance, Peters found conflicting stories among the locals about which river had been crossed, and where along the river. Then he measured the most likely site, and discovered it was neither as wide nor as deep as had been reported. Peters concluded that leaders of the revival had focused far too much on miraculous manifestations and had exaggerated some events in an effort to outdo one another. At the same time, he also found that some of the stories—particularly some physical healings—appeared to be well documented and true, a conclusion rendered meaningful by the care and seeming reluctance with which he reached it.

The Swelling of a "Third Wave"

The charismatic revival engineered a revolution in the worship styles of historic Protestant and Catholic churches. Millions of mainline, noncharismatic Christians soon were singing modern pop-style choruses during church services, a practice they borrowed from charismatics. The lifting of hands in praise, another charismatic trait, became commonplace in Baptist, Methodist, and Catholic congregations.

On the other hand, such Pentecostal practices as prophesying and "falling in the Spirit" continued for decades to be met with disdain. In the last few years, though, scholars such as C. Peter Wagner at Fuller Theological Seminary in California—an evangelical, non-Pentecostal school that is among the world's largest seminaries—have identified what Wagner calls a "Third Wave" of the miraculous Holy Spirit movement that is reaching deeply into denominations that previously rejected it. This wave is made up of mainline Christians who would decline to describe themselves as either charismatics or Pentecostals and yet have embraced everything from exorcism to prophecy to speaking in tongues. As a measure of the Third Wave, consider this: one academic article reports that in England, more Anglicans (68 percent) and Baptists (82 percent) say they have experienced such "gifts of the Spirit" as healing and supernatural knowledge than do Pentecostals (25 percent).

"That's kind of where I would put myself," said Steve Seamands, a United Methodist minister who teaches Christian doctrine at a mainline Protestant seminary. Miracles weren't part of his upbringing, Seamands told me, but in the last few years he's come to believe that God genuinely is performing wondrous works of power today. He laid hands on a friend who was dying in a coronary care unit. The man recovered against all medical odds. "But my style's different" from Pentecostals', Seamands said. He doesn't shout when he prays for people, for example: "I don't think God has a problem hearing."

A man named John Wimber served as Seamands's introduction to miraculous power. Wimber used to teach at Fuller Seminary and was quite skeptical of "faith healers" until about 1976, when he underwent a dramatic change of mind. He founded the Vineyard church movement, which has grown to include some six hundred churches that regularly practice the miraculous gifts.

Far and away the Vineyard movement's most incredible outpouring began at Toronto's Airport Vineyard church in early 1994. A spontaneous revival erupted there, spread across the Western Hemisphere into churches of all stripes, and continues today. It has drawn thousands of visitors to the original site, so many that *Toronto Life* magazine labeled the "Toronto Blessing" as Toronto's Number 1 tourist attraction of 1994. The "blessing" continues to be cited regularly in mainstream religious publications such as *Christianity Today,* which, in September 1995, described people at the Toronto Vineyard as having experienced such manifestations as "holy laughter, shaking, animal noises, and falling down, to name a few," as well as the appearance of angels who helped cure dyslexic children. "Others have testified that they have been healed of pain, headaches, long-term infertility, and severe emotional disorders." (In an odd twist, Wimber recently dismissed the Toronto Vineyard church from the Vineyard fellowship, essentially for letting its manifestations get out of hand.)

Seamands encountered Wimber, and subsequently the Vineyard movement, even before the Toronto revival started. Like many Third Wavers, Seamands had felt unfulfilled in his denominational ministry. "I began to get kind of hungry and thirsty for more," he said. Friends invited him to a 1990 conference in Michigan, where Wimber was among those who preached. At the close of his sermon Wimber issued an invitation for people to walk forward for prayer. Seamands stayed in his seat. He began to pray instead that God would heal hurt feelings among the faculty members at the seminary where he works.

"The next thing I knew, I was crying," Seamands said. "I don't usually do that." Then he began to groan and sob so loudly that people could hear him all over the gymnasium where the meeting was taking place. His stomach wretched as if he had the dry heaves. "I'd never had anything like that happen to me."

Two nights later, he did go forward for prayer. "Ever since then my life's been different," he said. "It's been an incredible adventure."

CHAPTER FOUR

ARGUMENTS AGAINST
MIRACLES

MOST OF US KNOW people who don't accept the miraculous at all, who continue to view miracles as the domain of the untutored, the gullible, and the dishonest. Some of these skeptics are our friends and next-door neighbors. Others sit in positions of authority and erudition, as professors, physicians, scientists, and even ministers. You have been influenced by their ideas, and so have I.

Among the more visible critics of the miraculous is James Randi, a professional conjurer, or magician, whose stage name is "The Amazing Randi." He's a longtime investigator of claims of the paranormal and in 1986 won a prestigious "genius grant," a MacArthur Foundation fellowship, for his work. He is a founder of CSICOP, an acronym for the Committee for the Scientific Investigation of Claims of the Paranormal. Randi's innovative work has been praised by scientist Carl Sagan, among others.

Randi has described himself as an angry man. What makes him the angriest, it seems, are claims of the supernatural, especially when they're propagated by psychics or television preachers such as W.V. Grant or Pat Robertson. You probably know who Robertson is. You might not remember Grant, because his audience always was more limited than Robertson's and in recent years, thanks partly to Randi and other investigators, Grant seems to have become even less prominent than before. Grant operated in the realm of faith healing, but also in spectacular "words of knowledge," in which he would stride through his audience, point to individual audience members he'd supposedly never met, ask them to stand up, and then tell them the details of their illnesses or their heartaches as clearly as if he'd been reading their mail. Frequently he knew the names of their loved ones or doctors.

Randi and several of his CSICOP associates went to great lengths to expose what they saw as deception in Grant's gifts, even digging through his garbage. In his book *The Faith Healers*, Randi exposes Grant's alleged methods. The words of knowledge, Randi argues, operated like this. Before each of Grant's worship services, Grant's wife and other members of his entourage would infiltrate the crowd and strike up conversations with people entering the auditorium. These plants from Grant's staff nonchalantly would inquire about the problems that audience members were facing.

Grant then would be supplied with crib sheets from these interviews, which he'd place in his Bible on the stage's podium to prod his memory. While ministering, Grant suddenly would seem to receive messages from God, then would call out audience members by name and tell them about their private ills. "He was relatively good at it," Randi said. After a Fort Lauderdale, Florida, meeting, Randi supposedly found one of the crib sheets in a Dumpster. He reprinted it in *The Faith Healers*. Grant, by the way, has disputed most of this.

Randi, who lives in Florida, told me he attributes the growing number of people who believe in the miraculous to the pervasiveness of such TV ministers, as well as TV psychics: "It's the availability of the media to the broadcasters." Preachers on television can reach audiences hundreds of times larger than they could ever hope to find when they were confined to tent meetings, he said. And many people want to believe the hucksters' illogical messages, he said: "They're looking for magic. They've always been gullible." Psychics and preachers infuriate Randi because, to him, they profit by taking advantage of human frailties.

I pointed out that some of the people I've interviewed who believe staunchly in supernatural healing are themselves physicians and others with extensive scientific training. That didn't impress Randi in the least. Postgraduate degrees in the sciences don't make people smart, he replied. Scientific training only makes them *educated*. They don't leave their universities with a guarantee they can actually use their learning toward logical ends.

It's not necessarily easy being a professional skeptic. There's no way of telling how many converts to skepticism Randi has made, if any. In some places—including Washington, D.C., he said—Randi's books receive short shrift from librarians, who are loathe to place them on public shelves. (In the Bible Belt city of Lexington, Kentucky, by the way, I easily found Randi's books. At the public library a couple of his titles were checked out the day I visited. The Lexington Theological Seminary library, no less, had several of his volumes on the shelves, available but not being used at that moment.)

Randi offered an analogy that he said explained his motives: He's standing on a street corner when he sees a person knocked head over heels by a hit-and-run driver. It's his duty as a human being to dash into the traffic, try to drag the injured person out of the busy street, and call for medical help. If the victim refuses Randi's aid? Well, there's not much he can do but try, he said. But clearly Randi sees himself as a rescuer. As a professional illusionist, he said, "I have specialized knowledge."

I asked Randi whether he'd ever seen anything he considered a genuine miracle. He grunted dismissively. No, he said, and he's never seen Santa Claus or the Tooth Fairy, either. Miracles by definition, he said, would be events with no logical explanations, and everything—everything—has an explanation.

"I'm a realist," he said. "I face facts as they are."

The Enlightenment

As a "realist" who sees himself as merely measuring claims of the supernatural against empirical data, Randi is a classic child of the Enlightenment. A brief history lesson is helpful here, perhaps, because until we look at the Enlightenment it's difficult to understand why some of us who were raised in Western society find it so difficult to accept miracles.

The Enlightenment was a scientific and philosophical movement that rose to prominence in the 1700s in Europe. It has remained the West's predominant intellectual paradigm ever since. Before the Enlightenment, most people—including theologians, physicians, and scientists—assumed the universe to be governed largely by unseen, supernatural forces. Angels, devils, and ghosts lived alongside human beings and, in some cases, competed for their souls. Illnesses might be caused by demonic curses, or else by God's judgment against sins a sick person had committed. As religion scholar Robert J. Miller said to me, Jesus' ancient enemies included men of enormous learning, but they never asked whether Jesus actually had healed a sick person or exorcised a devil, as we would today; their questions centered on whether Jesus had performed his phenomenal acts by Satan's power or God's. For obvious reasons, in the pre-Enlightenment world, priests, magicians, and shamans, those whose professions enabled them to discern and placate the spirits, enjoyed a tremendous political power that they sometimes abused.

The Enlightenment began as a much-needed intellectual revolution against the excesses of that system. It claimed many luminaries, including Denis Diderot, Voltaire, and Sir Isaac Newton. The guiding principle of the movement was that human reason, not superstition, should serve as the basis of authority.

The leaders of the Enlightenment valued scientific experiments and documentation, rather than uncritical obedience to any principle perceived to be divine law. For them, truth could be demonstrated empirically; that which couldn't be proven by logic or science automatically became suspect. The Enlightenment's leaders promoted tolerance for others' ideas instead of religious dogmatism. They asserted individual rights over the authority of the Church. Generally, they lampooned supernaturalism and assumed that the spiritual realm was an illusion. For them the material world accounted for all reality. Some leading figures in the Enlightenment were broad-thinking Christians; some became deists, believing in a distant "clockmaker" God who had created the universe then left it to run according to natural laws; and some were atheists. Many assumed that organized religion held people hostage to a false awareness of sin, and that humans could be elevated morally through education, apart from the church or synagogue.

The Enlightenment became trendy among the upper middle class and the intelligentsia. It spread across Europe and into the American colonies among progressives such as Thomas Jefferson. The American

Revolution stemmed in part from this new way of thinking, in that the Enlightenment tended to deny the "divine rights" given earthly monarchs. Most of the marvelous breakthroughs of contemporary medicine have resulted from the dispassionate, double-blind, scientific tests that grew from Enlightenment thinking.

Over the past two centuries, the assumptions of the Enlightenment have seeped into every nook and cranny of Western thought. As children, we are taught that only ignorant people believe in ghosts—because ghosts can't be seen or measured by scientific instruments. When as adults we get sick, our physicians assure us that the cause is a bacterium or a virus, not an evil spirit, and they prescribe antibiotics, not exorcisms. When a visionary announces she's talked with the Virgin Mary, psychiatrists speculate that the vision resulted from a chemical imbalance, wishful thinking, or a psychosis—but certainly was not due to an actual visitation from the other side.

A Doorway to Heaven—or Cheap Cameras?

The Amazing Randi and I share a mutual acquaintance who, like Randi, spends much of his life providing materialistic explanations for supposedly supernatural phenomena. His name is Joe Nickell. He's a lean, friendly man. His brown hair is thinning and he sports a narrow mustache. Philosophically they're poles apart, but Joe always has reminded me a bit in appearance and demeanor of conservative newspaper columnist Cal Thomas.

Nickell and I met in the early 1980s when we were graduate students pursuing degrees in English literature in the same university department. I ended my literary studies after receiving an M.A. and then transferred to a graduate program in communications. Joe earned a Ph.D. in English.

He's a fascinating guy: a former private eye and, like Randi, a former stage magician. Now he works for the Committee for the Scientific Investigation of Claims of the Paranormal in Buffalo, New York. "We investigate milk-drinking statues from India," Nickell told me in the self-amused tone he adopts when speaking about the supernatural.

Joe's made a name for himself as a professional skeptic, a term he insists upon as opposed to debunker. "I investigate claims," he said. "I don't have to resort to debunking." He's appeared widely on the national talk shows of Larry King, Sally Jessy Raphael, and others. He's published about fifteen books—and lost money on them all, he moans: "Skeptical books do not sell widely."

Like Randi, Joe tends to compare accounts of modern-day miracles with the appearances of popular mythical characters. Randi conjures up the Tooth Fairy; Nickell compares miracles with sightings of extraterrestrial aliens or the late Elvis Presley. Of course, there's one vital difference. The number of people who claim to have seen Elvis since his 1977 death is infinitesimal, and they mostly seem—as much as one can judge by watching them on tabloid TV shows—to be pinheads or publicity hounds. But millions of people say they've experienced miracles. The majority of them, or at least the majority of the ones I've met, appear to be fairly normal and to possess few ulterior motives.

Anyway, Nickell acknowledges that it's impossible to disprove all accounts of miracles, but he says that's not his job because he's not the person making the claims. The burden of proof, he said, always should rest upon the one who says that he or she has been touched by God.

We ran into each other several years ago in Cold Spring, Kentucky, a bedroom suburb of Cincinnati. A Roman Catholic visionary had announced that the Virgin Mary would appear at a church there, and seven thousand people, including dozens of journalists like me, had turned out for the event. Nickell clearly was in his element. All day long the church's parking lot had been filled with devout people, many of whom travel widely to attend these increasingly common apparitions. "Mary groupies" is what one wag among the reporters called them.

Some of the Marian followers liked to take photographs of the sun with those inexpensive cameras that develop pictures in sixty seconds. As I wandered among the crowd that day with my notebook and tape recorder, several folks eagerly showed me the images on those prints. The photographs appeared to show a clearly visible "door" in or near the sun. The Marian faithful told me this was the doorway to heaven, a sign of the Blessed Virgin's presence.

When I mentioned this to Nickell, he was amused. He assured me he could produce precisely the same effect by pointing a cheap camera at any bright light. The image wasn't the mythical golden door to heaven, he said. It was a reflection of the camera's aperture. Later, in his 1993 book *Looking for a Miracle: Weeping Icons, Relics, Stigmata, Visions & Healing Cures*, Nickell did just that: he created a "doorway to heaven" by aiming a Polaroid camera at a fifty-watt halogen lamp.

Among his best-known works is his investigation of the evidence surrounding the Shroud of Turin, the burial cloth said to have contained the body of Jesus. The fourteen-foot linen cloth bears the image, supposedly, of Jesus' bloody body, an image some had believed was burned into the cloth by the flash of power at the resurrection. Nickell wrote about his investigation in *Inquest on the Shroud of Turin* and again, briefly, in *Looking for a Miracle*.

He noted numerous inconsistencies in the cloth. For instance, the images of the body were flawed. The imprint of one leg showed it to be outstretched, and yet the shroud also contained a sole-print of the foot; to produce that print the leg would by necessity have been bent at the knee. Also, the imprint of Jesus' long hair was straight down toward his shoulders, as if he were standing instead of lying in a crypt. Roman Catholic scholars sympathetic to the shroud had themselves admitted to finding pigments of red ocher paint on it, indicating that the image could be an artist's forgery, Nickell said. Carbon-14 tests agreed that the shroud apparently dated to sometime between 1260 and 1390. Nickell and others concluded that it was the work of a medieval artist, not a miraculous relic of the Christ's resurrection.

The evidence for many other miracles is far shoddier, he told me. In cases where people claim to have been divinely healed, Nickell said, frequently the only source for the claim is the person who supposedly was cured, rather than, say, eyewitnesses and medical records. Just as often, there's not even that first-person testimony; the stories are told second- or third-hand. Time and time again, he said, the claims fall apart under tough scrutiny.

In addition, some sicknesses are emotional in origin. A person suffering from one of those ailments who receives prayer from a healer might indeed feel better afterward; that is, if she assumes the prayer will make her feel better, the power of suggestion probably will cause it to be so. "One wishes people well," Nickell said. Still, similar cures are common to every religion and to secular people, too, he said, and so are sudden changes in climate and near-accidents in heavy freeway traffic, which people also attribute to the hand of God. Some things just happen. "That's not proof it was a miracle." He said he wouldn't define miracles so loosely even if he believed in them.

"Clearly people are looking for some sort of personal dramatic involvement" with God, Nickell told me. "People are looking for sensations. Unfortunately, it's really an invitation for charlatans—or for delusion."

He doesn't doubt that many who claim to have experienced miracles are sincere. But they also are misled. We live in a land woefully undereducated in scientific methods, he thinks: "Science probably has outdistanced the population." Computers, satellites, and theoretical physics have progressed to a point that the general public no longer remotely understands them. At the same time, "There's this feeling that science and technology don't answer everything." That is, the science people do more or less understand appears to be a mixed bag. Some of the same scientific inventions designed to make our lives easier or protect us from foreign threats—such as military nerve gas—also created toxic pollution that has become a danger in itself.

So the supernatural, Nickell thinks, offers people a hopeful message they long to hear. "The message is, when you die, you don't die," he said. "You live on. All the paranormal offers something transcendent and wonderful that science does not offer."

What science does offer, Nickell said, is the truth. Science is empirical, testable, revisable. Unlike religion, it doesn't make claims it can't back up. Science, he said, promotes agreement among diverse people by demonstrating through well-defined, replicable steps what's correct and what isn't. Religion separates people with its "magical" dogmas. "People who engage in magical thinking are constantly pulling their guns out," Nickell said. "Or their Bibles."

Faith and the Enlightenment

Of course, there are varying degrees of skepticism. Not all skeptics dismiss every claim of divine intervention. Within organized religion, the Enlightenment has created serious tensions between belief in a supernatural God and reliance on rational materialism and human logic. Many religious scholars have struck a middle position that admits miracles are possible, but holds that they aren't likely. These thinkers usually find naturalistic explanations for most supposedly supernatural events, and in that regard aren't so different from Randi or Nickell except that they perform their work within the framework of a religious faith and sometimes for religious institutions such as seminaries.

Most of modern Judaism, for instance, that most intellectual of faiths, seems to hold little enthusiasm for supernatural events. One branch, Reform Judaism, arose during the early 1800s as an accommodation to the Enlightenment, in an effort to make Judaism more relevant to the modern world.

Jewish scholar David S. Ariel writes in his book *What Do Jews Believe? The Spiritual Foundations of Judaism* that Jewish thinking about miracles has evolved through the centuries. In the rabbinical tradition, Ariel says, God is portrayed as a caring parent. When children are small, parents frequently intervene in their arguments and act mightily to rescue them, because the children are unable to protect themselves. As children grow, parents who want their offspring to achieve self-respect and maturity must withdraw from the children's lives. Similarly, God may have acted miraculously among the Jews during their spiritual infancy. Today, Judaism has evolved beyond a need for miracles, even if they do exist. A miracle would violate the normal relationship between God and humans, and throw the relationship out of balance, because Jews have become accustomed to God acting indirectly. God leaves events to unfold according to the rules of science, the actions of people, and the tenets of Jewish law.

Even the ancient miracles reported in the scriptures are a subject of significant debate among Jews, said Tsion Ben-David, the Israeli who is an expert on Jewish and Christian history. Ben-David said that many

Jews would deny that the biblical accounts represent an active intervention by God. Instead, the stories are seen to contain an element of truth—but the events as recorded mainly are thought to have resulted from natural laws or from the prophets' superior human intelligence.

There's a story in the Hebrew Bible about the prophet Elijah, who found himself in a life-and-death competition with the prophets of the idol Baal over whose god was more powerful. The prophets of Baal built an altar to their god and Elijah built one to the Hebrew God. Then each side beseeched its respective deity to rain down fire from heaven and ignite its altar. Elijah was so certain that his God would oblige that he even asked his servants to douse his altar with water. As the Bible tells the tale, the altar of Baal didn't burn. Elijah's altar was consumed by smoke and fire. One modern interpretation of that story, Ben-David said, stems from the location of the contest. It was held on Mount Carmel, a mountain filled with carbonate rocks. If you pour water on those particular rocks, they tend to billow smoke, Ben-David said. Those who take a more modernistic view, then, argue that Elijah simply was smarter than the prophets of Baal. He understood the tendency of certain rocks to smoke when wet and outwitted his opponents.

Traditionalists, of course, would say that God intervened on Elijah's behalf, to save his neck and establish the Jewish God as the true deity.

"I'm a believer," Ben-David said. "I combine both of them together." Ben-David, like many modernistic Jews, thinks, Elijah did understand how water would affect those rocks. But it was God's favor that enabled Elijah to become so smart in the first place: "I say it was a miracle because God is taking care of us."

Psychological "Miracles"?

Within Christianity, too, and especially among the more progressive mainline denominations, a great many scholars have adopted rational materialism's explanations for what their forebears identified as miracles. One such group that has garnered much publicity is the Jesus Seminar, an interdenominational organization of more than fifty professors from colleges, universities, and seminaries throughout the United States and Canada. Members of the Jesus Seminar are trying to determine—using the techniques of critical scholarship—how much of the New Testament's accounts of Jesus' life and teachings is factual and how much is hyperbole, legend, and religious propaganda. They have cast doubts on much of what the Bible tells us, and even have suggested adding a fifth gospel to the canon, the Gospel of Thomas.

I talked with Robert J. Miller about the New Testament's accounts of Jesus' miracles. Miller, a Roman Catholic layman and a professor of religion, was editor of a Jesus Seminar volume called *The Complete Gospels*. He's a man who dresses in plain clothes and wears his hair in a ponytail.

"Christian scriptures rely very heavily on miracles to tell the story of Jesus," Miller said one sunny afternoon. We sat at his battered desk in a modest office located in an old building at Midway College, a women's school in the heart of Kentucky's thoroughbred horse country. "The New Testament is chocked full of that kind of stuff. That's not unique to the Christian religion."

But in Jesus' day, the natural world as we know it wasn't understood, Miller said. In our time, scientific breakthroughs have made many people skeptical about supposedly supernatural acts, he said, and rightly so. Science simply wasn't a barrier to belief two thousand years ago. Consequently, Jesus' Mediterranean world was full of faith healers, exorcists, and wonder-workers of all types. Again, the question in Jesus' day wasn't whether a supernatural act was really supernatural, but whether it was wrought by a good or a bad power.

Miller and others with similar views ask the opposite question today. They don't seem so much interested in whether a miracle proved to be good or bad. They are more interested in whether it was supernatural. Miller, echoing the modern Jews who believe that Elijah understood the properties of carbonate rocks, doesn't doubt that Jesus performed many of the mighty acts attributed to him. Ancient Christian and pagan texts alike are filled with testimonials to signs and wonders by holy men and women. In those cases, something noteworthy probably did occur, Miller said.

"Faith healing is real," Miller said. "It really does happen." The body and the mind work together, he said. Healing through prayer or the laying on of hands, then, "is the norm for medicine for human beings." Western society has been unique in denying that: "There's no good reason to be skeptical that Jesus actually sent people away after they'd met him, healed."

But here's the rub. Traditional religious leaders, and the writers of the gospels, attributed Jesus' powers to his divinity and to the supernatural presence of the Holy Spirit. Modern scholars tend to argue that Jesus' cures primarily were psychological and social, not supernatural. Two academic papers presented to a 1993 Jesus Seminar meeting in Sonoma, California, detail that point of view. One was written by John J. Rousseau of the University of California at Berkeley and the other by Steven Davies of College Misericordia in Pennsylvania. Rousseau's paper notes that Jesus employed curative methods frequently used by ancient magicians, such as rubbing spittle on an afflicted area of the body. Rousseau does note that Jesus seemed to successfully minister to ailments that other faith healers typically couldn't cure. To that extent, he might have ranked a notch above the run-of-the-mill wonderworker.

Davies's paper, "Whom Jesus Healed and How," argues that the central word in faith healer is "faith." That is, he says, contemporary medical experts speculate that 50 to 70 percent of all the illnesses for which people seek out doctors are psychosomatic. Faith healers, Davies says, are documentably effective at curing such diseases, especially ills that are known to often result from social disapproval or isolation, including deafness, blindness, paralysis, excessive menstrual bleeding, and dermatitis, the latter of which often was misdiagnosed in ancient times as leprosy. These ailments, Davies says, are the ones Jesus most frequently is recorded as having healed.

Davies's argument is that many of Jesus' patients were marginal people who had been stigmatized by their families or by society. Either a cause or a result of their isolation, depending upon the individual, was that these people suffered from psychosomatic afflictions such as dermatitis or excessive menstrual bleeding that led to their being considered sinners; these diseases were viewed as punishments from God. Jesus offered these outcasts forgiveness, acceptance, and a positive attitude of faith that helped soothe their minds, which in turn caused their physical conditions to improve. The results were dramatic, yet hardly required supernatural intervention.

Miller, like Ben-David, does see the larger hand of God at work in all this. Jesus seemed to possess a unique insight into human nature and the ability to tap into the curative powers of faith that reside in every person, Miller said. That, in a manner of speaking, was a miracle in itself.

Still, he downplays the specific supernatural aspect of Jesus' works. He doesn't think that Jesus performed some of the more spectacular acts recorded of him, the ones that would have required him to supersede the natural laws by which we all live. He doesn't believe that Jesus halted storms or walked on water. Those stories, he thinks, are the results of Christian myth-making. "It's possible I could walk on water," Miller said. "I don't think I can."

The Miraculous Dispensations

Miller and most members of the Jesus Seminar are theological liberals. Some theological conservatives accept the Bible's miracles as factual but are as akeptical as the liberals about modern-day wonders. Millions of grassroots evangelicals subscribe to a theological system called "dispensationalism." It argues that miracles largely ceased in the first century.

Dispensationalism began as an attempt in the 1800s by a Plymouth Brethren preacher named John Nelson Darby and, later, by a minister named Cyrus I. Scofield, to explain the future apocalyptic return of Christ to earth. Darby and Scofield held that God has divided history into several spiritual epochs, or dispensations, each of which heralds a key theological revelation.

The Reverend Walter K. Price, a Southern Baptist minister, has written eight books published by conservative Christian publishing houses such as Moody Press, Zondervan, and Broadman. Most of his books, such as *The Coming Antichrist* and *The Prophet Joel and the Day of the Lord*, deal with biblical prophecy surrounding Jesus' Second Coming. In an interview, he told me that wholesale miracles are ordained by God only when the Almighty introduces a new dispensation—and such dispensations are inaugurated only every few hundred or few thousand years. "Miracles come in cycles," he said.

When God led the Jews out of bondage in ancient Egypt, God was bent on revealing his divine Law and establishing an independent Jewish nation. To meet those goals, God smashed the Egyptians with a series of plagues, parted the Red Sea, fed the Israelites with manna from heaven—and on and on. Then miracles died out. The next epoch arrived hundreds of years later with the age of the great Old Testament prophets such as Elijah and his successor, Elisha. Again, God performed incredible acts, such as calling down fire from heaven. Again, miracles soon faded away.

The third dispensation began with the ministry of Jesus and his immediate disciples, whom Price calls "the Apostles with a capital 'A,'" men such as Peter, John, James, and Paul. They raised the dead, healed the sick, and cast out demons regularly, if the New Testament accounts are to be believed. God ordained these wonders, Price said, to kick off the dispensation that introduced Christianity to the world. The early Church founders exercised miracles at will, he said: "The gift of healing in the New Testament was the ability to heal anybody." Such "sign gifts" passed away after the first few decades of the Church, Price said. In one of his later epistles, Paul writes to Timothy, his friend and co-minister, that Timothy should drink a bit of wine as a treatment for his chronic poor health. "If Paul had the gift of healing, why didn't he exercise that gift?" Price said. "Particularly with Timothy, he couldn't do a thing with him except give him a little medical advice." In Price's view, the gift of healing already had begun to fade.

Miracles won't return on a large scale until the final epoch arrives, Price said: the period of tribulation dispensationalists think will precede the return of Jesus. Ours isn't that period.

It's complicated to talk about dispensationalism as a result of the Enlightenment, because if anything the movement has seen itself as a rebuke to modernism. Dispensationalists' arguments about miracles have, for them, rebutted the secularists and liberal theologians who have asked why, if the God of the Bible acted so powerfully and supernaturally, he doesn't part seas or raise the dead in the scientific age. The dispensationalists' response has been that this isn't one of God's dispensations for such miracles.

In the early 1900s, of course, Pentecostalism was born and its mostly conservative, mostly Protestant adherents began reporting mighty miracles worldwide. Ironically, dispensationalists ever since have found themselves in the uncomfortable position of denying the wonders reported by their fellow conservatives—in order to appear consistent, I suspect. Often they've dismissed contemporary Pentecostal miracles using precisely the same explanations as would their nemeses, liberals such as Miller or secularists such as Randi.

The phenomenon of speaking in tongues today, Price assured me, is a psychological manifestation, an ecstatic state that some people fall into when they allow their emotions to run away with them. Tongues-speaking has been documented among various groups, ranging from a pagan priestess at ancient Delphi to Mormons, Price said. "There's nothing specifically Christian about it." It isn't, he said, the supernatural gift that occurs in the New Testament.

CHAPTER FIVE

ARGUMENTS IN FAVOR
OF MIRACLES

IN A FASCINATING ESSAY that's part of a book called *The Kingdom and the Power*, psychiatrist John White pontificates on the supposedly supernatural manifestations reported during many of the great religious revivals, including mass weeping, divine visions, and being "slain in the spirit," an experience in which people spontaneously fall to the floor in a religious ecstasy.

Really, there are only four possible explanations for such experiences, White writes: they're psychologically based excesses in which troubled individuals act out their problems to call attention to themselves; they're produced by preachers through mass hypnosis and social suggestion; they're wrought by demonic forces bent on sidetracking people from the real message of God's love; or, else, they're acts of God.

White, a Christian, writes that his research and observations have led him to believe that some people do bring to revival meetings a need to seek attention through unorthodox behavior. But those people don't seem to make up the majority of worshipers affected by these "exercises." Certainly, mass brainwashing is a genuine phenomenon, he says, but can't account for the crowd's behavior in most revival meetings, because the standard catalysts necessary for brainwashing—physical exhaustion, a battering of the senses through incessant noise, control over people's ability to use rest rooms—simply aren't present. There are manifestations that White believes to be demonic, particularly in parts of the world where there's a widespread acceptance of witchcraft; there, the devil either tries to imitate what God is doing or to disrupt it, he says. Finally, White concludes that many of the exercises reported at revivals actually are works of God. The best test of which truly are performed by the Almighty, he says, is that when God acts supernaturally the results last for many years. The person affected doesn't necessarily continue to, let's say, fall on the floor, but is called to a lifetime of increased holiness.

What struck me as I read White's essay is that many psychiatrists, psychologists, historians, and sociologists wouldn't even have considered explanations three and four, the ideas that these revivalistic exercises might be provoked by demons or by God. And that, it seems to me, is a central flaw of the Enlightenment philosophy. It can't really address phenomena that are beyond the abilities of the sciences to test. As Robert Miller, the Jesus Seminar scholar, said when I interviewed him, science can document facts but it can't say much about the spiritual interpretation of those facts.

If, for instance, you rupture a disk in your back, X rays or other methods of diagnosis can show that the disk is bad. If you then ask your priest for prayer and later your pain dramatically eases, those same tests might show that the disk doesn't appear to be as badly damaged as your physician originally thought. The *why* is strictly a matter of interpretation. Your doctor might shrug and speculate that the first set of tests was poorly executed. You might be equally convinced that in answer to prayer God divinely improved your disk, lessened your agony, and spared you from surgery. You're entitled to your opinion and your doctor to hers, but there's no medical test that can prove whether God did or didn't come to your aid. Some doctors no doubt are dedicated atheists, but in my experience, at least, many physicians tend to wisely leave such questions of divine intervention alone.

Generalizations are tricky, I know, but psychologists, anthropologists, sociologists, and historians—those who specialize in the social sciences, which perhaps are even a bit more conducive to philosophical speculations than the medical and hard sciences—often seem more likely than physicians to deny the presence of the supernatural. They're entitled to their opinions. The problem arises when their opinions are stated as facts. To the contrary, they merely reflect the speakers' underlying assumptions about the nature of reality; namely, that we live in a closed, nonsupernatural universe in which God does not intrude, even if he exists.

C.S. Lewis lampooned the lengths to which historians of his day frequently went in order not to admit that an event demonstrated supernatural intervention. Even historians who admitted the possibility of a miracle wouldn't acknowledge the reality of one until all other explanations, no matter how absurd, had been exhausted, Lewis said in *Miracles: A Preliminary Study*: "Collective hallucination, hypnotism of unconsenting spectators, widespread instantaneous conspiracy in lying by persons not otherwise known to be liars and not likely to gain by the lie—all these are known to be very improbable events: so improbable that, except for the special purpose of excluding a miracle, they are never suggested." Still, he said, any of those seemed preferable to acknowledging a miracle.

Behaviorists and historians, and, for that matter, theologians and ministers, often are dealing with invisible human thoughts and motivations as much as with observable facts. They must rely upon their own philosophical assumptions about the nature of the world to explain certain behaviors.

If a psychologist has been educated to believe that rational materialism is true and that only the poorly educated, the neurotic, or the superstitious embrace the supernatural, then she almost certainly will develop her conclusions accordingly. Even though she might interview them afterward and take extensive notes, she might assume automatically that people who swoon to the floor during revival services are reacting to seeing others around them fall or to the suggestions of the preacher. If the psychologist is, like White, a former missionary who believes in miracles, she could just as easily conclude that these same people were dropped to the carpet by the Holy Spirit, or by some combination of supernatural power and psychological suggestion. One conclusion is about as provable as the other.

My point is not to insult social scientists, but to suggest that the assumptions the psychologist brings to the revival will play as big a role in determining her interpretation of what happened as will any physical facts.

As I said earlier, to an extent that's the case even when we are discussing miracles with physicians. Certainly some claims of divine help, such as healings, can be checked medically. If a man believes his brain tumor has been healed by God, an examination will reveal whether the tumor is now absent or present, the same size as before prayer or significantly smaller. But again, if the tumor is gone the examination can't necessarily determine why it vanished. So, the assumptions people bring to the discussion still will influence how they perceive and interpret the facts they encounter, even in a medical case.

It's just that all of this is doubly true in events that involve the obviously hard-to-test changes in the human psyche that result from many categories of miracles, such as religious conversions, apparitions, and deliverances from demonic oppression. Their genuineness nearly always lies in the eye of the beholder.

The Importance of Worldview

The single best authority I've found on this subject is Charles H. Kraft, an anthropologist and a specialist in intercultural communications who taught at Michigan State University and UCLA before joining the faculty at Fuller Theological Seminary in California more than twenty-five years ago.

As I've mentioned, the Enlightenment and the Reformation did a lot to raise doubts, some of them well founded, about many tales of supposedly miraculous events. Those movements taught us Westerners to think with our heads more than with our hearts.

Much good has come from a reasonable questioning of church myths and dogmas, Charles Kraft said, "but the pendulum swung too far." Secularists and some Protestant Reformers rejected not only preposterous claims of supernatural acts, but all claims of miracles. They threw out the baby with the bathwater.

All of us are limited by our cultures, our experiences, our personalities, and by sin, Kraft argues. We assume that our paradigm for understanding the world is the only reasonable way of understanding it. He says it would help us Westerners immensely to learn that our rational, empirical worldview isn't the majority one and never has been.

We need to humble ourselves enough to realize that the supernatural worldview is time-honored and that its adherents formed that view because it contains truth, just as there's a certain truth to the Enlightenment view.

Practicing Christians, for instance, ought to remember that their faith's founder assumed that he lived in a supernatural world, Kraft writes in his excellent book *Christianity with Power*. Jesus assumed there was a God who maintained ultimate authority over his creation—and who exercised that power. Jesus thought that demons were real. He believed that God led one kingdom on this planet and Satan another, and that those kingdoms were at war; Jesus repeatedly opposed the spiritual forces of the devil's kingdom through exorcisms. Jesus acted as if believing were seeing, rather than as if seeing were believing. To Jesus and his disciples, Kraft says, miracles weren't even really miraculous. They were part of the normal course of everyday living.

Today we use the word "miracle" to describe an event so far out of the ordinary that the very word implies an interruption of natural laws. For us, medicine is a normal and natural treatment; a dramatic improvement in a tumor that follows prayer seems to be a rare, extraordinary intervention. That's a mistake, Kraft says, one rarely made by other cultures.

In *Christianity with Power*, he maintains that Western Christians actually have more in common with Western secularists than with Christians who live in other parts of the world. Many of his fellow evangelicals in this country are practicing deists, he says; they believe in a God who really doesn't involve himself much in people's day-to-day lives.

The dichotomy first became clear to Kraft when he agreed to serve a stint several decades ago as a Bible translator in Nigeria. Quickly he saw that the evangelical missionaries there weren't meeting the Nigerians' needs for power over tragedies, bad weather, infertility, evil spirits, and broken relationships. The Nigerians might profess Christianity, Kraft realized, but as soon as they needed a genuine manifestation of spiritual authority they'd return to their animistic medicine men, because the missionaries were impotent in that realm and the medicine men possessed true power.

By the late 1960s, Kraft had joined the faculty at Fuller Seminary and was studying church growth. He was struck by the statistics: the fastest-growing churches worldwide were those of Pentecostals and charismatics. A good evangelical, he snorted at first and attributed the growth to contagious emotionalism. But the more he examined the subject, the more he became convinced that Pentecostals were searching for something more lasting than an emotional feeling. Like the Nigerians, they had tapped into a real power. Kraft's since become a Third Waver and has been involved in more than five hundred exorcisms, he said, as well as countless healings and other miracles.

Each winter quarter at Fuller Seminary, he teaches a spiritual "inner-healing" course. Each spring quarter he teaches a course in spiritual "power encounters," or miracles. "These are among the biggest courses at the seminary," Kraft said, and Fuller Seminary is among the largest seminaries in America.

An experiment Kraft regularly conducts with his students is to inform them that the room in which they're sitting is swirling with spirits—and gauge their reactions. Interestingly, he said, the students from North America tend to look at him as if he's slightly unbalanced. "We try to solve problems in a mechanical sort of machine-approach," he said. Most students from Africa, Asia, or Latin America have no problem with the idea of a room filled with unseen beings. Theirs are cultures that always have accepted the presence of the supernatural.

"It's the Western worldviews that are the odd ones," Kraft told me. "We say, 'Seeing is believing.'" Yet even science demonstrates that to be a limited view. The air around us contains radio waves that carry music into our automobiles, he said. We become nauseated because microscopic viruses have taken root in our stomachs. Kraft tells a story, perhaps apocryphal, about an insurance adjuster who was puzzled by a rash of deadly explosions involving "empty" gasoline drums. The adjuster's company had declared that empty containers were safe because they contained no flammable petroleum. As the insurance adjuster soon informed his superiors, "empty" wasn't necessarily empty. The drums contained no liquid—but plenty of fumes that were both real and lethal. Similarly, many things are quite real, but invisible.

Kraft, a mainstream Protestant, believes that unseen spiritual beings around us practice a "science" all their own; spiritual forces operate according to given laws just as gravity does. For instance, people must choose whether to cooperate with spirits or to resist them through skepticism, which partly explains why some people experience more supernatural events than others. People also can choose whether to cooperate with good spirits or bad ones.

A scholar himself, he is quite aware of the contentions of those who maintain that exorcisms and "faith healings" are purely psychological. "Psychological processes can be healing," he agreed. "But it usually takes a lot of time." Kraft said he's seen countless healings that occurred instantaneously after prayer. And the Bible's accounts of Jesus' healings say they happened immediately. "Even if he was a good psychologist, that's not the whole story."

A long-standing saw among students of biblical interpretation—hermeneutics is the technical name for that discipline—is that the simplest explanation for a text is the most accurate. Modern scholars frequently torture biblical passages to construct rationalistic explanations for Jesus' miracles, Kraft said. For him, the clearest interpretation is the one made by the texts: "This was the power of God, like the Bible says."

A common practice in some Christian circles today is to treat back or leg ailments by asking the person who is ill to sit in a chair and extend his legs. The person who is praying places the heels of the ill person's feet side by side to see whether the leg lengths are even. Usually they aren't. As the minister prays, one leg often appears to "grow" until both legs are of the same length and the heels are aligned. Frequently the person for whom prayer is offered reports that his pain is gone. The Amazing Randi photographed evangelist W.V. Grant performing this cure. Randi charged that Grant merely was manipulating the sick person's shoes, edging a shoe forward or backward on the heels to make it appear as if the legs had changed positions.

I've witnessed these "leg lengthenings," too, and I've had some questions about the practice as well. I can't speak about W.V. Grant, whom I've never met, but I believe Randi was incorrect in his estimation of how the cure usually is performed. It seems to me that the muscles of a person who is suffering, say, back pain almost certainly are tensed from the experience. If you extend his legs, they'll probably not match in length because of this tension, and the incongruity will be even more notable if the sick person happens to be sitting slightly off-center. If you then tell the person in pain that prayer will correct this condition, he is likely to unconsciously relax, straighten up, or otherwise move his legs until the heels are even. I've found this cure to be a matter of sincerity by both the person praying and the person receiving prayer—but used to assume the results were more psychological than anything else.

I suggested this to Kraft, who also has witnessed many leg lengthenings. He agreed they don't usually involve, say, the instantaneous growth of bones. Nevertheless, he said, people regularly report that their pain has disappeared after their legs were "adjusted." It's hard to know how much of that is divine and how much is psychosomatic, but to ask that is to miss the point, Kraft said: "When it happens right away, through prayer, I'd call that a miracle."

He's also been in church meetings where people reported that their headaches suddenly vanished after prayer. Again that might be a mere relaxation of bodily tension, he said. And some might consider a headache too trivial for the God of the universe to address. But again, if the headache disappears following prayer it should be seen as an act of God: "A headache's not a big problem unless it's yours," he said. "Then it can be a big problem."

It's not that Kraft would commit the mirror-image of the Reformers' mistakes. He's not rejecting science, technology, or critical thought. But he said an illness might have two causes, a germ and a spirit that directs the germ to a particular person. A mental disorder might be both the result of a chemical imbalance and demonic influence. We need to open our eyes to that other, unseen, world as well as to the "natural" world of Western science.

The Spirit World of the Melanesians

Another anthropologist told me that he had, through his own research, arrived at conclusions very similar to Kraft's. Darrell Whiteman spent seven years working in the southwest Pacific during the late

1970s and early 1980s. He wrote a book on Anglicanism in the Solomon Islands called *Melanesians and Missionaries*. By 1977 when Whiteman arrived in the Solomons, which are part of Melanesia, 94 percent of the islanders there had converted to Christianity, most of them in the previous forty years. Prior to becoming Christians, though, the Melanesians had been animists who believed strongly in good and evil spirits that inhabited the land around them.

As for Whiteman, he had grown up as the son of a college president in Kansas and Nebraska. Whiteman's father, G. Edgar Whiteman, died when Whiteman was twelve. "That's when I wanted a miracle," Whiteman recalled. "I kept thinking my dad might still come back to life—until he was put in the ground." Whiteman later reached adulthood as a rational, mainline Methodist for whom miracles weren't impossible, but neither were they part of his daily Christian walk. He began to view the world differently while working overseas.

His assignment in the Pacific was to interview Melanesians and determine how Christianity had affected their lives. At one point he lived in a nice leaf house on the island of Santa Ysabel in the Solomons. There, he attended a meeting local villagers had called with the area's Anglican bishop, Dudley Tuti, the paramount chief of Santa Ysabel and a Solomon Islander himself. The villagers, converts to Christianity, seemed bothered. "Before we were Christians," one man told the bishop, "if we needed rain we'd pray for it and we'd get it." That, of course, had been when they were praying to the spirits of their previous religion. "Now we pray and nothing happens," the man said. "What's gone wrong?" The Anglican bishop had little response. The intellectual, Westernized style of Christianity he'd studied hadn't prepared him for such questions.

After that, Whiteman began to ponder what he's come to consider a defining question of modern Christian faith: "Is there power in Christianity?"

There certainly seemed to be power in the animistic faith from which the Melanesians hailed. Whiteman interviewed some Santa Ysabel islanders about how they had selected the present site for their village a generation before. He discovered that, even though the islanders had converted to Christianity, they continued to consult mediums and shamans when they needed real spiritual intervention. The village headman told Whiteman that before the islanders decided to move to their village's present site, leaders visited a woman, also a Christian convert, who had been a pagan spirit medium before her conversion—and who continued to practice that craft. They asked her to "scout out the land" they'd selected and make sure it wasn't occupied by demons. About dusk, the headman was sitting in the medium's house, smoking a cigarette. The medium called up the various ancestral spirits at her disposal, which blew into the house like a wind. The headman heard voices. One spirit asked him audibly what his cigarette was, and the chief told it. The spirit snatched the cigarette from the headman's fingers, carried it across the room, and began to puff on it. The headman could see the glow of the cigarette's fire. Meanwhile, the medium asked the spirits whether the proposed village site would be safe. The spirits answered that it would, the headman recalled. "He told this story without any sense that it was unusual," Whiteman said.

Whiteman learned that islanders said they encountered angels and demons regularly; the spirits took various forms. "Melanesians see them all the time and describe them in vivid detail," Whiteman said.

He left the islands and returned to America with his own world-view permanently changed. He never actually witnessed these supernatural manifestations while he lived in Melanesia, but he heard so many matter-of-fact, firsthand accounts that he came to believe them. "I'm convinced that they are not made up," he said. "They are very, very real."

Today, Whiteman divides the world into three parts, which he illustrates by drawing a pyramid. The bottom third, the wide base of the pyramid, consists of what we can see with our human eyes, which he labels "sensory perception." That's where the Enlightenment world-view is based. The two top portions of the pyramid are the domains of the unseen, spiritual world. The highest, narrowest third is made up of "high religion" and the "other world" of heaven; this is the domain addressed by professional clergy, holy books, and abstract arguments about eternal destiny. The middle third, between the physical senses and high religion, is what Whiteman labels as "folk religion." It's invisible and spiritual, yet very much part of this world. Most modern

Christians are impotent here, Whiteman says, but it's really the area where most of the earth's population lives, a place of angels, demons, and supernatural visions. It's the world of Melanesian animists or, for that matter, Pentecostals. Secular materialists and intellectually minded mainline Christians may ignore it to their own peril.

Fortunately, many religious groups are acknowledging this lack. In the Roman Catholic Church, for example, Catholics who grew up before Vatican II were taught that the supernatural gifts of the Holy Spirit mostly ended with the first generation of Christians hundreds of years ago. Now, those same gifts are widely viewed as an indispensable part of the Church's life; they are seen as tools to help build faith and a feeling of community.

Scientific Evidence for Supernatural Intercession

As I noted in Chapter 1, there is a movement within science to study the supernatural using empirical methods. Some findings have been startling. The most widely cited of dozens of academic studies of the supernatural is one conducted by cardiologist Dr. Randolph Byrd at San Francisco General Hospital, who published the results in 1988 in the *Southern Medical Journal.*

In Byrd's study, some 393 coronary-care patients were randomly divided by a computer into two groups: one (192 patients) that would be prayed for daily by Christian home prayer circles and one (201 patients) that would not be prayed for. The prayer circles were given the patients' first names and a succinct description of their conditions. No one in the coronary-care unit, including doctors, nurses, or patients, knew who was to receive prayer. The study lasted ten months. At its end, writes Dr. Larry Dossey in *Healing Words: The Power of Prayer and the Practice of Medicine*, patients who had received prayer were five times less likely to need antibiotics and three times less likely to develop pulmonary edema than the group not prayed for. None of the prayed-for group needed an endotracheal tube inserted into their throats to breathe, while twelve of those not prayed for needed tubes. Fewer members of the group that received prayers died.

The results apparently were dramatic. The study was scientifically conducted to prevent bias in the testing procedures; it was a randomized, double-blind test. Immediately, though, some experts pounced on Byrd and his study, Dossey writes. Critics complained that only "born-again" Christians had been recruited to pray and wondered whether Byrd had some ax to grind. Byrd, they said, had not determined whether the members of the prayer circles actually prayed daily for the patients, as they'd agreed they would. Byrd hadn't asked the people what kinds of prayers they used, either. Some critics complained that giving the prayer circles the patients' first names violated the confidentiality of double-blind tests. Others said Byrd hadn't measured the comparative skill of the patients' doctors, to see whether the group that fared better happened to have been placed in more competent medical hands.

As I read Dossey's book, and even more so as I researched my own book, it became exceedingly clear to me again that no scientific analysis is likely to convince hard-core skeptics, who will find flaws in any study that purports to show that supernatural forces influence our lives. Similarly, no effort to debunk miracles will dissuade those who believe in divine intervention. Worldview is everything here.

The Most Convincing Evidence

I freely admit I have come to believe in miracles—not in every report of divine intervention, but in many. There are two central reasons why.

First, I'm a skeptic myself by inclination and by training. I'm a professional journalist with secular graduate school degrees in the liberal arts and the social science of communications, both of which attract cynics and naysayers of all types, many of whom were my teachers. My inclination always is to find an empirical reason for any unusual event. Yet I've both witnessed and participated in events I can't explain rationally, events that I must, if I'm to be honest, say that I think involved supernatural forces. So I'm convinced by my own experiences. And, as a preacher once said, a person with an experience is never at the mercy of a person with an argument.

The second reason I believe in miracles is the overwhelming body of evidence comprised by the millions of people who say they've witnessed them. How could that many people be that deluded for that long? The belief in miracles is both universal and historical; it cuts across all societies and dates to the earliest days of humankind. In working on this book, I've run into dozens of people just like me who are by nature and education leery of the supernatural, but who have been changed permanently by the things they've seen with their own eyes or felt in their own hearts. Among them are writers, professors, anthropologists, housewives, lawyers, physicians, chemists.

Even most of those I've interviewed who cast doubts on certain kinds of miracles admitted that they believed in other supernatural acts. For instance, Walter Price, the Baptist dispensationalist, with great patience explained why the age of miracles in Christianity has passed away. But he also said something I found interesting, given his resistance to most modern reports of supernatural intervention. "I think God still works miracles today," he said. When I asked what he meant, he said he personally knew people who had been healed through prayer. His objection, as I gauged it, wasn't to individual accounts of modern miracles, but to manifestations that disagreed with his own theology—such as speaking in tongues—and to claims that miracles are taking place daily. "God answers prayer. Miracles occur in answer to prayer," Price said. "People are healed. But it's not this wholesale stuff."

In the end, there's no proof that any event is miraculous. As I began compiling the stories that make up the next seven chapters, my initial goal was to document them as thoroughly as possible, to cover all the nonsupernatural explanations. I soon changed my mind. I did try to verify information wherever possible. I talked with eyewitnesses, looked at videotapes, examined crucifixes that people assured me had changed from silver to gold. Quickly I realized that neither I nor anyone else could ever lay to rest all the possible counter-arguments. And I decided finally just to let the people tell you their own stories and explain the ways in which the wonderful things that have happened to them changed their lives. Then you can judge for yourselves.

CHAPTER SIX

MIRACULOUS CONVERSIONS

T HE AUTHOR OF THE GOSPEL of John tells a story about a religious leader, Nicodemus, who one evening slipped into the camp of Jesus of Nazareth. As in many of the gospels' stories the writer supplies few details, but Nicodemus appears to have been both attracted and perplexed by Jesus' teachings and supernatural powers. In John's anecdote Nicodemus opens his conversation politely: "Rabbi," he says, "we know that thou art a teacher come from God; for no man can do these miracles that thou doest, except God be with him."

Jesus isn't comfortable with small talk. He cuts to the marrow of his message: "Except a man be born again, he cannot see the kingdom of God."

Nicodemus is taken aback. "How can a man be born when he is old?" he asks. "Can he enter the second time into his mother's womb, and be born?"

"Except a man be born of water and of the Spirit, he cannot enter into the kingdom of God," Jesus says. "That which is born of the flesh is flesh; and that which is born of the Spirit is spirit."

What Jesus meant, and what the lives of his disciples would bear out, is that some people, if not all, apparently need to experience a life-altering spiritual conversion, in which they leave behind their old doubtful ways of looking at the world and begin to observe the cosmos through the eyes of faith. Then they can enter that realm of the supernatural that Jesus called the kingdom of God. Such conversions of the heart make up the most ubiquitous category of miracles. A recent Roper poll found that 37 percent of American adults say they've experienced a life-changing revelation of Jesus Christ. Conversions are so common that we often don't consider them miracles at all.

They are. Some religious authorities say that conversions might be the greatest of all miracles. Charles Kraft called a conversion "the basic freeing" of the soul—an act of deliverance that looses us from a faithless worldview to worship God. "That's *the* big miracle," he said. Conversion often is the first step on the journey to receiving other kinds of divine intervention.

Conversions can take many forms, but generally are sudden events rather than gradual ones, writes Peter McKenzie in *The Christians: Their Beliefs and Practices*. They often occur during a period of stress, upheaval, or uncertainty in a person's life. The epiphany that changes the convert's worldview might be merely internal, in the form of a dramatic, private insight. Or, it sometimes includes an actual, temporary ability to see supernatural spirits or the ability to hear a divine voice, or both. The results, in any case, are quite visible. An atheist becomes devout. A brutal man becomes a pacifist. A shy woman receives the zeal and courage to testify about her faith.

Conversions, under one name or another, are common to many faiths besides Christianity. Buddha, for example, received a powerful illumination while sitting under a fig tree. That surely was a kind of conversion.

Still, the most famous conversion ever was that of a zealous, legalistic religious official named Saul of Tarsus, a member of the Pharisee sect of leaders in ancient Palestine. Saul had taken it upon himself to persecute the fledgling group of Jews who had formed a splinter movement called Christianity. He imprisoned many of them. When the deacon Stephen was lynched for his faith Saul heartily approved the execution and, by his own admission, guarded the cloaks of those who stoned the Church's first martyr.

As Luke, the New Testament account's author, tells it, Saul eventually set out for Damascus, in present-day Syria, with letters from the high priest that authorized him to arrest any Christians he found there, whether men or women, and return them in shackles to Jerusalem. But something happened to Saul along the dusty highway to Damascus: "Suddenly there shined round about him a light from heaven: and he fell to the earth, and heard a voice saying unto him, 'Saul, Saul, why persecutest thou me?' And he said, 'Who art thou, Lord?' And the Lord said, 'I am Jesus whom thou persecutest . . .'" By this time Saul, Luke tells us, found himself "trembling and astonished."

Interestingly, those in Saul's entourage heard the voice, but didn't see the light that Saul saw, a light so piercing that it blinded him. His companions led him by the hand into Damascus. Days later, a Christian named Ananias arrived to minister to the feared persecutor. With his help Saul regained his sight and received the Holy Spirit.

After that wrenching experience, Saul of Tarsus became St. Paul the Apostle. The man who once had vigorously tried to destroy the early Church spent the rest of his life working as a missionary to enlarge it. Far more important, he wrote several of the letters that became the Christian New Testament—exactly how many of the epistles he wrote remains in dispute, but he may have written nearly half the new Christian canon. In having done that, Paul became the most influential Christian in history other than Jesus. It was a remarkable and instantaneous turnaround.

"Once an Infidel and Libertine"

If Saul's conversion ranks as the most famous, just as poignant is the conversion of an eighteenth-century sailor named John Newton. Today Newton is remembered as the composer of the beloved hymn "Amazing Grace." The song was autobiographical, a snapshot of Newton's life.

John Newton was born July 24, 1725, in London, the only child of a harsh shipmaster, Captain John Newton, and a devoted mother, Elizabeth Newton. Newton later would say that his father might have loved him, "[but] he seemed not willing that I should know it." His kindly mother, on the other hand, filled his days with religious instruction and taught him to pray. She died when Newton was seven, though, leaving him to his father and, soon, a neglectful stepmother as well. By age eight Newton was shipped off to boarding school at Stratford in Essex. The sadistic schoolmaster there, writes biographer John Pollock, "was a tyrant of the cane and birch-rod" who thrashed Newton mercilessly.

By his eleventh birthday, in 1736, Newton was withdrawn from the school and assigned to his father's ship. During their six years together at sea, the elder Newton brutalized the boy, apparently to make him a tough, knowledgeable seaman.

By the time old Captain Newton retired from the sea in 1742, the body and the spirit of his teenaged son had hardened considerably. The younger Newton possessed a keen mind and read widely, but his tastes ran to pornography and treatises by atheists. Newton became an atheist himself.

His life already had been difficult, but soon it took a severe turn for the worse. In 1744, war was declared between France and England. Just before the declaration during a walk along the English dockyards, Newton was kidnapped and pressed into service on a nearby ship. Later, faced with a pending five-year voyage to the East Indies, Newton deserted. He was captured, paraded through the streets of Plymouth in chains, then thrown in jail. When at last he was returned to his ship he was demoted, stripped, spread-eagled, and flayed with dozens of lashes of a cat-o'-nine-tails before the assembled 350 men of his ship. A marine fainted just watching the horrendous beating, but Newton refused even to whimper, and somehow survived the torture. Afterward he considered himself "degraded." He alternately contemplated committing suicide and murdering his captain.

When his ship arrived at Madeira, Newton changed vessels with his captain's permission and joined a slave ship bound for Sierra Leone. There, he eventually became partners with a slave dealer. He learned to judge the value of men and women offered for sale by their fellow Africans. Exceedingly bitter and profane, he delighted in offering up blasphemous mock "prayers" to a God in whom he didn't believe. Years later he would recall: "I sank so low that the Negroes thought themselves too good to speak to me."

Over time, Newton became the mate of another slave ship, the *Greyhound*. While aboard this vessel he happened to find a copy of the Christian treatise *The Imitation of Christ*, by Thomas à Kempis. Bored, he picked up the book several times and, while reading it, asked himself, "What if these things be true?" Not that he believed they were.

Then, returning to England on a seven thousand mile voyage, the

Greyhound was caught in a devastating storm. Newton lay asleep in his bunk when the first icy wave ripped into his cabin and soaked him. He dashed for the deck. As he climbed the ladder, the captain ordered him below to fetch a knife. He stepped from the ladder and another sailor hurried in front of him to climb the rungs instead. As the other sailor stepped onto the deck's planks, a wave broke across the deck and washed him out to sea. Newton soon was frantically pumping water from the reeling, battered ship. At one point, he took the wheel.

The situation seemed hopeless; everyone aboard believed the ship was sinking. As the distraught Newton prepared to die, he remembered the God about whom he'd read in *The Imitation of Christ* and about whom his mother had told him so long ago. "Too late! Too late!" he cried. "For if these things be true, what mercy can there be for me?" He recalled his blasphemies against the God on whom he now was dependent for his eternal soul. In desperation he wailed, "O God, the God of my mother, have mercy on me!"

That night, March 10, 1748, marked John Newton's conversion. The winds slowly died away. The ravaged ship survived, and limped on toward an Irish port, four weeks away. Even after the immediate danger had passed, though, Newton couldn't shake God from his thoughts. He now found a Bible on board and began to pore through it, looking for hope that he could be forgiven his innumerable sins. His famous hymn would one day proclaim that he been blind, and now had begun to see.

Converted or not, Newton later became the captain of a slave ship and remained in that occupation for a half-dozen years, narrowly escaping death several more times in troubled seas. When the waters were calm, he took advantage of his slack time to study Latin, Hebrew, and the Bible. Newton later said that some of his sweetest communions with God took place while he was piloting ships whose cargo consisted of humans chained in the hold.

Today, it seems improbable that a devout man could remain the captain of a slave ship. But Newton, like all of us, was a product of his times. Among most British subjects of his day—and Americans, too—slavery was accepted as part of the natural order. The Bible mentioned but didn't explicitly condemn it. Europeans commonly were taught that they were a superior race, and that superior people had been ordained by God to rule inferior ones. There also were slavery's economic benefits: the health of the economies of such cities as Liverpool and Bristol hinged on the slave trade. For some time, Newton's profession didn't seem incongruous to him at all, although he did try to deal more mercifully with his crew and his African cargo than in his days as a scoundrel.

Slowly, though, over a period of years, his conscience awakened. He found himself "sometimes shocked" to be fastening the chains that bound other people. At last he begged God in his prayers to provide him with another means of earning a living.

Newton successfully found employment as the tide surveyor in Liverpool, a job that, like his former captain's position, afforded him time to study religion. He held that position for nine years, all the while becoming increasingly active in church affairs and making friends with men who now are legends in Protestant Christianity, including the evangelist George Whitefield and John Wesley, the founder of Methodism.

In 1764, at age thirty-nine, sixteen years after his initial conversion, Newton was ordained a priest in the Church of England and was assigned to the drab village of Olney on a miserable stipend. There Newton and his neighbor, the mad, suicidal poet William Cowper, composed hundreds of hymns, including "Amazing Grace." Newton also established himself as a preacher of ability, and his small congregation grew to more than two thousand in attendance on Sundays.

In his mid-fifties, Newton became rector of St. Mary Woolnoth, London. By then, he was speaking against slavery, which from his own experience he had come to regard as "vile." In London in 1785, a wealthy playboy, gambler, and member of Parliament named William Wilberforce fell under Newton's influence. After two years of counseling—and many discussions of Newton's days as a slave ship captain—Wilberforce became a Christian convert. His new faith led Wilberforce as well to oppose slavery.

Despite vehement opposition and derision from several sides, Wilberforce soon introduced into the House of Commons a movement to free England's slaves and halt the slave trade. In support, the much-respected Newton wrote *Thoughts on the Slave Trade* and testified before England's Privy Council against slavery. Over time, the abolitionist movement gained momentum. Parliament abolished the slave trade in March 1807; slavery itself finally was abolished throughout the empire in 1833.

Newton died on the last day of 1807, just months after the human bondage he'd once promoted had been struck down, partly through his own tireless campaigning. Afraid that well-meaning friends might "falsify" him with a "eulogizing epitaph," the elderly minister already had composed the inscription for his own tombstone. It said, simply:

JOHN NEWTON

Clerk

Once an Infidel and Libertine,

A Servant of Slaves in Africa,

Was by the Rich Mercy

Of Our Lord and Saviour,

Jesus Christ,

Preserved, Restored, Pardoned,

And Appointed to Preach the

Faith

Which He had Long Labored to

Destroy

❦

"Born Again"

The descriptive term that Jesus used for experiences such as Saul's and Newton's—being "born again"—recently has fallen into disrepute. That fall might have been unwittingly accelerated by Charles Colson, the infamous special counsel to President Richard Nixon, who allegedly once said he would run over his own grandmother to get Nixon re-elected.

During the Watergate debacle, Colson was implicated in various crimes, most of which he denied having committed, but he resigned from the White House under pressure in March 1973, as the Watergate scandal was peaking and Colson, his colleagues, and even the President were being exposed as Machiavellian infighters. Of all Nixon's men, Colson ranked among the most despised and feared. Ultimately, he would serve time for helping smear Daniel Ellsberg, who had leaked the Pentagon Papers.

A few months after he'd resigned, on a Thursday morning, Colson quietly revisited the White House. He was spotted. During a routine press briefing later that day, CBS correspondent Dan Rather tore into Assistant Press Secretary Jerry Warren, demanding to know why Nixon was speaking to Colson again. After some hemming, Warren explained that Colson hadn't been there to visit Nixon. He'd come to the White House to attend, of all things, a prayer breakfast. The White House press corps erupted in mirth—and skepticism.

Soon, what Colson had hoped to keep secret had become public. That is, under the influence of a Massachusetts business executive, Tom Phillips, and having read C.S. Lewis's piercing defense of faith, *Mere Christianity*, Colson had experienced what he claimed was a heart-felt Christian conversion. He later wrote about it in *Born Again* and other books. In the immediate aftermath of Colson's conversion, a period wracked by the national cynicism that followed Watergate and the fall of Vietnam, his insistence that he'd been "born again" became synonymous in some quarters with hypocrisy.

Yet Colson's conversion has stood the one critical test, the test of time. After serving his prison sentence, Colson founded a respected nonprofit ministry to prisoners, Prison Fellowship, that continues to act as a benchmark for other jail ministries. He has won the Templeton Prize, the church world's equivalent of the Nobel Peace Prize. He has become a respected author and defender of the faith much in the mode of C.S. Lewis. By any outward measure, Colson's conversion would seem as real as John Newton's.

Another Watergate Figure Changes Vocations

Colson's change of heart wasn't the only one among Watergate's infamous personalities. Jeb Stuart Magruder—public relations adviser in Nixon's White House, deputy director of the Committee to Re-elect the President, admitted felon—experienced an equally remarkable transformation.

Jeb Magruder is a tall, husky man with neat, graying hair. He wears glasses and looks more like a senior accountant than the Presbyterian pastor that he is today. A proper mainline Protestant, he's not quite comfortable describing himself as "born again," he told me as we sat at a round table in his tasteful office in the urban church where he serves as senior minister.

"I see it as 'born anew,' " Magruder said—which seemed to me to be a minor difference. But that's a better translation of the early Greek words used in John's gospel, he insisted. "I see it more as 'renewed' for someone who has been a Christian." Which is to say, somebody like Magruder, a man who was brought up in church. He always intended to do right, he said, and always possessed a conscience, but found himself easily seduced by the power, vanity, and moral ambiguities of Washington during the tumultuous 1970s.

Magruder was born in November 1934, and grew up on Staten Island, New York, during the Depression and World War II. He describes his parents as straight-arrows. "They weren't zealots," he said. "They were good, Christian people." His father, Donald D. Magruder, a transplanted Southerner, owned a printing business and stationery store. The Magruder family attended a Reformed church until the war began. Then gas rationing forced them to walk to a nearby Episcopal church. There, Magruder became active in a youth group and served as an altar boy. He attended public schools in New York City, and discovered himself to be a rare WASP among ethnic Italians, Irish, and African-Americans. Knives were common in his high school: "It was a rough place."

He was a bright young man, and his mother, particularly, drilled into him that people who are given gifts in life owe a debt of responsibility and duty in return. Magruder won acceptance to prestigious Williams College, where most of his classmates seemed rich. For the first time, he observed the many benefits of wealth and power, and decided he wanted them for himself.

Magruder spent two years at Williams, then left school for a stint in the Army. When he returned to Williams to finish up his degree in political science, the Reverend William Sloane Coffin Jr., a famous liberal minister, arrived on campus as chaplain. Magruder studied under Coffin, became friends with him, and briefly considered entering the ministry. He also considered careers in politics and business, eventually choosing the latter.

He went to work in California and married a well-to-do woman from that state. He later temporarily left the West Coast to earn a master's in business administration degree at the University of Chicago, where faculty luminaries as George Shultz, later U.S. Secretary of State, taught that it was the students' obligation to climb the ladder of success. That would lead them to positions of influence from which they could make beneficial changes in the world. "Which I bought into completely," Magruder said. "I was very upwardly mobile."

After business school, he became an executive and an entrepreneur in California, and grew increasingly active in planning political campaigns. Among other things, he served as Southern California coordinator for Nixon's successful 1968 presidential bid. He served as an elder in a Presbyterian congregation in Los Angeles, too.

Magruder was the model of success: handsome, educated, hardworking, politically active, and ambitious. In 1969, in his mid-thirties, he was offered a job serving at the highest level of government, as a presidential adviser. He never considered turning down the offer: "That's what I was taught to do." He quickly learned to love his work in the White House; it offered him power, intrigue, and the career contacts for unlimited future success.

And then his life suddenly fell apart. He had been assigned an important job as deputy director of the Committee to Re-elect the President, reporting directly to Attorney General John Mitchell and White House Chief of Staff H.R. Haldeman. There, Magruder took part in the plan to break into the headquarters of the Democratic Party. When the burglars were caught, Magruder helped engineer a cover-up—which succeeded for a while, until burglar James McCord told Judge John Sirica that perjury had been committed during the Watergate trial. As one of those who had lied, Magruder realized he was in deep trouble. He likely would lose his job and his reputation. He might go to prison. Magruder anguished over what to do, and finally decided to admit his deeds to the Watergate prosecutors.

Even today, Magruder doesn't believe that he had become terribly immoral back then. At the time, he was troubled by the attitudes of maverick Watergate figures such as G. Gordon Liddy and Colson. "I wouldn't walk over my grandmother," Magruder said, referring to Colson. But without realizing it, he had managed to compartmentalize his life. He and others had committed unlawful acts in their jobs they never would have considered in their private lives. They convinced themselves they were acting for the greater public good. Such is the duality of human nature.

As his personal and professional universe imploded, Magruder's photograph was strewn across national newspapers and network TV. Reporters camped out on his lawn and harassed his wife and children. He was berated by vindictive prosecutors. He began to hate venturing out in public. Afraid that people would point and whisper, he no longer felt he could even go to church. Worse, Magruder began to believe that God must be nauseated by his crimes and decided it was better to keep his distance from the Almighty.

One day, after he had testified on television before the Ervin Committee, which was investigating Watergate, he received a supportive letter from the Reverend Louis Evans and his wife, Colleen. Evans was the minister at National Presbyterian Church in Washington, D.C. Magruder once had heard Evans preach and had been greatly impressed. The couple, as it turned out, lived only a few blocks from Magruder. In their letter they invited him and his family to visit should they ever feel the need to talk or pray with someone.

Desperate, Magruder uncharacteristically did just that: he drove alone to the Evans home one afternoon, knocked on the door, and introduced himself to Colleen Evans. Louis Evans wasn't home, but Magruder would later write, in his book *From Power to Peace,* that Colleen Evans imparted to him what had become a rare feeling for Magruder, the sense of "all-rightness." The next week Magruder returned to the home and met Louis, or "Louie," as most people called the minister. Over time, Magruder emptied his troubled soul to the preacher. They talked about the ups and downs of human life, about how people can know what is the right thing to do but refuse to do it. They talked about God as well, but Evans never pressured Magruder into making any kind of commitment to faith or repentance. He simply became Magruder's friend, and treated the Watergate conspirator as if he were a brother.

Under Evans's guidance, Magruder began to meet also with a small group of Christian men. He talked with them about the scandal in which he was embroiled and couldn't help but contrast their attitudes with the attitudes of the federal prosecutors with whom he also was meeting. The prosecutors considered him to be scum. His new, religious friends didn't agree with the wrongs he'd done, but neither did they judge him; they accepted him as he was.

Caught in this crucible, Magruder reconsidered his whole life. Slowly, he realized that something always had been missing. No matter how many successes he'd achieved, how many steps he'd ascended on the ladder, he'd felt incomplete. He remembered how unhappy a man he'd always considered Richard Nixon to be. When Nixon finally was elected president in 1968, Magruder had thought to himself that at last Nixon now would be at peace. Working in the White House, though, Magruder had seen firsthand that Nixon remained engaged in some hellish internal war. Temporal power, in and of itself, could never satisfy a person, Magruder decided.

The devoted Christians he'd met seemed to possess happiness. Magruder talked with Evans about this. He wanted God to become real in his life, he told the minister, but he'd committed dreadful wrongs. He'd failed himself, his country, the Almighty.

One frigid Friday night, Magruder rode with Evans in the minister's subcompact Toyota to help Evans organize some new Christian groups. They were late returning. Outside Magruder's house the two large-framed men sat packed into the tiny car. Pensive, Magruder asked Evans whether, given his Watergate infamy, he should become involved with the new groups; his presence might discredit them.

Evans asked whether Magruder still found it difficult to believe that God could accept him as he was. Yes, Magruder admitted. *God already has forgiven you*, Evans said. *He'll tell you that if you'll listen.* Evans asked if he could pray for Magruder, and Magruder agreed. There in the car Evans asked God to remove Magruder's fear and his unbelief. As Evans prayed, Magruder found himself talking to God, too. For the first time ever, he spoke aloud as if God really were present, right in the little Toyota with them. Magruder told God that he wanted to surrender his life, and asked if Jesus Christ would help him. And somehow, not audibly, but as clearly as if the voice were audible, Jesus said, "Yes." Peace poured through Magruder. He felt bathed by a supernatural love.

He told Evans what was happening to him. Evans replied that, if he had really given his life to God, Magruder would have to start living life God's way rather than his own way. Magruder said that was no problem. Now he wanted more than anything to conduct his life according to God's plan, whatever that might prove to be. He didn't want prestige or power anymore.

His encounter with Evans, and that night with Jesus, "changed my theological and philosophical direction dramatically," Magruder says today.

Magruder, like others, went on to serve time in prison for his Watergate-related misdeeds. After his release from jail, he eventually enrolled in Princeton Theological Seminary, earned a divinity degree, and returned to California as a minister. Even after he was ordained, he continued to suffer fallout from the scandal and stresses of Watergate. In the 1980s his rocky first marriage fell apart. (He has since remarried.) He discovered that working in the church could entail its share of problems and personality conflicts, too: "Life doesn't become perfect," he said, "because we as humans are imperfect."

Nevertheless, Magruder said he's never regretted his dramatic change of vocations. He insisted that he's been able to perform far more genuine service from the pulpit and the pastoral study than he ever did in the White House. God's even used the Watergate debacle for good, he said. People feel comfortable confiding their wrongs and their fears and their failures to him—and he knows how to respond when they do—because he's been there, in spades. More than two decades later, he continues to believe that he truly encountered God that night in the Reverend Louis Evans's tiny Toyota.

"It was the trigger for all that's happened since then," he said. "But the path wasn't straight and smooth and without its own difficulty."

"In God We Trust"

Not everyone finds God while suffering catastrophes. Ken Silvestri, a real estate agent in his mid-thirties, found God in the midst of materialistic success. In 1994, he and his two partners in the Silvestri Team sold $40.9 million worth of properties. To put that in perspective, consider that the average U.S. real estate agent lists or sells about 7 properties each year. In 1994, Silvestri and his friends handled 309 total real estate transactions.

Silvestri's a handsome, friendly guy whose sales reap him a personal annual income well into the six figures. Like Magruder, he's always considered himself a good person; in his youth he was an Eagle Scout. He admits to one central character flaw: he has at times felt consumed by the desire for professional and financial success. He was raised a Roman Catholic, but he'd never given much real attention to religion. "Churchgoing was sort of an on-and-off thing," he said. Typically he went to services four or five times a year.

In 1995, Silvestri held a series of business meetings with some of the building contractors with whom he worked. There was one guy, Kirk Seeberger, who'd long impressed Silvestri. His houses were well constructed. His customers loved him. One day over lunch at a restaurant Silvestri asked Seeberger, "Kirk, what is it that drives you?"

Seeberger's response wasn't what Silvestri had expected. The builder said that, while he didn't consider himself terribly religious, he'd embarked on a real relationship with God. Sometimes when he was working, the builder said, he'd look up and ask, "How am I doing?" Often, he'd imagine he heard these words from God in reply: "You are my son whom I love. In you I am well pleased." That was his goal, Seeberger said: to actually hear those words someday. He'd stopped working to please other people and was trying instead to please God.

"I remember just sort of gulping," Silvestri said. "It was a profound kind of statement I'd never heard before. I remember just kind of sinking down in my chair." In the days and weeks to come, he thought about how he'd long taken God for granted in his own life.

Then, one beautiful fall Sunday morning—October 1, 1995—Silvestri had held an open house at a property he was trying to sell. He came home and worked on an exercise machine in his family room. Tammy, his wife, was cooking. Impromptu, Silvestri decided he needed a jog. The Silvestris live in an upscale community connected to a golf course, and after Ken had run perhaps a half-mile from his home, he veered onto a golf cart path. It was seventy-eight degrees out. The sun shone warm on his face. "It was just a glorious, glorious day," he said. "You couldn't help but feel so alive."

No more than one hundred yards down the golf cart path, he jogged past a penny lying on the ground. For some reason, he felt compelled to turn around and go back. He stooped and picked up the penny. It was a worn coin, minted in 1975; its copper finish had turned brown. His eyes caught the inscription: "There it was," he said, "'In God We Trust.'" Four words he'd seen countless times.

Silvestri, clutching the penny, turned and began running again under the warm sun, but now his thoughts meandered. He realized how blessed he was. He was healthy. He had a great job and great friends. And those words kept pounding in his mind with each step: "In God We Trust. In God We Trust."

A need filled him. An awakening: "In God We Trust."

Then Silvestri spoke to the Almighty. "I said, 'Hey, I believe that up there,'" Silvestri said. "'I want to have that.'" The next thing he knew, as he continued to run, tears welled in his eyes and trickled down his face. Silvestri, the good guy, the Eagle Scout, found himself confessing his sins and begging forgiveness. He asked God to give him a task to do, to prove his sincerity. He asked for courage to complete that task, whatever it might prove to be.

A powerful sensation overshadowed him then. "It just seemed like I felt this warm glowing spirit," Silvestri said. "There was this wonderful feeling of forgiveness. . . . I was weeping. I felt so good. I just knew I'd been forgiven."

Silvestri promised God that for the rest of his life he'd never eat breakfast or any other meal until he'd first read the Bible each day. "All of a sudden it was just like this newfound power I had. I was just floating, almost."

Two weeks later, Silvestri was baptized at a Christian church he'd attended sporadically. He told his friends what had happened to him, too. The jogging experience even affected his marriage. Before, "there was just a lot of friction and stress," he said. He'd been more focused on his career than on his wife. "Now it's just totally different. It's just totally transformed our marriage." One day he wrote Tammy a note that said, "I've loved you for years, but now I'm *in love* with you."

There's an even more remarkable result. In 1991, a man had bought a small business that Silvestri owned and had written him a bad check for ten thousand dollars as a down payment. The guy later paid off the bad check, but still hadn't paid the remaining eighty-five-thousand-dollar debt he owed Silvestri—and, according to Silvestri, had driven the business into the ground. Silvestri owned a lien on the man's personal property. There were hard feelings between them.

After his conversion, Silvestri, who felt as if he'd received God's forgiveness, contacted the man and made him a deal. Silvestri told him he was going to forgive the bill for the remaining eighty-five-thousand dollars. But he asked that, as a way of paying off the debt, the man write a two hundred-word essay each day for one hundred days and mail it to Silvestri. The topic for each missive: forgiveness.

The man accepted the offer. As his letters began to arrive, Silvestri perceived a subtle transformation in him, too. The man said he'd been trying for twenty years to forgive a member of his own family, and that now, as he'd considered the subject of forgiveness, his heart finally had begun to soften.

Silvestri said that before his experience on that golf cart path, he didn't see his life in terms of white and black, God's ways versus his own ways. His life was filled with grays. "I've come out of the gray area," he says. "I want everything to be exactly white. Every day now, I look at it as a blessing."

And he carries that 1975 penny with him everywhere, to remind him.

An Encounter with Antiquity

Dr. Jud Chalkley, like Ken Silvestri, never had given God much serious thought. The anesthesiologist—"I pass gas for a living," he
jokes—describes himself as "quite rebellious and very much living for
Jud. Until I got sick."

A native of Columbia, Missouri, he was a graduate of the University of Missouri Medical School. Lean and athletic, a runner, he competed in a mini-marathon in the spring of 1978. By that fall he couldn't
walk up two flights of stairs without his fingernails turning blue. He'd
been stricken during the summer with sarcoidosis, an inflammatory
lung disease. For the next eighteen months Chalkley was too ill to practice medicine. By 1979 he and his wife, Robin, moved to New York City,
where they hoped Jud might establish a new career as a writer, because
it looked as if his medical career had been permanently ended by his
disease. "I was really seeking, trying to figure out what I wanted to do,"
he said. "I only had a couple of good hours a day."

Among other things, Chalkley began to explore religion, but in his
own reserved, intellectual way. In June 1979, he was reading one book
by a conservative Protestant, Catherine Marshall, and simultaneously
another by a liberal European Catholic. Their approaches to faith were
polar opposites.

One day during his couple of good hours, Chalkley went out for a
walk. While strolling near the southwest corner of Central Park, he
happened to see the headquarters of the American Bible Society. On a
lark, he stopped in. The second floor contained a museum that included exhibits of biblical materials. Chalkley wandered around there.

He came to an exhibit that featured a copy of the ancient Isaiah
scroll that had been among the Dead Sea Scrolls, the vital, chance dis-
coveries unearthed in the Middle East in 1947. Chalkley stood alone,
reading about the old manuscript. The Isaiah scroll was uncannily faithful to the other, more recent works that had been used in forming both
the Jewish and Christian canons of scripture.

Without warning, with no expectation that such a thing might happen, the young physician found himself in tears, rocked by a spiritual revelation. He sank to the floor, weeping.

"The realization that God's word was authentic and real and ever-lasting just overwhelmed me," he said quietly in late 1995, still a re-served man. He chose his words carefully. "I no longer hovered in that abyss between knowing and not knowing and doubting, but I believe by the Holy Spirit's presence I had that assurance of truth. . . . I real-ized that I'd been living for me and that almost everything I did was selfish and self-centered and sinful, and that I really needed to get my focus on living for the Lord."

Ultimately Chalkley returned to his medical practice. But as with St. Paul, Newton, Colson, Magruder, and Silvestri, his life never has been quite the same. He became an active churchgoer. Today, he and Robin host prayer meetings in their spacious home. Chalkley has com-pleted several trips as a volunteer medical missionary to Africa.

It all began with that summer day's revelation in a building near Central Park in New York City. "I believe with all my heart that God loves each and every one of us," Chalkley said. "God has a plan for each and every one of us that he longs to impart to us." The physician pointed out that Jesus once said he came to earth so that people might enjoy life abundantly. "I really believe those things," Chalkley said.

CHAPTER SEVEN

HEALINGS

AFTER DR. JUD CHALKLEY experienced his dramatic conversion in a museum at the American Bible Society, the young anesthesiologist discovered another benefit to his newfound faith. For nearly two years he had been debilitated by sarcoidosis, a lung disease that had left him barely able to breathe.

One evening in the spring of 1980, he ate a heavy steak dinner. A long-distance runner before being stricken by his disease, he still tried to keep in as good a trim as possible, so he drove to a university track to walk off his meal. As he stood on the track, he said, a voice spoke to him. It wasn't audible. It was an internal voice. Chalkley understood it to be imparting to him a message from God. "It's okay," the voice said. Somehow, Chalkley knew immediately what that meant: he was healed. The doctor began to run down the track. He ran on and on. "I wasn't short of breath," he said.

Later, he visited his own physician, who agreed that Chalkley's lungs had improved significantly. This second doctor ordered X rays; they confirmed what Chalkley had felt. His lungs were clear. He was able to return to his medical practice full-time, something that before had seemed impossible.

The healing was most amazing to him in that it was totally unexpected. "I'd never knowingly seen anybody healed," he said. The spiritual effects have been long-lasting, too. "It really drew me to the Lord in terms of Bible study, prayer, commitment, trying to change the things that needed changing in me," he said. "That's not to say that I've arrived at that lofty pinnacle."

Interestingly, the spiritual effects of Chalkley's recovery remained longer than the physical ones. A year after that healing on the track, his sarcoidosis reappeared. Chalkley submitted to a lung biopsy, which confirmed the recurrence. This time he underwent two years of treatment with the drug prednisone, from 1981 to 1983. The medicine sent the disease into remission again. Sarcoidosis struck him a third time in 1983, while he was serving a residency and studying on a fellowship at the University of Virginia. "It's a disease that waxes and wanes over its course," Chalkley said.

Chalkley's recovery in 1980 sounds like a spontaneous remission, albeit a temporary one. Such remissions occur occasionally, for reasons that are open to debate. They happen to religious people and the nonreligious alike. But more than fifteen years later, Chalkley was certain it was God who touched him that day on the track: "I just had an impression in my spirit."

In November 1991, Chalkley's wife, Robin, woke up with a sore throat, and soon was diagnosed with acute adult epiglottitis, a rare and serious throat infection. "She has been sick ever since," Chalkley said. She suffers from an unidentified virus that has damaged her immune system; her diagnosis now is chronic fatigue syndrome because no one knows what else to call it. She's undergone extensive evaluation and exploratory surgery at the University of Virginia, to no avail. She functions in her daily life at one-third to one-half her normal capacity. That makes it tough for the Chalkleys because Jud is a busy physician and Robin, a pleasant woman with medium-length blond hair, is the primary caregiver for their three children. It was one thing when he was ill, Chalkley said. "When the mother gets sick, it's desperate. We got desperate."

Medicine couldn't mend Robin's body or really even identify her sickness, so the Chalkleys decided to try the ministry of Benny Hinn, a controversial television evangelist known for his high-energy crusades, during which many people fall to the floor, under the power of God, they say, and others claim to have been spectacularly healed. "We believed in healing," Chalkley said.

The couple first attended a Hinn crusade in Tulsa, Oklahoma, then Robin went to one in Chicago alone. Together they traveled to Charlotte, North Carolina, and later to Hinn's home church in Orlando,

Florida. By 1993, Chalkley had volunteered to serve at Hinn's rallies in Kansas City, Chicago, Cincinnati, and Louisville. The services usually begin with up to two hours of praise and worship music that includes a three-thousand-person choir made up of people from the cities in which Hinn is appearing. "It's just incredible," Chalkley said of the music. Then Hinn preaches. The climax takes place when people in the congregation stream to the stage to report the miracles they believe God has performed for them during the evening. Ushers screen them initially. "They try to keep people off the stage who just want to be on the stage and fall down, or whose stories don't make sense, or who are obvious phonies," Chalkley said. "Most of it's for attention, I think. The media have planted people. They have faked miracles to expose the whole ministry as fraudulent."

Those whom the ushers believe might really have been healed of serious diseases are directed to an interview room away from the action, where volunteers such as Chalkley ask them to sign release-of-information forms, to describe what ailments they suffered, and then to tell why they think they've been cured. Chalkley isn't working there officially as a physician, but his medical training helps. "We just take their story and try to be precise," he said. The volunteers warn those who've come forward to consult their doctors at home. "They're advised to continue all their medications and not to do anything foolish," Chalkley said. The information from each night's rally is compiled and forwarded to another physician who works for Hinn researching the healings that appear legitimate, Chalkley said.

The vast majority of the supposed healings aren't real, in Chalkley's educated opinion. "I'm pretty skeptical," he said. Some who come forward merely want attention. Often there's no hard evidence they ever suffered from the diseases they claim. Many more are genuinely ill, get caught up in the emotion of the moment, and think they've been cured—but haven't been. Any number of AIDS patients have said they felt healed. "I'm not God," Chalkley said. "I don't know, but to my knowledge those have not been documented."

In every service there are special sections of the audience reserved for ill children, including those in wheelchairs. "It's heartbreaking, too," Chalkley said. "You so hope that they would be healed, but I've never seen any of those terribly, terribly afflicted kids restored while I was working."

Neither has Chalkley's wife, Robin, been healed.

In his work for Hinn, Chalkley has interviewed between three hundred and four hundred people, he said. He's seen five to ten he believes truly were supernaturally restored to health, as best as he could determine from the evidence available to him. He met a girl from St. Louis who had been healed earlier at a Hinn crusade. She had been wheelchair-bound and carried a documented diagnosis of multiple sclerosis. Chalkley knows her and her whole family. "The last time I saw her, about a year ago, she was fine," he said. "She believes she was touched by the power of God—and I have no other explanation, as a physician, for an instantaneous cure of MS."

In one rally in which he was working, Chalkley interviewed another young girl wearing Coke-bottle glasses. She believed her eyes had been healed. "We tested her vision and it was 20/20." Skeptics might argue those weren't really the girl's glasses, that it was a hoax—"and they might be right. But she was one eleven-year-old that acted like her vision had been restored. She either had to be an Oscar-winning actress or something really had happened to her."

Hinn's spokeswoman, Sue Langford, refused to confirm any of this: Chalkley's voluntary role or the numbers of documented healings in Hinn crusades. "It's just our policy" not to comment, she said.

Chalkley said he's often disturbed by Hinn's extravagant showmanship. Hinn learned his craft by working with the late, eccentric Kathryn Kuhlman. "She was extremely flamboyant and quite a show-type person," Chalkley said. "Benny Hinn apprenticed under her and he has a lot of that flamboyance as well. . . . But there's no doubt in my mind that God has used him."

Faith Healing Versus Divine Healing

Next to conversions, healings probably are the most commonly reported miracles of our time. Mention miraculous healing and you're likely to conjure up images for many people of big-time "faith healers" such as Hinn, or of old-fashioned tent meetings, sawdust floors, and impassioned pleas for money. The names of healing evangelists are part of the lore of twentieth-century American folk religion: the fictional Elmer Gantry, the real-life Sister Aimee Semple McPherson, Oral Roberts, and Kuhlman. The stars of the movement always have been controversial. Their meetings combine as much melodrama as piety—wrenching music, pathos, light shows. Some, such as McPherson, were linked to scandals of one kind or another.

These tent-and-arena revivalists nearly all are Protestants. But Roman Catholics have their own variations, such as the healing apparitions at Lourdes, where pilgrims flock by the tens of thousands. In rural regions of Africa, India, and Asia, Islam and Hinduism boast also their healers.

But most miraculous healings don't take place among large, rowdy meetings. The number of people who might have been healed at a rally of, say, Benny Hinn, is tiny compared to the number of people who say they've been healed at home. Still, we should be careful before we reject even the most flamboyant healers. Many of them have succeeded in their ministries partly because there is an inexplicable force around them—which they usually attribute to God—that produces extraordinary manifestations of power.

Prizewinning poet and playwright Daniel Mark Epstein in 1993 published a first-rate biography, *Sister Aimee: The Life of Aimee Semple McPherson*. Epstein writes as a secular rationalist, one who is sympathetic to McPherson but leery of her ecstasies and miracles. Always, Epstein poses nonmiraculous explanations for the supposedly supernatural phenomena that were attached to McPherson's emotional preaching. For instance, one well-known healing in Sister Aimee's ministry involved Louise Messnick, a woman pitifully and obviously crippled by rheumatoid arthritis. McPherson prayed for Messnick. In plain view of a large revival crowd, Messnick's clawlike hands straightened. Her chin, once locked on her chest, raised to a normal position. She was instantly cured of all her disfiguring symptoms. Epstein acknowledges this, yet explains in some detail that rheumatoid arthritis is a disease of the immune system, which doctors say can respond amazingly to the power of suggestion. Messnick reportedly had been in a deep depression and McPherson filled her with the hopeful possibility of a cure, Epstein suggests.

However Epstein, eminently fair, also admits that McPherson's many healings pose a conundrum for secular historians. It's clear that the reported miracles numbered in the thousands, he says, that mountains of contemporary press clippings bore witness to them, that McPherson actually didn't want a healing ministry and tried to avoid it—and that there is no evidence whatever of fakery. Epstein stops short of saying that the healings were true miracles. Still, his observations should give pause to any thoughtful reader.

Similarly, prizewinning British journalist and author John Cornwell investigated the world of religious visions, apparitions, and miracles in his 1991 book, *The Hiding Places of God*. Cornwell reports on one modern cure at Lourdes that actually made its way into the English *Journal of the Royal Society of Medicine*. A twelve-year-old Sicilian girl, Delizia Cirollie, was diagnosed with a bony metastasis of neuroblastoma on her right knee. A physician recommended that the leg be amputated to stop the cancer's spread. Cobalt treatments also were recommended. Cirollie's family refused medical treatments and her condition continued to decline. A teacher suggested she be taken to Lourdes. She spent four days bathing in the water there, praying and attending religious ceremonies, but returned home without showing any improvement. A few months later, the girl's cancer suddenly disappeared. Even the damaged bone of her stricken knee repaired itself. Subsequent examinations differed on whether the condition she'd originally suffered was neuroblastoma or Ewing's tumor. In either case, there were no recorded spontaneous remissions of neuroblastoma in a child over the age of five and no recorded spontaneous cures of Ewing's tumor at all. Clearly something remarkable had happened.

However, Cornwell rightfully points out that of the two million ailing pilgrims who have visited Lourdes since 1858, a mere sixty-five are recognized by the Roman Catholic Church as having been miraculously cured. On the other hand, it should also be noted again that the Catholic Church's criteria for declaring a miraculous healing are the most stringent in the religious world.

I believe people are sometimes healed at these large rallies. But most miraculous healings are private, unexpected ones. Usually when people receive a spiritual cure it's not in the presence of an evangelist. It's simply a gracious gift of God. Most healings aren't faith healings so much as divine healings.

Allergies Are Healed at a Catholic Meeting

Carol Sparks, a housewife, calls herself a cradle Catholic. She was a nominal churchgoer, though, until the early 1980s, when she attended a "Life in the Spirit" seminar designed to teach Catholics how to tap into the supernatural power of the Holy Spirit. There, she invited God to play an active part in her life. "It was a commitment prayer," she said. "I felt an immense power and an outpouring of his love. The Holy Spirit, he is love. It just felt like a washing of water over me. . . . I felt clear and fresh and renewed." Immediately she became more active in her faith and experienced a new joy in it.

She still had one problem that could make her life miserable at times. Carol suffered from severe allergies. Tree pollens set off her agonies: "You can't get away from the outdoors," she said. Even the nickel in jewelry could cause her eyes to swell shut, her nose to pour, and rashes to erupt on her body. Carol asked her Catholic friends to pray for her. They prayed time and again, and she felt as if she were improving slowly. Very slowly.

Then one weekend she and some friends drove to a "signs and wonders" seminar held at a Catholic college in Steubenville, Ohio. Signs and wonders is another name for divine miracles. Unfortunately, Carol was sick all weekend. Her allergies had flared up, and she spent most of the trip fending off a terrible headache, one so bad that even her ears and neck hurt. She really couldn't pay attention to the lessons the seminar's teachers tried to impart.

Organizers had erected a striped tent on the campus, and near the end of the weekend some two thousand worshipers crowded into it. The seminar's leader, a priest, asked other priests and lay healers to encircle the tent for a period of prayer. As they prayed, Carol left her seat and walked forward to a Father Wade. She can't recall his first name now, but she definitely remembers what happened. The priest placed his hands on her head and shoulder. The next thing she knew Carol was lying on the ground, knocked off her feet by God's power. "It was a very peaceful feeling," she said. As she'd walked to the front her ears, neck, and head had throbbed. "When I got up, there was none of that. It was like a burden had been lifted. I knew I was healed."

That was more than ten years ago. Since then, Carol's had some minor flareups with her sinuses. But her eyes have never again swelled. Her nose doesn't run constantly. All other serious symptoms have vanished, too. "The Lord has taken the severity away," she said.

God Mends Teeth

Like Carol Sparks, Ray Grachek is a Roman Catholic. He's a retired mechanical designer for the federal government and a native of Fremont, Ohio, where he graduated from a Catholic high school. Like Sparks, Ray experienced a significant deepening of his spiritual life when he was well into adulthood. At forty, he says, God favored him with a hunger for the scripture. "I devoured it," he said. He even began taking his Bible to the army depot where he worked so he could read it during his breaks and on his lunch hours. He started an interdenominational prayer group of men at the depot who met once a week. It grew to include up to fifty men by the time Ray retired. "Our common denominator was Jesus Christ," he said.

A few years ago, Ray was at home. He'd recently had some periodontal work done and his mouth was sore. Worse, four of his front teeth were so loose that they were, in effect, dangling in their sockets—so loose Ray had to chew food on the sides of his mouth to avoid them. The periodontist already had told him the teeth needed to be extracted.

This particular day, in 1991, Ray sat in a chair in his family room. On the floor beside his chair lay a circular from a Protestant evangelist. The headline on the publication said, "God is grieved with the world's sin today." Ray glanced at the headline, and as he did somehow the thought came to him—he believed it was an inner voice from the Holy Spirit—"What would you ask me that I would do for you?"

Ray couldn't answer. He hadn't considered asking God to do anything for him. "I said, 'Lord, you know more than I'—never thinking of my teeth."

The inner voice spoke to him a second time: "Would you believe I'm grieved over the sin of the world if your front teeth were healed? Then they are!"

The crazy thing? "They just tightened up," Ray said. "They just gradually tightened up." When he returned for his next examination, the periodontist was amazed. The teeth didn't need to be extracted after all. The dentist said, "'Wow! Beautiful!'" Ray said. "I didn't tell him."

But ever since, Ray has taken it as his duty to pray for the sins of the world daily, "many times during the day." He believes that's what God was calling him to do when God tightened his teeth.

A Buddhist Healer Helps a Businessman

Donn Hollingsworth had been superintendent of the American School in Kuwait and a private school headmaster in the United States. He also was a Protestant minister. In Kuwait he picked up parasites that attacked his blood supply. When he returned to America, he learned he'd suffered a major heart attack without knowing it. Doctors said his heart was so enlarged that no diet or therapy could help. To make matters worse, Donn and his wife, Ann, discovered their insurance policy didn't cover medical care in the United States. The couple soon exhausted their savings.

Ann, a stately woman of aristocratic bearing, recalled recently what those days were like. "I found you can't take each day at a time without some hope," she said. "I cried each day and night for a year and a half."

Donn decided he must do something other than sit down and wait to die, and a new overseas opportunity presented itself. An international electrical company—founded in Kuwait and based in England—needed an English-speaking coordinator to manage its operations in mainland China. Its subsidiary there, China Products Co., exported refrigerators, dishwashers, and other electrical appliances from China to other parts of the world. The company wanted someone who could keep its various British, Kuwaiti, and Chinese nationalities talking with one another. Donn and Ann accepted the task. In 1988 they moved to Guangzhou and were assigned an apartment in the elaborate Garden Hotel, a residence for foreign nationals.

No sooner had the Hollingsworths arrived in China than they found that their company was beset by problems. Despite Donn's best efforts, the people of various nationalities involved in the project couldn't communicate. Worse, Donn suffered severe angina that left him weak for days at a time.

Then Ann was invited to a tea at the American consulate general's office, which also was housed in the Garden Hotel. Donn remained in their apartment. At the tea, "A Chinese woman came across the room, and she starts talking to me in Chinese," Ann recalled. A second Chinese woman interpreted: "She said, 'This woman says she can help your husband.'"

As far as Ann could ever determine, the woman who approached her never had met Donn and knew nothing of his condition. Her name was Madame Moe. Puzzled, Ann agreed to take Madame Moe and her interpreter to the Hollingsworths' apartment on the hotel's twenty-first floor. As they entered it, Madame Moe looked at Donn and started bowing. "I said, 'What's she doing?'" Ann recalled. The interpreter informed her that Madame Moe, a Buddhist, had declared that Donn, the Christian minister, must be a spiritual master.

Madame Moe walked over to Donn and placed her hands over his chest and back without touching him. Her hands radiated warmth like heated irons. Donn's heart immediately improved. The pain stopped. His energy returned.

The Hollingsworths soon became friendly with Madame Moe, who, as it turned out, was a member of a special unit of Buddhist chi gong healing masters based in Beijing. The Chinese believed them to possess wondrous curative powers, even though Buddhism isn't a theistic religion. Members of Madame Moe's unit frequently were called in to treat elderly Chinese government officials before their summits with American leaders—despite the fact that the Communist officials supposedly were hostile to all religion.

Madame Moe began showing up unannounced at the Garden

Hotel a couple of times a month, just when Donn was feeling his worst. It was as if she could sense his pain, Donn once told me. Ann agreed. "She would come and his energy level would get such a boost. His angina would just disappear."

The chi gong healer became something of a minor celebrity—and a novelty—among the foreign nationals at the Garden Hotel. She offered her powers to Ann, who suffered from neck and back problems, as well as to members of the American consulate. Ann Hollingsworth has a photograph of the small, black-haired woman ministering to Prescott Bush, the elder brother of President George Bush, who happened to visit the hotel during a trip to China. Bush is sitting in a chair as Madame Moe, wearing sunglasses, runs her hands over him. "She said she could see the energy better with sunglasses," Ann said.

That same night, some Kuwaitis attended a lavish Arab meal prepared in honor of Bush and his American delegation. One Kuwaiti complained that his arm hurt and that he couldn't raise it above his shoulder. The Americans asked Madame Moe to help him. "He came out doing jumping jacks," Ann said. "He was so excited he wanted to take her to Kuwait. He said he'd set her up."

The Buddhist healer would perform tricks, too. "We'd say, Madame Moe, cook an orange," Ann said. The Americans would hand her a cold orange from the hotel deli's bin. She'd grasp it in her hands a few minutes—and turn it into a squishy, cooked mass of pulp.

The most amazing thing, though, was how Madame Moe seemed to intuitively know when Donn was sick. "Her ability to work with Donn was just extraordinary," Ann said.

Despite his poor prognosis, Donn led an active life for a number of years, largely due to his experiences with Madame Moe and his fervent belief in the powers of spiritual healing. The Hollingsworths returned to the States in 1990, and Donn became pastor of a small independent Presbyterian church. I first met him there in the early 1990s and heard his unusual story. At the time, he appeared quite healthy and vibrant. When I visited him and Ann late in 1995, though, his heart problems had flared up again and he was bedridden in their modest home, unable to talk much. He died peacefully in February 1996.

Ann, a Christian, said she'd often thought about what she saw overseas. "My lord and master is Jesus Christ. There is no question in my mind," she said. Yet in her travels she encountered good, loving, and spiritually powerful Muslims, Hindus, and Buddhists. "It was a real awakening to me," she said. "They were such spiritually attuned people. It's the first time I realized that Christianity is the minority religion. . . . God is so much more than my intelligence can sort out. I know who my lord and master is, who my advocate is. But I can't tell you that yours isn't true to you."

A Missionary's Daughter Sees Cancer Disappear

Sue Philpot is a trained nurse, a homemaker, and the wife of a Kentucky state senator. She's a personable, blond woman in her mid-forties. Sue grew up in Africa, in what is now called Zaire, the daughter of missionaries.

In 1962, when she was twelve, her family returned to the United States on a furlough and lived temporarily in Wilmore, Kentucky. Sue complained to her mom, Doris R. Davis, that her leg hurt. "Oh, it's just growing pains," Doris said, and didn't give the matter much consideration. But Sue kept whining. Finally, Doris had to take one of her sons to a local physician and, almost as an afterthought, told Sue to come along so the doctor could look at her leg, too.

To Doris's horror, the general practitioner took one look at Sue's leg and announced that he must call an orthopedic surgeon in Lexington.

Sue quickly was shuttled off to the surgeon, who X-rayed her leg. He called Doris into a nearby room to look at the images. "Sure enough there was this lump on the bone coming up the middle of her leg," Doris said. The lump was the size of a half-dollar. The doctor said it almost surely was a fast-growing osteosarcoma. Bone cancer. "It just zooms through your body," Doris said. As she remembers it, the physician "blew up" at her for ignoring Sue's pleas for so long. Sue remembers hearing her mother in the next room, sobbing. The doctor scheduled surgery for the following Monday.

"I'll never forget that," Doris said. "It was such a traumatic event." Likely, Sue's leg would be amputated. If that prospect by itself weren't bad enough, the Davises also knew that Sue's illness might prevent them from returning to their beloved mission field.

The only one not terribly frightened was Sue. She had recently undergone a conversion experience after watching a Billy Graham film at her boarding school. "I was still on that high," she said. The young girl understood the situation's gravity, but figured that if she died, she'd just go to heaven and that would be dandy.

She was admitted to Lexington's Good Samaritan Hospital on a Sunday. Her uncle, the Reverend David Seamands, then was pastor of Wilmore United Methodist Church. He asked the congregation to pray a special healing prayer for Sue that day, even though she wasn't present at the service.

Monday, after her surgery, Sue woke up from the anesthesia. She saw the surgeon shaking his head in wonder. Her leg was still there.

The doctor's exact report remains a matter of debate among the family, thirty-some years later. Sue recalls that surgeon found no cancer. As Doris remembers it, a biopsy showed the presence of cancer, but to the doctor's astonishment the disease hadn't eaten deeply into the bone and hadn't spread elsewhere. The surgeon merely removed a small portion of the affected bone. One thing is sure. When the surgery was over, the cancer was gone—quickly and easily. Sue kept her leg, with only a thick scar than runs upward from her ankle to show for her trouble. The cancer never recurred. The Davises returned to their mission field in Africa.

Whatever the details, Sue believes she was divinely touched because of the prayers offered on her behalf. So does Doris. "It's nothing but a miracle," the grateful mother said.

The Miraculous Morgan Family

Sometimes miracles run in families. Frank Morgan's family is one of those fortunate clans. Like many Appalachians, Morgan's parents moved north with their children during the first half of this century, hoping that Frank's father, Monroe Morgan, could find work. They settled first in Indiana and later near Dayton, Ohio. The Morgans belonged to the Anderson, Indiana-based Church of God. It isn't a

Pentecostal denomination, yet Monroe and Maude Morgan, like many of their fellow church members, believed in divine healing.

It was a good thing they did. By the time young Frank was in the sixth grade he had become sickly and enervated. His parents took him to a doctor who tested his spittle and found that he had been exposed to tuberculosis. X rays followed, and what they showed couldn't have been more grim. Frank had contracted TB in both lungs. The five other children in the family also were tested for tuberculosis, but none of them had been infected.

In those days, the 1930s, doctors possessed few treatments for the dreaded TB. "It usually was a deadly disease," Frank said. There was a sanatorium near Dayton, but it was filled to capacity.

There seemed little hope for Frank. As a last resort, Monroe and Maude Morgan wrote to a minister in Indiana, the Reverend E.E. Byrum, who was said to possess the gift of healing. They asked the preacher to anoint a handkerchief with olive oil and mail it to them so they could place it on Frank. In the Bible, St. Paul sometimes healed people that way. Byrum obliged.

After the handkerchief arrived, young Frank sat in the living room in a chair. "They unfolded it and laid it on my chest and prayed for me," he said. "They just prayed that God would heal me." His brothers and sisters were present. Frank didn't feel anything special as they prayed. "But from that day on, I began to recover." When I interviewed Frank, a retired insurance supervisor now in his seventies, he cried as we sat at his dining room table. "I can't talk about these things without getting emotional," he said by way of apology. "I do think God spared my life."

By the eighth grade, Frank Morgan was playing sports. He was still pretty scrawny, but his health and strength just improved and improved. By his last years of high school at Brookville High School in Brookville, Ohio, where the family had by then moved, he was an outfielder on the baseball team, and a forward on the basketball team; he competed in the high jump, the broad jump, and the hundred-yard dash on the track team. He was named the outstanding boy athlete in his senior class. "That was quite a change," he said.

During World War II, Frank was called up for military service. A doctor conducting his Army physical exam found evidence of his past disease. After some wrangling pro and con, and another, more rigorous exam, Army physicians decided not to accept Frank for the armed forces. "Both lungs were pretty badly scarred," he said. "So the evidence was there." Clearly, he'd once had a severe case of TB. But everyone agreed the disease itself was gone.

That wasn't the end of miracles in the Morgan family.

Frank eventually married and his wife, Wyvonna, developed crippling arthritis. By age thirty-four, the young mother of four was virtually an invalid. Her hands were gnarled. The family was quite religious—Frank taught Sunday school for fifty years and believes a calling to that lay ministry was one reason God had spared his life from TB—but Wyvonna couldn't kneel beside her children's beds to say their nightly prayers with them.

About 1956, the family was attending a Church of God in Marion, Ohio. It was a small, brick church built with donated labor. The average attendance on Sundays ran between 100 and 125. A traveling evangelist came to speak at the church. Frank can't even recall his name forty years later. "He went from church to church," he said. The evangelist spoke about healing. At the end of one service, the minister asked those who were sick to approach the altar, where he would anoint them with oil and pray for them. Wyvonna hobbled down the aisle, bent and in pain. She couldn't kneel as the others did, so she sat on the front pew. The evangelist never even made it to her. A lay woman from the congregation anointed Wyvonna instead. "She said there was something like an electric shock that went from the top of her head clear through to her toes—and the pain and stiffness was gone instantly," Frank said. Wyvonna's hands still were drawn and knotted, but otherwise she was totally, instantly healed.

As the Morgan family walked home down Congress Street in Marion that night, a neighbor glanced out her window. She was so shocked by what she saw that she came to the Morgans' home the next day to find out what had happened to Wyvonna—why she was walking normally. Soon the word spread. "When she'd walk down the street you'd see the neighbors peeking out their windows and peeking out their doors to watch her," Frank said. "They couldn't believe the change that had occurred. She walked like a young girl again."

Wyvonna passed away in 1986, a victim of lymphoma. But several other eyewitnesses confirmed her instantaneous healing. One was Fred Morgan, Frank's brother, a retired professor of biological sciences who taught at colleges in Indiana and Florida. He was present at the service that night. "I'm sort of a skeptical person myself," Fred said. "I think it was a miracle. I was there when it happened. She was able to go ahead with her life from that point on."

Frank and Wyvonna's daughter, Diana Davis—no relation to Doris R. Davis in the previous story—holds the most poignant memory of that night. At forty-eight, Diana suffers from the same crippling arthritis that afflicted her mother. "I don't have that kind of faith," she said of her mom's healing. "I don't think that could happen to me." Still, she recalls her mother's cure well. The evening Wyvonna was healed, the young mother prepared Diana and her sister Barbara for their evening prayers. "Our mother knelt by our bed that night for the first time ever," Diana said. "That's what I remember. We sat straight up in bed."

There's one more twist to this story. Barbara, the other daughter in the bedroom with Diana that night, as an adult developed a lymphoma similar to the one that eventually killed Wyvonna. Barbara's prognosis was equally grim. A malignant tumor the size of a cantaloupe had wrapped itself around her colon. Her doctor gave her about three years to live and started her on a chemotherapy regimen. One Sunday morning she walked forward in her mainstream, evangelical church and asked for prayer. When the minister touched her, "I felt like a little shock go through me," she said. "I just got better." In fact, with the help of continued medical treatments, she fully recovered and has been cancer free for ten years. She credits both prayer and medicine. "I think God works through the doctors," she said.

CHAPTER EIGHT

MIRACLES OF DELIVERANCE

M Y FAVORITE SONGWRITER, John Prine, once composed a light-hearted if fatalistic tune called "It's a Big Old Goofy World."
Well, it's a big old dangerous world, too. Not infrequently, people find themselves tumbling into the maw of terror: muggers surround them on big-city buses; they're even attacked by demons, some say. Just as the hand of the Almighty seems to appear unexpectedly during periods of individual soul-searching and during illnesses, it also appears during great calamities. God or his emissaries sometimes show up to rescue fortunate people from death, injury, and the fires of hell itself. I call these acts miracles of deliverance.

Deliverance from Hell

You've heard about near-death experiences, where people's hearts stop on operating tables. These folks travel through a tunnel with a light at its end. As they approach the light, they feel incredible peace. They see Jesus or an angel or their dead relatives.

Well, Kathy Bland died in 1989, and she experienced a near-death experience of another kind. She went to the bad place. As in a lake of fire. As in a horned devil of greenish brown. "It was real," Bland says. "I just suddenly found myself there." In hell.

In 1994, for Easter Sunday, I wrote a newspaper story about what clergy and scholars say happens when we die. In it, I cited a *Time*-CNN-Yankelovich poll that found that 74 percent of rank-and-file Americans believe in hell. My interviews with ministers and academics, on the other hand, showed them to be divided on whether hell really exists.

Bland, a woman in her mid-thirties who lives in rural Jessamine County, Kentucky, called me later to say she could settle that debate. She'd *been* to hell.

After talking with her, I checked out as much of her story as I could. The Hades part, of course, I couldn't verify. But her account stood up to as much scrutiny as I could give it. Her mother, Barbara Bland, who lives on a Bourbon County farm, said Kathy apparently is of sound mind. So did Barbara's Roman Catholic pastor. Kathy's physician confirmed that she had been desperately sick and had hovered at the point of death, just as she'd told me.

Kathy had led a tough life. At the time of her illness, she'd been partying hard. She didn't go to church. She'd never given much thought to the afterlife, she said. Then she came down with a staph infection that spread to her heart. She ended up gravely sick in Lexington's Central Baptist Hospital, in need of heart surgery. Evidently Kathy clinically "died"—or coded—two or three times during her ordeal, depending upon whether her memory or her mother's is more accurate. The Reverend Thomas P. Farrell, a Catholic priest, said he administered last rites.

One of the times she died, Bland awoke on a furnace about six feet long by three feet wide: "I was laying on it, burning," she said. Terrified, she jumped to her feet and fled through a nearby door, only to find herself facing a lake of fire where lost souls writhed in the flames. Beside the lake was a cliff on which stood Satan himself. The tormented people in the flames were forced to praise him. "They would make you worship the devil," Kathy said. "But I wouldn't."

As soon as she refused to worship Satan, she found another exit. She fled again and suddenly was walking down a path in a peaceful green pasture, which she believes was purgatory.

Kathy was resuscitated in the hospital and survived against the odds, "our miracle child," her mother called her. She spent months recuperating in a hospital for the disabled. Until our conversation, she'd told hardly anyone about her visit to the netherworld. But she'd never shaken the images. She realized that some might say she'd only had a hallucination set off by chemicals her brain released as it closed down. She disagreed. "I was definitely in hell." Kathy said she was allowed to return because her family had asked a lot of people to pray for her. She went to hell because "I hadn't been a very good person. I'm just trying to take warning from that incident."

Today, more than seven years after her visit to the fiery lake, Kathy continues to believe she was spared by God from an eternal damnation. "It's given me more of a positive outlook on life," she said. "I've just made steps to make a better life. It's definitely something God did. For sure. There's some reason for me to still be here." Kathy says she prays a lot these days. She's become a dedicated mother to her child. She doesn't want to ever return to that dreadful place.

A Girl Outruns Charging Animals

Joann Poppleton grew up on a farm near the historic town of Concord, Massachusetts, and later lived in the Midwest for more than forty years. She's a retired reading teacher, outgoing and articulate. She's a Roman Catholic.

Miracles began happening early in her life. The first one saved her from serious injury when she was eight years old. She was running near the barnyard on her family's farm, toward her house, when she heard the thump of hooves. Looking back, Joann saw that someone had left open a gate—and that a cow and two horses were charging at her. "They were all chasing me," she said. "I thought, 'I'll never make it to the kitchen door.' It was terrible."

The spooked animals were right on top of her and the house was fifty yards away. Joann's mother and the Poppletons' housekeeper happened to look outside and see the small stampede. They rushed to the kitchen door and held it open. Joann's mother screamed, "Jesus, help her!"

Little Joann ran faster than anyone thought she could. She dashed through the open door and into the safety of the house, mere steps ahead of the galloping animals. The cow crashed into the porch and the horses slammed into the cow, a three-animal pileup. "My mother said, 'That *had* to be a miracle! How could an eight-year-old outrun a cow and two horses?'" Joann said. "That's the first time I ever heard the word 'miracle.'"

She believes today that the Lord interceded and somehow gave her an extra boost of speed that delivered her from a certain trampling. But the near-tragedy was so traumatic that she never could shake the fear. At least once a week for years and years afterward, throughout her youth and into adulthood, Joann suffered nightmares of being chased by cows and horses. "It was torture," she said. For decades, she dreaded going to sleep at night, not knowing whether an awful dream would await her when her eyes shut.

Then, when she was nearly seventy years old—more than sixty years after that near-miss in the barnyard—she received a deliverance of another kind. One evening her nightmare returned yet again. This time she was being chased by horses bent on stomping her beneath their hooves. But this dream was different from all those other hundreds of nightmares. This time a supernatural voice said, "Step aside and let the horses around." She stepped to the side and the horses galloped past her. Really, it was that simple.

That ended the bad dreams. "I don't have those nightmares anymore," Joann said. "I know that was a healing. I don't have nightmares. I thank God all the time that I can go to bed and not worry about having nightmares about cows and horses chasing me."

Saved from Marauding Skinheads

He looks like an aging biker, stocky, but with shoulders that are beginning to round and a thick mustache that is graying. His complexion is rough enough that it borders on leathery. He still wears his dark hair in a ponytail, favors black shirts and black jeans and motorcycle jackets.

John Smith has spent much of his adult life among notorious biker gangs in his native Australia. But he's not a Hell's Angel himself. In a way he's a heaven's angel, a rebel, an intellectual, and a former atheist who was astonished to find himself converted to Christianity several decades ago. John helped found and lead the Jesus Movement in Australia. A radical Christian with long-standing ties to the counterculture of the 1960s, he's always seen it as his calling to minister among society's misfits and outcasts, the people "normal" churches find it difficult to accept. He says it's not easy being a dedicated Christian in his home country. About 23 percent of Australia's people are church members, he said, but attendance is only 5 percent at best.

The Lord, John says, had delivered him many times. This is one story he tells. The racist skinhead movement, imported from Great Britain, had grown very large in Australia by 1974. The skinheads, for whatever reasons, quickly declared themselves hostile to all bikers—and Victoria, where John lived, then had more than seventy motorcycle gangs. The skinheads and bikers clashed several times. So the stage seemed set for trouble when large groups of skinheads and motorcycle gangs both converged on that year's Sunbury pop festival, a sort of Australian Woodstock. John, who attended the outdoor concert with God's Squad—his small group of ragtag biker converts to Christianity—found himself caught between the warring parties.

Early on, fights broke out. The police couldn't distinguish the genuinely aggressive skinhead gangs from nonviolent fans who simply dressed in skinhead fashions. So they decided on another tactic: they tossed all the bikers out of the concert because they were easier to identify; they all wore black leather jackets bearing large patches that stated which gangs they belonged to. But the police overlooked God's Squad and a band of maybe forty Hell's Angels, who were allowed to remain. The Hell's Angels had camped near a river.

As the weekend wore on, word reached the Hell's Angels' camp that the skinheads were massed on a nearby hillside and planning to attack them, as well as God's Squad, since they also were bikers. The skinheads numbered in the hundreds, perhaps in the thousands. They were armed with clubs, chains, metal bars. Altogether, there were about sixty bikers, including the Christians.

The "father" of the Melbourne Hell's Angels, Doug Scott, approached John and asked whether God's Squad intended to help them defend themselves. The skinheads wouldn't care whether John's group was religious, Scott said. They would massacre the Christians alongside the Hell's Angels. John replied that he and his friends would have to discuss the matter.

"We went away to pray about it," John recalled. Some of the members of his group were former warriors themselves and were inclined to take up arms. But after prayer, God's Squad returned to the Hell's

Angels' camp. It was nearly dark. John told Scott that his group's members, being Christians, would not fight the skinheads. Yet he understood, he said, that the vastly outnumbered Hell's Angels couldn't retreat without losing face. On the other hand, God's Squad wasn't worried about losing face, John told Scott. As the skinheads charged down the hill, the members of the God Squad would go up the hill and try to talk with them, to see if they couldn't negotiate a peaceful settlement. John still remembers one of the Angels, a dark-skinned six-foot-seven Torres Strait Islander named Affy, standing there with a chain in one hand and a metal fence post in the other, shaking his head in disbelief.

Various Angels replied that the skinheads would rip the God's Squad apart. "I don't think it's going to work out that way," was John's reply, as he records it in his autobiography, *On the Side of Angels*. "We believe God's with us and somehow he's going to sort this out."

John considered the battle inevitable. It was like a form of tribal warfare, he said: everyone's reputation was on the line. The skinheads had boasted they were coming, and so they couldn't back off. The Hell's Angels couldn't retreat without being humiliated. God's Squad had promised to go up the hill first, a brave stand, and now they couldn't leave.

God's Squad and the Hell's Angels sat down in the Angels' camp to nervously wait for the fight. As for the Christians, "We sat there and prayed," John said. The wait stretched on and on, into the night and then into the wee hours of the morning. About 4 A.M., one of the Hell's Angels stood up and said, "The skinheads aren't coming." He announced he was leaving. Scott, the Angels' leader, said that if he deserted and the skinheads did come, the Angels would hunt him down later and bash his brains out with an iron pipe as revenge for his cowardice. The man sat down, and they all waited some more.

"We just waited all night—and they never came," John said. More than twenty years later, he doesn't have any rational explanation for why the skinheads didn't show up. He does know this: the Christians' courageous stand apparently touched some of the Angels deeply. God's Squad developed lasting friendships with several of them.

John's not a big advocate for contemporary miracles. Nevertheless, he considers the skinheads' failure to attack a miracle of Old Testament proportions, like one of those stories in which God turns away an invading army before it can launch a single arrow or spear. He said God seemed to remind him after the Sunbury festival about a Bible verse that applied to his situation: "When a man's ways please the Lord, God makes even his enemies to be at peace with him."

Muggers Flee

Eunice Irwin, whom we met earlier, is a seminary assistant professor of Christian mission and contextual theology who has conducted much of her research and church work in the Philippines. In 1983, she was riding across Manila in a commercial Jeepney, an open-sided vehicle with a covered top that can seat up to twenty people and serves as a form of public transportation.

At a stop, four young men boarded the Jeepney and spied Eunice, an American woman, traveling alone. Two of them took seats on her right and two sat across from her. As the bus started on its way again, one of the youths beside her leaned toward Eunice, flashing a knife. He expertly slashed the side of her purse and jammed his hand inside it, rummaging through the contents. A couple of weeks earlier in Manila an American woman had resisted such an attack—and had been stabbed. Eunice couldn't fight, couldn't scream.

She did the only thing she knew to do given the circumstances. She prayed. She wasn't so much frightened, she said. "Somehow I was enraged, feeling my rights were violated." This was her prayer: "Lord, you can stop this." When she'd finished, she lifted her eyes and looked straight into the eyes of the mugger with the knife. Eunice felt a sharp zing almost like a jolt of electricity.

Evidently, so did the mugger. "He got zapped. He just jumped," she said. "He was scared. I was scared."

The fellow with the knife quickly popped to his feet. His buddies did, too. They stopped the Jeepney and fled as hastily as they could. As the vehicle pulled away, the four youths stood at the curb staring at Eunice through the Jeepney's open sides, as if dumbfounded. It all happened so fast that Eunice needed a moment to take stock. Her purse was cut, but none of her money or possessions had been stolen. She was unscratched.

"I believe God did that miracle," she said. "I really think that God has the ability to protect." She doesn't know exactly what it was that happened when her eyes met the mugger's, whether it was psychological or angelic or what, but she speculates that something in that electric gaze pricked the young man's conscience and reminded him that he was committing a sin. "I didn't do anything. I just prayed," she said. "Somehow God just used that look."

Delivered from Demons

Eric Holmberg came of age during the 1960s and 1970s. He was, by his own description, a problem child. Even so, he won an appointment to the U.S. Naval Academy—only to be dismissed for using drugs. Later he graduated from the College of William and Mary. While he was there, his drug use intensified. He especially liked LSD, which he thought was a spiritual substance that was helping him become god-like. And he equally disliked Christianity. "I considered myself something of an apologist for agnostics," he said. He led the life of a hippie, living in the country with several other rebels.

After graduation, Eric ended up in Jacksonville, Florida, working for a company purportedly researching alternative fuels. The company later turned out to be a scam, although he didn't know that when he took the job.

There he met a co-worker named Steve Hall. Steve was another wild-child, who now describes his early life as that of an "insane, hippie, drug freak—to the max." Steve once had been jailed for using the facilities of the University of Florida's agriculture college to grow marijuana. But by the time Eric met him, Steve had undergone a Christian conversion and was, to use a euphemism, high in the Spirit. He wanted to tell everybody he knew about God, including Eric.

The two young men had enough in common that they became friends, even though Steve had quit using drugs and simply considered that to be part of his background. "It wasn't Eric's background," Steve said. "It was his life."

For months they ate and worked together. Steve told Eric what a difference his new faith in Jesus had made. "I came from a lifestyle he was still in," Steve said. "That got his attention."

At the time Steve commuted daily to Jacksonville from Gainesville, more than seventy-five miles each way. He had moved into a converted fraternity house at the University of Florida that had been taken over by the Maranatha Christian Center, a charismatic ministry to students. The group used part of the house as a worship center, and some members of the fellowship, such as Steve, lived in dormitory rooms upstairs. His daily drive was lengthy, but Steve felt he needed the constant fellowship of other dedicated Christians to educate him in the faith and prevent him from sliding back into his old, drug-addled ways.

One weekend, Steve persuaded Eric to accompany him to Gainesville. Eric agreed, partly to see Steve's church and partly because he wanted to find and meet a novelist named Harry Crews, who taught at the university and whose work Eric admired.

The man who then was associate pastor at Maranatha Christian Center, John Rohrer, remembers the evening that Eric and Steve arrived. It was the weekend of football homecoming at the University of Florida. John had just finished music practice in the converted fraternity house his church had occupied. It was about 9:30 P.M. Steve walked through the door with Eric, both of them hulking men who stood six foot four. John looked at Eric. "I've never seen a more perplexed and angry—just tormented—man," he said. "I thought to myself, 'I don't know if I'm up for this.'"

John is a former basketball coach. A lifelong Southern Baptist, he'd fallen into a hedonistic lifestyle. He'd nearly committed suicide before rededicating his life to God during a tearful session alone one evening in his living room. After becoming serious about his faith again, he took a job as head coach at a small Baptist college.

During his tenure there, his sister had led him into contact with a Maranatha group in another state. He'd spent two years quietly attending the charismatic meetings—his contract at the Baptist college forbade him to, among other things, speak in tongues—before he asked for the "baptism in the Holy Spirit." When he did that, the presence of God's supernatural, miraculous power poured into him. "All of a sudden my life changed," he said.

One gift that began to manifest itself through him, he said, was the ability to discern spirits, which is mentioned in the New Testament. Although John barely had heard of demonic spirits during his upbringing and training as a Southern Baptist, he found himself with an uncanny ability to see into the spirit world and to know when demons were present. He soon decided that God had called him to a vocation more meaningful than winning basketball games. He resigned his coaching position and eventually was ordained by the Maranatha Christian Church, an affiliation of congregations that mostly ministered to college students.

Other gifts of the Spirit also became particularly potent in John's life, he said. He was strong in the word of knowledge and the word of wisdom. The definitions of those two gifts vary from scholar to scholar, but John understands them as the ability to tell people hidden things about themselves that John couldn't otherwise know unless God had shown him—and then to tell people how to respond after God had revealed these matters.

Because his ministry involved working on a university campus, the gifts had proven invaluable to him, John said, looking back. Daily he was dealing with intellectuals, many of them hostile to Christianity and especially to John's brand of supernatural, charismatic faith. He thinks of himself as a jock, an ex-coach, and said he couldn't refute his critics intellectually. "I've never been considered a particularly intelligent person," John said. But the insights given him by the Holy Spirit more than compensated for his lack of erudition when dealing with smart people. "They're blown away because I'm such a dumb guy. We'll never reach the intellectual mind with intellectual things. They already think they know it all. God takes the base things to confound the wise."

That night when Eric Holmberg walked into the converted Greek house with Steve Hall, John figured he had his work cut out for him.

The three men talked for perhaps an hour there in the Maranatha house, then moved to a Denny's restaurant. It was packed with loud, drunk homecoming revelers.

"Tell me about yourself," John, the minister, said to Eric. And Eric did. He expounded his theories on religion and why it didn't make any sense. "There's just no God or anything," John remembers Eric saying.

John was struck by Eric's intelligence. Despite his youth and his drug use, the young man already had become an expert on alternative fuels such as gasohol. "I mean, he's brilliant. He's a genius," John said recently. "I saw the absolute hopelessness in his eyes. The cynicism and the sarcasm." Then, John said, the Lord spoke a message inside his heart: "He said, 'Eric just needs to see a demonstration of me.'"

Eric kept talking, while John wrestled with the words he felt welling inside him. Finally, John broke in. "The Lord just literally began to minister to Eric's life," he said. John told Eric about Eric's relationship with his father, about his childhood, his searches for meaning and for God. He told him specifics about his sense of disgust toward the world, his hopelessness. "I was just in the flow of things," he said. "It was more than a word of knowledge. It was God opening up this man's life. I realized the Holy Spirit was doing a number on this guy." John looked across the table and saw goose bumps on Eric's big arms. Steve saw them, too.

"Nobody, not even Steve, could know these things," Eric admitted. "I know there's a God."

"Then let's pray," John said. As he recalls it, he began to lead Eric in "the sinner's prayer," a prayer of repentance, in the crowded restaurant. Not wanting to cause a scene, John whispered, "Lord Jesus, come into my life."

Eric shouted: "Lord Jesus come into my life!"

People at the tables and booths around them stopped talking. Some started to laugh. Eric kept going, shouting every line that John whispered.

Abruptly, John said, Eric's whole countenance changed. The anger reappeared in his face. He didn't want to pray anymore. "It was as if an entirely different spirit came upon him," John said. "I thought, 'Oh, my word, what's going on here?'" Upset and confused, John told Eric and Steve, "Let's go." With the restaurant's other patrons still staring and laughing at them, the three men rose, paid their checks, and returned to the Maranatha house. Eric and Steve left the house around midnight. "I'll be praying for you," John told Eric.

Sunday morning, though, Eric and Steve showed up for the church service. Pastor David Houston delivered a sermon that Eric says struck him at the time as meaningless—"but God was just all over me." When Houston gave an altar call at the service's end, Eric went forward to try again to give his life to God. Eric was assigned a counselor, another member of the congregation, to talk with him. Steve accompanied Eric and the counselor to Steve's room.

"My mood quickly changed," Eric said. He became hostile again. He argued with the counselor. The counselor said he thought Eric might be possessed by demons. The idea sounded crazy to Eric. The counselor said Eric needed to surrender the pride he placed in his intellect. Eric mouthed off some more. The counselor soon gave up and left the room.

"Screw this," Eric said. He told Steve he was going to go try to find Harry Crews, the writer. "Screw this Christian stuff."

Steve had had enough of Eric, too. He'd decided that Eric's central problem was that he was a jerk. "I said, 'Man, the heck with you. I don't care what you do. That's it.'" Steve, angry, stalked to the bedroom door, opened it—and there stood John Rohrer.

"What's up?" John said. He looked into the room at Eric. "Eric, I want to ask you a question. Have you ever had any experiences with demons?"

Here we go again—demons, demons, demons, Eric thought.

But Steve knew better. He'd been around John long enough to trust his insights. "He was into a level of ministry that most people don't ever see," he said. Still, Eric had really gotten under his skin. So Steve went down the hall to a friend's room to read his Bible and pray. Within minutes he fell asleep.

Meanwhile, John stared straight at Eric. "Your problem is that you've cursed God."

"You mean like using bad words?"

"No," John said. "I mean to his face."

"You mean like Faust?"

"Who's Faust?" John replied.

Eric explained about the character in a play who sold his soul to Satan. And no, he added, he'd never cursed God. "I'm innocent of that."

"Well, God told me you had," John said.

John asked if he could pray for Eric again, and Eric agreed. John walked into the room, placed his hands on Eric's head, and began to bind any demonic spirits from masking the young man's memory. Then John began to pray in tongues.

Within ten seconds, Eric said, his memory seemed to compress. His mind zeroed in on one long-forgotten moment. When he'd lived in the Virginia countryside while attending William and Mary, he'd regularly dropped LSD. For a time he'd begun to think that God was everywhere, in everything, and that he himself was being transformed into God. One night, he'd sat in the front yard on an old car seat that he and his housemates used for a bench. This was in late November or early December. The trees above him were bare, a full moon shone in the sky, and stars glittered everywhere. Eric was tripping.

Suddenly that night he'd experienced a devastating revelation: he wasn't God. Instead, Jesus Christ was God. "I just had this epiphany," he said. "Maybe God in his mercy was trying to get hold of me." But instead of thanking the Almighty, Eric had done just the opposite. He'd screamed profanity. "I don't need you!" he'd yelled toward the heavens. "You might be great, but I'm going to live my own life!" He'd danced maniacally around the yard and even had spoken in tongues— demonic tongues, he believes now. By the next morning, having returned from his chemical trip, he'd forgotten all about the experience until John had placed his hands on him. Nevertheless, Eric realized that from that night on his life had taken a wrenching downward spiral. He'd started lying and stealing, had treated people cruelly. He'd become so wicked and abhorrent that by the time he attended his last party at William and Mary his former friends had grown to detest him. They'd thrown their drinks on him.

Now he told John about his memory. He was guilty, he said. He had cursed God to his face.

"That's a spirit," John said. "When you did that, a spirit of the antichrist came into you." John decided to pray for Eric again. He placed his hands on Eric and rebuked the demon inside him. Using Jesus' name, John commanded the demon to loose Eric and come out of him.

Eric felt as if a frantic cat were clawing his stomach from the inside, trying to get out. The ripping pain doubled him over. He fell to the floor and began to gag. John went right down after him, rebuking the demon. Steve, asleep in the room down the hall, was jarred awake by an otherworldly voice that erupted from Eric; it was that loud.

Eric's eyes were clenched tightly, but something shadowy leapt through them and flew out the room's window. "I felt this enormous sense of release," Eric said. "Just this enormous sense of release."

John left the room. Eric struggled to his knees and prayed, "Here I am, if you want me." Yellow wisps of smoke poured in through the window. "This presence just came into the room," he said. "It was like liquid love was being poured over me." It felt as if he were being drugged, only better, purer.

As John told me: "The rest is history." Today Eric lives near Pensacola, Florida, where he leads a small Christian organization called Reel to Real Ministries. Its main mission is to provide social critiques of contemporary mores—on dating and sexuality, abortion, rock music, movies, television—from a thoughtful Christian perspective. Eric has produced videos on such subjects, and he's been a frequent guest on conservative religious TV programs such as "The 700 Club" and "100 Huntley Street."

His experience with John Rohrer and Steve Hall in that former Greek house took place more than fifteen years ago. The three men have long since scattered. John is the pastor of New Hope Christian Church in Columbus, Ohio. Steve is senior pastor of Faith Christian Church in Tucson, Arizona. I contacted the three men separately, yet they all vividly remembered the incident in Gainesville, and, while some of the details of their memories differed, as is to be expected, their stories were remarkably similar. None, as far as I could see, had anything to gain by exaggerating.

Eric is the most reserved and analytic of the three. He volunteered that there might be rational, psychosomatic explanations for all his behaviors that weekend in Gainesville. He doesn't think what happened to him was merely psychological, though. For one thing, the results were lasting. The former apologist for agnostics has devoted the last fifteen years of his life to serving God. For another: "It's not my personality to behave like that at all. I really believe this thing was very, very genuine."

CHAPTER NINE

APPEARANCES

I SAT IN THE DEN OF Dr. Patrick Schneider's modest home, drinking a cup of flavored coffee. He asked if he could show me a videotape he'd made. I agreed, and he popped the tape into his videocassette recorder. A night scene appeared on the TV screen, bearing the date on which the tape was made, August 31, 1995, near the screen's edge. The camera panned across a huge outdoor crowd standing in the shadows before a massive, forbidding gray building. The people recited a "Hail Mary" with a priest who spoke over a loudspeaker. There were fifteen thousand people there, Schneider said; the site was an old Roman Catholic seminary in Cincinnati. "Now, watch," he said. "It's almost midnight."

Suddenly, the black sky around the seminary erupted in lights that flashed and pulsated on either side of the gray stone building, above it, in front of it. The lights seemed to strobe forever, although they couldn't have lasted more than perhaps a minute, maybe much less, before dying away. Remarkably, the crowd remained quiet, as if it had been expecting this all along. Schneider told me the lights erupted while the Virgin Mary, supposedly dead for more than 1,900 years, appeared at the seminary to a visionary named Sandy, who is able to see her. When the visionary's view of Mary ended, the lights stopped.

"I think anyone who goes there with a reasonable mind will conclude that these are not natural events," Schneider said. "There are no strobes doing those lights. Anyone can go up and look around."

Schneider drolly refers to himself as "Mary's jerk." He's Mary's jerk, he said, because people of his station aren't supposed to believe in apparitions of the Blessed Virgin. "I was sort of called," he explained, meaning that his qualifications make it difficult for others to dismiss him as a flake or a particularly gullible observer. Schneider's a physician with a medical degree from the University of Kentucky and a master's degree in public health from Harvard. He's a Phi Beta Kappa. He's completed, by his own count, twenty-five years of formal education, much of it in the hard sciences. He's chair of the department of medicine at respected St. Joseph Hospital in Lexington, Kentucky. I wouldn't call him Mary's jerk, but I might suggest that he's becoming a Mary junky, which is not necessarily a bad thing.

Schneider's interest in apparitions began in 1992. Before that, in December 1991, an Arkansas visionary had written Father Leroy Smith, a Catholic priest, saying she'd received a message from Mary. The Blessed Virgin had told the visionary, Cyndi Cain, that she intended to appear at St. Joseph Catholic Church in Cold Spring, Kentucky, a bedroom community of Cincinnati where Smith then was pastor. A second visionary from a Cincinnati suburb, apparently Sandy, confirmed the message to Smith. Soon the word had leaked out to the general public. Mary had even set a date for her arrival: August 31, 1992.

Reporters immediately pounced on the impending apparition, which became front-page fodder for newspapers and the lead item on TV newscasts throughout the region. The visitation promised everything that makes for good feature writing: a large crowd, strong feelings pro and con, colorful quotes, and a certain air of wackiness (the Virgin Mary wants to come to *Kentucky*?). In the end, up to fifteen hundred people crowded into St. Joseph Church in 1992 and another five to seven thousand gathered outside in the church's parking lot, some reciting the rosary, some holding lighted candles.

One of those present was Schneider. He'd fallen away from the Christian faith in his youth, then at age thirty had experienced a religious conversion and had started attending church again. Now in his forties, Schneider, like many of us, didn't know what to make of the brouhaha over Mary's prophesied visit. So he'd decided, out of curiosity, to drive from Lexington north to Cold Spring and see what happened.

I, too, was there in 1992, at midnight, when Mary's presence supposedly filled the inside of St. Joseph Church. When Mary appears anywhere from Medjugorje in the former Yugoslavia to Cold Spring, Kentucky, typically no one actually sees her except one, or a few, pre-selected visionaries. But her presence is said to manifest itself to others in various ways, particularly during the moments when the visionaries are communicating with her. Lights flash, the chains on crucifixes change from silver to gold, a smell of roses permeates the air, and, during daylight appearances, the sun dances and spins.

That night in Cold Spring, I, a skeptical—and Protestant—reporter, didn't witness anything out of the ordinary from my vantage point in a fenced, closely guarded media pen in the church's yard. However, in the parking lot, Schneider found his attention captured by a sudden flash of lights in a nearby tree. He walked over to inspect the tree and determined that it wasn't rigged with electric bulbs. Intrigued, he managed to obtain a videotape of the lights from someone else who had taped it. By the time he watched the tape, he was hooked. He began attending apparitions that kept popping up in our region: the one at Cold Spring, which recurred there annually on August 31 until it was moved in 1995 to the old seminary in Cincinnati; another one that began at nearby Falmouth, Kentucky, on the eighth of each month.

Carrying along his video camera, he taped apparition after apparition. He never captured Mary on tape, of course; she doesn't pose for cameras. But he logged several other striking effects. On May 8, 1994—Mother's Day—an estimated thirty thousand worshipers and curiosity seekers crowded around a white statue of the Blessed Virgin on a rolling hillside near Falmouth. Speaking over a microphone, Sandy recited the message given her that day by Mary. "No mother aches more for her children than I do for all of you . . ." the visionary said. She urged people to convert their lives to God's ways, to pray daily. As Sandy talked, Schneider pointed his video camera straight into the sun.

I also watched the tape he made that day. In it, the sun suddenly starts to throb and jump. Schneider pans the camera down to the crowd again. My first thought was—as professional skeptic and investigator Joe Nickell had told me about the "door to heaven" effect on stills from Polaroid cameras—that if you pointed a video camera at any light as bright as the sun, the resulting image likely would look eerie. I mentioned this to Schneider, who said that was his initial thought, too. So he'd pointed the camera back at the sun again as soon as Sandy finished delivering her message. We watched that segment of the tape. The sun now is surrounded by a reflective halo, the kind most of us likely have seen on television when cameras are pointed skyward. But the throbbing and jumping are gone. The sun looks normal compared with the previous images in which it pulsates. Schneider said that after he went home that weekend, he took his camera out again and pointed it at a blazing sun, just to see again whether he could reproduce the throbbing effect. Nothing happened out of the ordinary. "I've done that a number of times," he said.

He showed me tape he'd shot during another Falmouth apparition. "Watch, the sun goes nuts," he warned. It does. Not only does it pulsate, but in this tape streaks like star bursts shoot out from it. The sky around the sun turns black. To Schneider, Falmouth seems to be the site of an especially strong Marian presence. "I do believe it is holy ground," he said.

I explained to him Nickell's experiment with the "door to heaven." You'll recall that some of those who visit apparition sites point their instamatic cameras at the sun and snap pictures. Frequently the resulting prints contain an image over the sun in the shape of a door; some of the doors even bear what appear to be hinges. Many Catholics believe this to be a miraculous sign of the "golden door" to heaven. Nickell, who makes his living investigating claims of the supernatural, had said he obtained an identical image by pointing a Polaroid at a halogen lamp. The "door," he said, is merely a reflection of the camera's aperture superimposed on the film by the brightness of the light.

Schneider wasn't too impressed by Nickell's experiment. At one apparition he ran into a nun conducting her own experiment with the heavenly door (Schneider said the proper term is "gate of heaven"). The nun had shot twenty or more images of the sun at regular intervals and numbered and dated them as they rolled from the camera. The pictures she'd taken before the moment of that day's apparition contained no gate. The photos shot during the visionary's communication with Mary clearly contained the gate. The pictures of the sun taken after the apparition didn't show a gate. "Many of these people are pretty thoughtful people," Schneider said. "They're studying things for themselves."

He said the thousands who attend apparitions have at times been labeled as fanatics by those, including other Catholics, who believe all apparitions are silliness and superstition. But the crowds invariably are well behaved, not fanatical, he said. No one except the designated visionaries ever claims to see Mary. "Why didn't a lot more people run up to say, 'I saw her, too'?" he asked about the thirty thousand people who were present in Falmouth on Mother's Day, 1994. Neither has he seen any attempt at self-aggrandizement connected to the apparitions he's attended. Sandy, the visionary who presides at northern Kentucky and Ohio appearances by Mary, has diligently avoided media attempts to interview or publicize her. "She was not interested in going on talk shows or anything," he said.

Schneider, a bright man, finds more reasons to believe in the apparitions than to disbelieve. But neither does he think hard-core skeptics would ever be convinced, regardless of the evidence. "I don't hold much faith for debate," Schneider said. "People either believe or they don't. Faith is a gift."

Appearances Everywhere

Visions, touches, or messages from beings who are not breathing, flesh-and-blood humans—such as ancient saints, angels, and dead loved ones—are phenomena common throughout history. Christianity, the world's largest faith, was born of a belief in just such events. Jesus' conception and birth were attended by angels who were seen by, and who spoke with, Mary, Joseph, shepherds, and others.

The most remarkable supernatural appearance of all was the resurrection of Jesus following his crucifixion. Five hundred people reportedly saw the risen rabbi on one occasion, days or even weeks after he'd been publicly crucified as a heretic. His closest friends proved so certain of their post-execution encounters with him that they were themselves transformed, albeit in a different way. Before the resurrection, Jesus' disciples had run away in terror when he was captured. They had hidden in locked rooms. One had denied that he even knew

Jesus. After the resurrection, those same people stalked boldly into the synagogues and public squares of Palestine, proclaiming that Jesus was alive again. Most eventually were killed for their faith. You've got to believe in an apparition pretty strongly to give your life for it. Indeed, faith in Jesus' resurrection remains widespread today. A Gallup poll found that 82 percent of fifteen hundred Americans asked said they believe Jesus rose from the dead.

However, most modern-day reports of supernatural appearances don't concern visions of Christ himself, but of lesser spiritual beings. Without question, the most notable phenomena are the multiplying reports of apparitions by the Virgin Mary and by angels. According to figures compiled by the International Marian Research Institute at the University of Dayton, almost 80,000 apparitions of Mary have been claimed since the 200s C.E. So far only a handful have been officially recognized by the Roman Catholic Church. They include, among several others, Guadalupe, Mexico, in 1531; Paris, France, in 1830; La Salette, France, in 1846; Lourdes, France, in 1858; and Fátima, Portugal, 1917.

Unofficial appearances by Mary, though, have become almost ubiquitous. One report in *Our Lady Queen of Peace* newspaper, a Pennsylvania publication devoted to news about apparitions, cites an academic study that found that 232 Marian apparitions were reported in thirty-two countries between 1923 and 1975. By another estimate, 300 apparitions have been reported in this century. Some have become major tourist attractions. Mary supposedly began manifesting herself in 1981 in Medjugorje, a village in the war-ravaged former Yugoslavia. Twenty million people since have visited that site. More interesting to me is that Mary now pops up in what, to my American mind, are far less exotic locations such as northern Kentucky and Conyers, Georgia.

Some followers say that Mary most frequently and powerfully appears just before, or during, periods of great tribulation. The Fátima apparition, for instance, started in Europe during the darkest days of World War I. Medjugorje, some say, heralded the disintegration of Yugoslavia and the slaughter that has followed it. Mary comes to prepare and comfort people, her followers say. If that's the case, you can't help but wonder what's in store for the American South, given the ongoing apparitions in Kentucky and Georgia.

In addition to the Marian phenomenon, the last few years have witnessed a proliferation of reports of angelic intercessions. Much of that movement began with Sophy Burnham's *A Book of Angels,* first published in 1990. Burnham's book was released without much fanfare and with modest expectations by her publisher. It became a word-of-mouth best-seller and has been widely imitated. Bookstore shelves now are glutted with angel titles—hundreds of them. There are network TV news segments devoted to tales of angelic appearances, as well as at least one dramatic series, "Touched by an Angel," that airs in prime time. Angel collectibles are big sellers in gift stores.

A Yogi Sees His Former Master

Clearly, though, apparitions aren't just Christian events. On March 9, 1936, Hindu guru Sri Yukteswar passed away at age eighty in an ashram in Puri, India. His disciple, the yogi Paramahansa Yogananda, was away on a trip. Precisely at the hour when witnesses said Yukteswar had died, 7 P.M., Yogananda was on his way to catch a train for Puri. He saw a black astral cloud cover the sky, but didn't understand its meaning. When he arrived at Puri train station, he was met by a friend who told him Yukteswar was dead. Distraught, Yogananda rushed to the ashram, where he found his guru still sitting in the lotus position in which he had died. The next day, Yogananda himself conducted the funeral, he writes in *Autobiography of a Yogi.* Yukteswar had lived a long and glorious life, but his death proved an emotional blow to his disciple, who loved him intensely.

Three months later, at 3 P.M. on June 19, 1936, Yogananda—who traveled a great deal giving lectures—sat on his bed in the Regent Hotel in Bombay, meditating. A beautiful light filled the room and waves of joy washed over him. He looked into the light, and there stood Yukteswar before him.

Normally it had been Yogananda's practice to fall to his knees at Yukteswar's feet, but he now was so overcome with euphoria that he rushed across the room and threw his arms around the guru. The man's presence wasn't a vision or a spirit, he said. He could feel Yukteswar's flesh.

"My son," Yukteswar said.

The guru explained that he had resurrected himself in a new body and had taken up residence on an astral planet. He liked the residents there better than most of the people on earth, Yukteswar explained, and he invited Yogananda and his family to come live with him someday. Then he asked his disciple to loosen his grip on the guru's body, because it was uncomfortable.

Yukteswar talked about the nature of life, death, and the afterlife, an in-depth discussion that lasted two hours, Yogananda says. When he had finished, Yukteswar said, "I leave you now, beloved one!" and vanished from Yogananda's arms. As he departed, he promised to return again once Yogananda had reached a state of perfect spiritual consciousness.

A Nineteenth-Century Law Student Sees Jesus

The Reverend Charles G. Finney ranks among the more famous preachers in modern Christian history. Born in Warren, Connecticut, in 1792, to a family that wasn't religious, he moved later with his parents to upstate New York. In 1818 he decided to study law with an attorney in the town of Adams.

A devout but, to Finney's mind, ineffectual band of local Christians set out to convert him, he recalled in his memoirs. He attended a few of their services, and when they asked whether they might pray for him he impertinently answered, "You have prayed enough since I have attended these meetings to have prayed the devil out of Adams, if there is any virtue in your prayers. But here you are, praying and complaining still."

Nevertheless, their witness gradually worked on Finney's heart and he grew troubled about the state of his soul. He spent the morning of October 10, 1821, walking in the autumn woods, praying and seeking spiritual revelation. Ultimately he confessed his many sins to God and was filled with a sense of peace for the first time. Yet by the time he returned to town he was plagued by doubts. He wasn't certain whether he'd actually pleased God or offended him. Finney had been such a sinner, he said, that he wondered whether God might have become angry with his willingness to presume that God would accept him.

He returned to his law office and found that the attorney with whom he studied had gone to eat. Not hungry, Finney took down his bass viol and started playing sacred music. As he played and sang, tears streamed down his cheeks. He was so overcome with emotion that he couldn't continue. Finally, he put away his instrument.

That evening, Finney built a fire in the office's open fireplace. He hoped to spend the night alone, because he wanted to try praying again, to see whether he could obtain some answer from God as to whether he had been forgiven. His attorney friend announced he was going home for the night. As Finney shut the door behind him, he wrote later, "my heart seemed to be liquid within me." He rushed into a dark back room to pray. Suddenly the unlighted room filled with light. "As I went in and shut the door after me," he wrote, "it seemed as if I met the Lord Jesus Christ face to face. It did not occur to me then, nor did it for some time afterward, that it was wholly a mental state. On the contrary, it seemed to me that I saw him as I would see any other man."

Jesus didn't speak, Finney said, but gazed upon him with such a look "as to break me right down at his feet." Finney fell to the floor and, sobbing like a child, poured out his soul to the apparition. "It seemed to me that I bathed his feet with my tears," he said, "and yet I had no distinct impression that I touched him, that I recollect."

Finney never knew how long he lay on that floor. When the apparition ended, he returned to the front office and discovered that the healthy fire he'd built had nearly burned out. He was about to sit down by the fire, he said, when "I received a mighty baptism of the Holy Ghost." The Spirit coursed through his whole body "like a wave of electricity going through and through me. Indeed it seemed to come in waves and waves of liquid love; for I could not express it in any other way. It seemed like the very breath of God. . . . I wept aloud with joy and love; and I do not know but I should say, I literally bellowed out the unutterable gushings of my heart. These waves came over me, and over me, and over me, one after the other, until I recollect I cried out,

'I shall die if these waves continue to pass over me.' I said, 'Lord, I cannot bear any more;' yet I had no fear of death."

Finney went on to become one of the great Protestant evangelists, a man who led thousands to the Christian faith.

An Angel Watches over a Dying Man

Jim and Joann Poppleton were vacationing in Colorado Springs, Colorado, visiting their son's in-laws. It was not a happy period for the Poppletons. Six months earlier, Jim had been diagnosed with Lou Gehrig's disease, which slowly causes its victims to lose control of their motor skills, their limbs, and ultimately to lose their lives. Jim already was having difficulty walking.

While the Poppletons were in Colorado Springs, they and their hosts visited the U.S. Air Force Academy's spectacular campus, which includes an unusual, picturesque chapel that rests on a small mountain. The only way up was a steep flight of stairs. Joann wanted to see the chapel, but was certain Jim would never make it up the steps. After some discussion, they all decided to give it a try. With some help, Jim did climb to the top of the stairs. He got to see the chapel, too.

The small party started out of the church and down the stairs. Joann took one of his arms to support him and their son's father-in-law, Jerry, took Jim's other arm. They'd descended only a few steps when Jim stumbled and pitched forward. Joann and Jerry snatched at him. "I panicked. I really panicked," Joann said. Then, as if from nowhere, a big man dashed from the side of their view. "This huge human being came down and caught Jim as he hit the first landing," she said. "We didn't know where he came from. He was just there. . . . I didn't see his face. I just saw his form."

Wordlessly, the fellow scooped Jim up in his massive arms and carried him to the bottom of the steps. Joann and Jerry, hearts pounding, rushed to catch up. By the time they reached Jim, the man had set him down. Joann checked out Jim to make sure he was okay, then turned to thank the man. He had disappeared among the other campus visitors. She never saw him again.

Two years later, Jim's condition had worsened. He was confined

to a hospital, unable to talk or walk. But he did still possess some control over his hands. When he wanted to communicate he wrote messages to Joann.

One day she walked into Jim's hospital room and saw him gazing
into what looked like a broad column of light in one corner of his
room. As the light faded, Jim took his paper and began to write. When
he handed the message to Joann, she could hardly believe his words.

A man, a big man, had walked into Jim's room as he lay there
alone, Jim had written. "Do you know who I am?" the man had asked.
Jim had nodded that he did. He'd instantly recognized the fellow: it was
the man who'd rescued him two years earlier on the steps of the Air
Force Academy chapel. "I'm your guardian angel," the big man said.
"I'm going to be with you through the rest of your experiences here.
And I'll be with you when it's time to go to heaven."

Afterward, Jim seemed filled with an almost otherworldly peace,
his wife said. He died four months later, still at peace with himself and
with God.

Touched by God

The table was set for a Kentucky Derby party. It was May 4, 1974.
Donald Hillenmeyer owned a nursery business that had suffered financial reverses. His life and career hadn't always been easy, but this
weekend he was thrilled. Earlier, one of his sons, David, had quit college and had gone off to work in South Carolina as a night auditor at
a hotel. Hillenmeyer always had harbored high hopes for David, had
wanted him to finish college and build a successful career. That Derby
weekend David had come home for the race and then had told his father he intended to stay for good. He wanted to finish college. On the
way out of the house to visit friends, David said to his mom, Margaret,
"Daddy was so happy."

After David left, Donald told Margaret, "You're a millionaire."

"If I am, I'd like to know where the money is," she said.

Donald explained that as far as he was concerned, the news about
David was as good as receiving a million bucks.

This is how fast matters can change. "Donald was dead fifteen minutes after he said that," Margaret said. He went in to take a bath and suffered a heart attack.

After the funeral, as Margaret, then forty-nine, tried to sort out what had happened, she barely grieved. "I was so happy for him," she said. Donald had worked so hard and nothing had gone right for him in his business. "He probably went to Mass every single day. He really believed wholeheartedly in God." Margaret figured Donald was happier in the next world.

Then reality set in. Within a few months she found herself alone—and lonely. She had little money and was working in the dress department of a large retail store. Two of her children, David and daughter Janie, were enrolled in college at the same time, a big expense. All Margaret could see ahead of herself was work and more work, loneliness and more loneliness.

She lived then in a large old Victorian duplex, and was sitting one evening on a chaise lounge, in the dark, staring out a window. Her predicament overwhelmed her. This was more than a case of the blues. It was nearly despair. "Everything just seemed insurmountable," she said. She'd tried to pray, but God had seemed remote for such a long time. Her faith had wilted.

Margaret cried out, "God, where *are* you? Are you really there?"

That's when a remarkable thing happened. "All of a sudden I just felt—something very gently brushed my shoulder," Margaret said. It was as if a person had walked into the room and touched her in a kind, reassuring way. Only there was no one in the room but Margaret.

Then a voice spoke to her, directly. "Don't you worry," it said. "Don't you know I'll take care of you?"

Peace wafted over her like a cool breeze. She recognized the voice. It was God speaking. To her. "It was an internal voice," she said. "It was not audible. Nobody could have heard it but me, but it was very much there. It was God, that's all I can tell you."

After that, Margaret's life changed for the better. "Nothing 'miraculous' happened," she said. But life's knots gradually untied themselves. She managed to help her kids finish school. She met another man, Bob Bohan, and remarried. "That made it a lot easier," she said. An aunt unexpectedly left her a bit of money.

The true impact of that gentle physical touch—and the message that accompanied it—struck inside of Margaret, not in her outward circumstances. "I just felt very peaceful from then on," she said. For a full ten years, she felt as if she were in control of whatever problems arose day to day, "which is not my nature," she said. "I just knew that if I called on God he would come." After a decade of this uncanny serenity, she gradually allowed some of her routine worries to slip back into her life.

Margaret isn't the kind of person who is comfortable discussing her faith publicly. She's mostly kept her personal visitation to herself. "I've not told a lot of people," she said. "But I have told people when they're having problems." Her advice to them: "Ask God to help you." She knows from experience that he will.

The Sun Spins in Bosnia

Barbara Kincaid's story holds some elements in common with Margaret Bohan's. She was forty-eight when her husband, Ray, died of cancer. Her son was married and her daughter left soon after Ray's death to join the Air Force. Barbara was alone. "I cried all the time," she said. She did her best to find solace in her Catholic faith. "I've always had a great love for the Blessed Mother," she said. Barbara works as a secretary for a Catholic diocesan office.

In 1993 she decided to take a trip with a group of friends to Medjugorje, the site of the famous, although unofficial, Marian apparition in Bosnia-Herzegovina. "I didn't ask to see any miracles," she said. "I just wanted peace."

Soon after the group had arrived in Medjugorje, they hiked up the mountain called Podbrdo where the apparition was said to have first appeared to several children in 1981. "I just went into tears. I just cried and cried and cried," Barbara said. But this weeping wasn't from a sense of desperation. Rather it felt to her like an internal cleansing, what some call "inner healing."

While they were in Medjugorje, Barbara and the others stayed in the homes of Croatians. One day she was sitting on the porch of the house where she boarded when it occurred to her that she inexplicably was gazing into the blazing Bosnian sun. "It dawned on me, 'I'm looking directly at the sun and it's not bothering me,'" she said. Then the sun began to move in a circle. "It had all the different colors behind it, like a rainbow." She had traveled to Medjugorje in a group of sixty-five people, some of whom she knew and others she didn't. Just then a man from the group, with whom she wasn't acquainted, hurried over from the house where he was staying and said, "Hey, look at the sun!" Barbara still can't quite comprehend what she witnessed. "It astounded you. You don't really believe you're seeing what you're seeing."

In a second episode, Barbara and other pilgrims set out well before dawn to climb another hill near Medjugorje, Mount Krizevac, which includes a pathway marked with the stations of the cross. She and the others prayed the stations as they went, so it took them three hours to ascend the mountain. They reached the crest of the hill just as the sun rose.

Barbara looked out at the sky. "Here was the sun dancing in the sky again," she said. She gazed at it intently. "I saw the Blessed Mother holding a baby inside the sun." Mary was smiling proudly, as if she were a mother saying, "Look at my baby." Then Mary moved aside and Barbara saw an adult Jesus behind Mary, hanging on a cross. The image of Jesus faded. He was replaced with a white dove, which symbolizes the Holy Spirit.

"I just didn't think I could stand any more," Barbara said. She didn't feel worthy to see such visions, so she started down the steep hill. She reached a cove where area residents sold religious artifacts. A man there said, "Wait a minute." Barbara paused, assuming he wanted to sell her a souvenir. Instead, he handed her a big walking stick to help her return down the curving, rocky slope. He refused to take any money for it. She thanked him.

As she rounded the next corner in the path, silent words formed in her. She believed they were given to her by God: "I am your rod and your staff. I will always take care of you."

Those words were true. When she returned to the United States her loneliness and fear had lifted. "And he truly has taken care of me," she said.

A Chemist Finds Comfort in Mary

If there's anyone who would at first seem unlikely to become a believer in Marian apparitions, it's Richard Watson. He grew up in the conservative branch of the Church of Christ, a Protestant sect so strict that it doesn't allow musical instruments to be used in its worship services. Conservative Protestants place hardly any theological significance at all on Mary. Frequently—and incorrectly, by the way—they sometimes accuse Roman Catholics of worshipping Jesus' mother, which Protestants consider heretical.

In addition to his non-Catholic background, Watson makes his living as a clinical chemist, so you'd assume him to be analytical and dubious of claims of dancing suns, "doors to heaven," and crucifixes whose metal elements change colors. Indeed, he's not particularly gullible, he said. "I'm pretty skeptical."

Watson earlier in life was quite active in the Church of Christ. He'd worked as a volunteer missionary while in college, and later as a medical missionary, in Nigeria, Haiti, and Jamaica. There came a time, though, when he didn't feel he was growing spiritually and so he started searching for other avenues in which to express his faith. He and his wife had built a home in a middle-class subdivision that happened to be within sight of a new Roman Catholic church. Watson visited the church and eventually, at age thirty, converted to Catholicism, despite opposition from his family and friends.

"It's quite a change," he said. Many things about his new denomination appealed to him, particularly the church's teaching that the communion elements actually are transformed by the Holy Spirit into Christ's body and blood. On the other hand some things bothered him, too—such as his fellow Catholics' affection for Mary, which he didn't understand at all.

At work Watson talked with a friend who had grown up as a Catholic. He asked her about the rosary, a series of prayers of devotion to the Blessed Virgin. His friend said she'd prayed it as a child but couldn't remember how it went. However, she soon brought in a catalog that offered religious paraphernalia, including rosary beads. Watson leafed through it. At his confirmation he'd taken as his Christian name "Andrew," because St. Andrew is the patron saint of Scotland. Watson's family originated in Scotland. In the catalog he saw a rosary that included a medal of St. Andrew, so he ordered it.

A year passed. He'd switched parishes, and at his new church became involved with a small faith "family" of believers who fellowshiped together within the large cathedral congregation. In 1992, Watson heard people there discussing Medjugorje. A few people in his church group considered embarking on a pilgrimage. Watson loves to travel, and the idea of a religious pilgrimage intrigued him. Not long afterward, though, the church's rector said that with a war raging in Bosnia, a trip to Medjugorje probably would prove too dangerous. The rector already planned to lead a group vacation to the Holy Land that fall, so Watson decided to go there instead.

It was a great vacation. While they were traveling Watson met some people in the group who were enthused about Marian apparitions. They taught him how to pray the rosary. He liked the Mary folks quite a bit, and when they returned home Watson joined their home prayer group. He began to say the rosary regularly, too.

One day he noticed that the delicate metal links connecting the beads on his St. Andrew rosary, which was silver when he bought it, had changed colors. "Almost immediately all the chains turned goldish, a gold color," he said.

That annoyed Watson. He'd paid good money for what he thought was a high-quality rosary—and it had turned out to be so cheap that the silver finish had rubbed off as soon as he started using it. The next time he went to church, he pulled the rosary from his pocket and showed it to his friends. "Look what happened," he said. "I thought I had a good rosary."

His friends' response surprised him. They didn't think he'd gotten stuck with a cheap rosary at all. He'd received a "signal grace," they said—a supernatural sign of Mary's presence in Watson's life. People commonly reported that their rosaries' chains turned gold when they attended apparition sites, Watson's friends said. He'd never heard of such a thing.

As he continued over time to pray the rosary with his friends, Watson began to put aside his Protestant reluctance toward the Blessed Virgin, he said. He found that his friends weren't being sacrilegious, they weren't worshiping Mary. They were merely showing her the respect they considered due her as the Mother of God. After all, the Bible itself prophesied that all generations would call her blessed. The Catholic Church, he said, talks about what it calls "the church triumphant." Part of the idea is that no one who truly believes in Christ ever dies. Those who pass from this world simply go to live in another, heavenly realm, but they remain a part of the daily communion of all Christians. So Catholics often asked Mary or other saints—whom they consider very much alive—to pray for them during times of need, just as people here ask their earthly friends in the church to pray for them.

By the following year, 1993, Watson had decided to take a trip to Medjugorje after all. He and his tour group happened to arrive there during Mary's Feast of the Assumption. In a Medjugorje gift shop, Watson spied two attractive, identical rosaries for sale. They were made up of small wooden beads connected by silver chains and both rosaries had silver crucifixes. The rosaries were so pretty that he bought one for himself and one for a friend back home.

He returned to his room, laid his friend's rosary on the nightstand, and stuck his rosary in the front pocket of his jeans. That evening, he went to Mass at St. James Church, where Mary appears to several visionaries. As he walked into the church, he pulled his new rosary from his pocket for the first time, glanced at it—and saw that the chain and crucifix now were gold, not silver.

He waited until after Mass to make any judgments. "I'm a scientist, I like to look at things factually," he said. At work, when he and other chemists conducted experiments, they always used two identical test groups: the first one to be acted on by the catalyst with which they were experimenting, and a "control group" that was not tampered with. By comparing the two groups later, they could gauge the catalyst's effects by seeing how much the first group differed from the untouched control group.

In his room lay the other rosary that had been identical to the one in his pocket. It would serve as his "control," the one not acted upon—which is to say, the one he hadn't taken to St. James Church.

When Watson returned to his room he picked up the rosary he'd bought for his friend back home. He compared it with his rosary. The chain and cross on his friend's remained silver. The chain and crucifix on his rosary now were gold. This time he couldn't attribute the transformation to any natural effect, as he had when his St. Andrew rosary changed colors. He couldn't have worn the finish from this new rosary—he'd hardly touched it; it had been crammed in his pocket all day.

"That was a signal grace," Watson said.

CHAPTER TEN

PROPHECY

Tʜᴇ ʙɪʟʟʙᴏᴀʀᴅ ᴏɴ Iɴᴛᴇʀsᴛᴀᴛᴇ 68 just outside Frostburg, Maryland, cries out for attention from passing motorists: "Noah's Ark Being Rebuilt Here." It's difficult to pass it by. You're drawn to see just what kind of person would reconstruct a 450-foot boat smack in the middle of the Maryland countryside. It's kind of like building a pontoon bridge across an Iowa cornfield.

That's precisely the reaction Pastor Richard Greene expected to provoke when he erected the billboard—and when he and his church, called God's Ark of Safety, began construction on their landlocked ship twenty years ago. Strangers regularly exit from the four-lane interstate and wind around to the site, where the foundation for the ark has been poured and 110 massive concrete support pillars have been set into the ground. Often Greene or a member of his congregation is waiting to greet them. "We just ask them, 'Are you ready today, should Jesus come?'" Greene said. "Right there on the ark site, I've led many people to Christ."

Greene doesn't really expect a deluge to wash Frostburg into the distant Atlantic Ocean. The ark, should it ever be completed, isn't designed to float. Actually, it will be a nonbuoyant worship building for Greene's medium-sized charismatic congregation, which averages between 130 and 170 people on a typical Sunday morning.

This boat is, like the billboard, a signpost. Greene says God entrusted the idea to him through a series of wrenching prophetic dreams he endured in 1974. The message: Jesus Christ soon will return to judge the earth. The planet and many of its inhabitants are headed for destruction and only those who have put their faith in God will be spared. The last time God similarly judged the world was in the time of Noah, when an angry Almighty wiped out humanity with a flood; only righteous Noah and his family survived. Greene's ark is calculated to remind sinners that a similarly awful day of reckoning looms ahead. According to the Bible, God will again destroy a large portion of the earth, this time with fire.

If you're thinking by this time that Richard Greene is one giraffe shy of a full ark, you'd do well to consider matters more carefully. Nothing about him, other than his boat-church, would strike any visitor as terribly odd. No one could be more aware of the incongruity, perhaps even the silliness, of Greene's ark than Greene himself. Neighbors have snickered at him for two decades. So have various journalists dispatched to Greene's ark in the hinterlands. Greene's desire in life was to become a missionary to foreign nations, not an apocalyptic shipbuilder. He's simply doing what he must, he said, which is to prove obedient to the prophetic message God gave him: "I know that I *know* this thing isn't of me. Otherwise, I'd have gone to Africa years ago to hide."

Greene was born about sixty years ago in Pontiac, Michigan, and spent his early work life as an engineering analyst for Pontiac Truck and Coach, a General Motors plant. During the 1960s he began to feel an internal tugging toward the ministry. He thought the Lord might be leading him toward a call as a foreign missionary. He attended Detroit Bible College and trained to become a registered nurse so that he would qualify for medical duty overseas. There was only one hitch in his plans. He interviewed with missions organizations all over the country, but couldn't find one willing to hire him, even though by this time he'd spent six years preparing for such a post.

After a period of discouragement, prayer, and soul-searching, he decided that God must have some other plan for him. Perhaps he might become the pastor of a small congregation somewhere that couldn't afford a full-time minister; he could support himself as a nurse and avoid putting a financial strain on his church. Again, he began the interviewing process, this time with various churches hither and yon. The only one that offered him a pastorate was a small church of about twenty people in Frostburg. It was the one place he didn't want to go, because Frostburg was the hometown of his wife, Lottie. He'd always felt as if the good Lord expected him to work someplace more remote from family and friends. But the Frostburg pastorate being the only job available, Greene accepted it in 1973. He went to work in a local hospital, too.

"The visions started April, May, and June of 1974," he said matter-of-factly. Greene would lie down in his bed at night, nod off to sleep—and find himself staring at a vivid ark. It would be as if someone had flipped on a movie projector. "I watched Noah build the first ark as clear as if I'd been there," he said. He saw a present-day ark, too, an attraction for people of all races and nationalities; they'd pull onto the site in tour buses and mobile homes.

The dreams turned ugly. He'd see Noah's first ark again, finished. God would slam its door shut and the rain would begin to pour. Frantic people would pound on the ark's sides, trying unsuccessfully to get inside as the water bubbled up around their waists, their necks, and over their heads. "It was the most traumatic thing I've seen in all my life," Greene said.

This went on night after night, for three solid months. Seemingly the real revelation came to him a bit at a time. He remembered a passage from Matthew 24: "But as the days of Noah were, so shall the coming of the Son of man be." And another scripture, from Acts 2, which prophesied that in the last days before Jesus' return, God would begin to once again pour out divine revelations through visions and dreams.

Greene began slowly, over the weeks, to understand that he was experiencing a modern-day vision. Jesus had promised in Matthew 24 that the days before his return would be just like the days of Noah. "What happened in Noah's time?" the Holy Spirit seemed to ask Greene. Obviously, Noah had built an ark, Greene realized. "I want you to build an ark, too, as a sign and warning of Christ's return," God seemed to tell him.

This went on and on. The problem was, the preacher didn't want to build a modern-day ark, regardless of what God said. "I wouldn't yield," he explained. "I knew I was setting myself up to be called crazy, just like Noah did."

Finally, as a last resort, unable to gain any peace or make the dreams stop, Greene decided to make God prove that it was in fact God who wanted this ark built. He asked for two signs. First, God must send an artist to draw a rendering of the ark. Second, when Greene told his little congregation this wacky idea, God would see to it that they agreed that God was in it.

Within days an artist showed up practically at Greene's doorstep and, once Greene had explained the idea, volunteered to sketch Greene's ark. Then Greene, in fear and trembling, approached the lay leaders of his church. They'd been hoping to construct a new building and already had purchased a few acres of land. Now he told them about his recurring dreams. He thought God wanted them to build a replica of the ark, he said. To his astonishment, they agreed.

Soon the little congregation started preparing their land. Clearly this was a project far beyond their abilities. Greene's plans kept expanding—or being expanded. Eventually he would estimate that the entire construction might cost as much as $10 million, including a two-thousand-seat auditorium, a Christian school, a Bible college, a medical and counseling complex, a food center. "That's probably why God picked us," he said. "We're so small we can't do it." Any aspect of the venture that succeeded would require obvious, divine aid.

At the same time his vision became clear, Greene felt God urging him to tell the world what he was doing—and why. "I don't even know how to tell Frostburg," the flustered minister replied in his prayers.

He needn't have worried. Word quickly leaked out on its own. Almost before Greene could comprehend what was happening to him and his meager congregation, a reporter asked permission to interview him for a story about his proposed ark. Then another reporter followed up on that story. And another. And another. And another. Today, Greene can't even remember all the media outlets on which his ark has appeared: the *Washington Post,* the *Baltimore Sun,* the Associated Press, United Press International, NBC News, ABC, CBS, "The 700 Club," Trinity Broadcasting Network. Countless smaller newspapers and local TV stations also have picked up on the story of the offbeat preacher in rural Maryland who is proclaiming, in effect, "The end is near!"

As the news accounts spread, Greene began receiving mail and even unsolicited donations from across America and from foreign countries. "I knew people around the world didn't know where I was," he said, again amazed. Among the more puzzling responses was one from a person who claimed to have watched Greene's story on national television in Australia. "I've never been to Australia," he said.

But he's been plenty of other places in the last two decades. Christian groups around the planet have asked him to come to their churches and tell his story. He obliges as many as possible—trying to remain obedient to God's instructions to spread the ark's message. He's visited twenty-one foreign nations, smuggled Bibles into China, and stood in Moscow's Red Square, he said. The more places he's spoken, the more invitations he's received. On the twentieth anniversary of his prophetic dreams he found himself preaching in western Africa. He's taped segments for national television and radio programs in Ghana, Nigeria, and Zimbabwe. He now spends seven months a year on the road; an assistant runs the church while he's gone.

All those years earlier, while he still worked for General Motors, he'd felt as if God was calling him to some remote, Third World mission field. He'd been heartbroken when no one would hire him as a missionary and he ended up as the part-time pastor in Frostburg, instead. "Not knowing God was going to open up the largest mission door I could ever walk through."

Of course there have been difficulties along the way. Many of the journalists who have reported on his ark have done so tongue-in-cheek. He's had some down times, he admitted. Money for the ark project has been slow coming in. "As God provides, I build. No banker would loan me the money," he said. "I owe no man nothing. . . . I've never asked for money anywhere." Still, over twenty years he's raised enough to sink that $300,000 worth of concrete in the ground. The church is creeping toward the $200,000 it needs to build one major section of the ark itself.

He believes the construction and fund-raising have taken such a long time because God is as patient today as he was in the days of Noah. When God spoke to Noah, God promised to give sinners 120 years to mend their ways before the ark was finished; then it would be too late. Not that Greene expects his ark to take 120 years to complete, or that he expects to be here that long himself. But God doesn't want to destroy the earth this time, either, Greene said, and he's giving people time to repent again, just as he did before.

Given all the remarkable things that have transpired over the years, especially the fact that his ark has, of its own volition, been publicized all over the earth—nearly always with Greene's admonition that it is a sign of destruction to come—Green is even more certain of his dreams' prophetic accuracy today than he was in 1974. "It's a warning of the Second Coming. It's got to be," he said. "It's really an end-time warning."

Proclaiming God's Word and Will

The term "prophecy" covers a broad range of manifestations. Generally, though, it is a phenomenon by which a person, through one of several forms of revelation, delivers to others a message from God. It can involve dramatic dreams, visions, or omens, as in the case of Richard Greene and his Maryland ark. On the other hand, in the ancient world prophetic oracles often were shouted in public by prophets caught up in frenzies. Today, prophecy sometimes follows a comparatively low-key, internal prodding—a "knowing," as some call it—that the prophet attributes to the Holy Spirit or another spiritual force and shares quietly with other people.

Many people assume that prophecy always involves foretelling the future. Often it does. But just as frequently it's a matter of "forthtelling," or revealing and solving through divine guidance some hidden problem that's bothering a person. Some scholars contend that prophecy can include the ability to keenly understand holy texts with an insight not available to the average student, and that a minister's sharpest sermons might well be the products of the prophetic gift. In the Hebrew Bible and throughout much of the Christian tradition, prophecy frequently includes a courageous and biting criticism of the prevailing culture's mores. When the Reverend Martin Luther King Jr. preached so eloquently against racial injustice, some Christians interpreted his behavior as prophetic. Founders of most major religions—including the Persian holy man Zoroaster, founder of Zoroastrianism, and Muhammad, the founder of Islam—are considered great prophets by their followers.

Joseph Smith started the Mormon Church based upon visions, texts, and ideas he said had been imparted to him by Jesus Christ and an angel. His early disciples also reported receiving prophetic revelations. For instance, Benjamin Brown, a nineteenth-century high priest in the Church of Jesus Christ of Latter-day Saints, wrote of a remarkable prophecy spoken by Elder Heber Kimball in 1847, as the Mormons struggled to survive in the valley of the Great Salt Lake.

Mormon pilgrims from the East had arrived in the valley in such numbers that the Saints' meager crops and food stores quickly were exhausted, Brown wrote, as recorded in Cathy Luchetti's book *Under God's Spell*. People ate roots and killed their livestock for food. Their clothes wore out and they had to wear animal skins. Their wagons broke down, and they had no materials with which to fix them. In the midst of this crisis, Brown says, Elder Kimball "stood up and prophesied that 'in a short time' we would be able to buy clothing and utensils cheaper in the valley than in the States. [We] only hoped it may be so, but without an absolute miracle, there seemed no human probability of fulfillment."

Soon, though, the discovery of gold in California became news in the East—and America's most famous gold rush was on. Hoping to capitalize on the lust for gold, various corporations in the Eastern states hurried to supply the thousands of new California prospectors with food, clothing, and mining tools. These companies, sparing no expense and at inflated prices, bought up all the supplies they could find and loaded them on wagons bound for the West. They expected huge profits in California. Unfortunately for them, after the wagons had crossed the plains, and just before they reached the valley of the Salt Lake, the entrepreneurs learned that businessmen from all over the world had sent ships nearly foundering from the weight of supplies for California—and had beaten the wagons there. The goods on the wagon weren't needed, but they were too far west turn back. Desperate to unload their wares, the owners sold their supplies to the Mormons instead, for half the price the goods would have brought back East. Kimball's prophecy had been startlingly fulfilled.

Much, much earlier than the Mormon migration to Utah, St. Paul had implied in the New Testament book of I Corinthians, Chapter 14, that many if not all Christians possessed the ability to prophesy, a wondrous gift that he described as edifying, exhorting, and comforting the congregation and which he called the most important of God's supernatural works among church members.

But as with many miraculous manifestations, today you are more likely to find the more supernatural varieties of prophecy practiced among Pentecostals, charismatics, and Third Wavers than among other, more traditional Christian groups. Christians who exercise this kind of prophecy use several terms for the various manifestations of prophetic gifts, based upon a passage by Paul in I Corinthians 12: "prophecy," "words of knowledge," or "words of wisdom." At the grassroots level you find the words used almost interchangeably, although scholars continue to debate their exact meanings and uses. (Speaking in tongues, along with the ability to interpret messages in tongues, also can be prophetic; we will look at them in the next chapter.)

In my experiences among Pentecostals and charismatics, "prophecy" usually refers to a message that is meant for an entire assembly, such as those attending a specific church worship service. A "word of knowledge" or "word of wisdom" more typically is a message intended for an individual, although it might be delivered to that person during a public gathering.

There's always a potential for the abuse of such "gifts" by dishonest or self-aggrandizing ministers. And many well-meaning people also misuse prophecy; they easily can mistake their personal opinions or background knowledge of situations for messages from God. So anyone who is given a message "from the Lord" by another person would do well to test it thoroughly before taking it to heart. Yet I've seen uncannily accurate instances of this gift.

When I was a young man in my twenties I recommitted my life to the church after several years as a dedicated wastrel. This was just after my father had recovered from cancer, left his Southern Baptist congregation, and founded a charismatic congregation. I was uncomfortable with much about the charismatic renewal, but other parts of it I liked, particularly the genuine love for God and for each other that I sensed among the worshipers. Also, I felt that out of family loyalty I should attend my dad's new church, at least until he had it running well. I soon was confused about various religious issues, though—everything from doctrines about God's forgiveness to warnings about the eternal judgment; such ideas seemed foreign to me after my lengthy stints as a beer-guzzling high school jock, college fraternity boy, and ne'er-do-well dropout.

One sunny weekday afternoon I happened to be walking outdoors when, without any warning, I received what struck me as a remarkable insight on one doctrinal question that had troubled me a great deal: God's grace, or his sovereign power to love people, accept them as they are, and ordain ahead of time beneficial plans for their lives. I felt as if I suddenly perceived the truth of this grace clearly, much in the same way you can wrestle with an obtuse algebra formula until you're frustrated enough to bang your head against a staircase and then, in an instant, understand it perfectly.

I was so happy about this exhilarating insight that I wanted to tell my friends at church. In those days I sometimes served as a substitute teacher in an adult Sunday school class, or even spoke in evening worship services when my dad, the pastor, was away and had no one better to fill in for him. The next several times I was given an opportunity to talk, I shared my newfound understanding of grace—and was vigorously shot down by other, older church members who had been taught differently.

Because I was young, inexperienced, and already confused by my Christian faith, I grew discouraged. I'd been so certain of my new knowledge. Now I wondered whether it had been a self-delusion. However, I didn't tell anyone about my frustration except my wife, Renee, who always kept my confidences. We didn't want to cause a problem in the church, particularly because my father was the pastor—and because he disagreed with me, too.

Not long afterward, a guest minister from Texas traveled to our church to hold a scheduled series of services. As I said, no one but my wife and me knew how frustrated I'd grown over the opposition to my flash of supposed insight, but it had become a big deal to me. I'd been so certain I'd learned a spiritual truth for once, and now I wondered how I could have been so badly mistaken.

Near the end of one service the guest evangelist, whom I'd never met before that weekend and never have seen since, asked those who wanted prayer to come forward. As several people walked down the center aisle and formed a line, the preacher began ministering to them using what he believed were the supernatural gifts of the Holy Spirit. He prayed for some to be healed. He prophesied over others. I didn't go forward but my wife and I, as I recall, happened to be sitting on the front row of the crowded sanctuary.

As the period of ministry wore on, the evangelist unexpectedly walked up to Renee and me, placed one hand on Renee's shoulder and the other on my chest, and began to pray aloud. Then he spoke a "word of knowledge" to me. I can't tell you the precise words he said because I didn't write them down, but his message went very much like this: "Son, the Lord says he's given you a powerful insight," the evangelist said. "He's revealed his truth to you on a subject, but you've questioned whether it was from him because every time you tried to share it, somebody told you, 'That's not true.' Well, the Lord says that the word you have is from him and it is true. 'Don't worry about those who don't receive it now,' the Lord says. 'At the proper time I will bring it forth, and when I do, the people who I've prepared to receive it will receive it.'"

You could have knocked me over with a cork gun. The guy couldn't have spoken any more plainly to my situation if I'd written him a letter beforehand explaining it. Yet he had no way of knowing what I was going through.

A year or so later I was asked to become one of a series of temporary speakers who would rotate on Sundays at a nearby church that was without a pastor. It was the little church in which my wife had been raised. I summoned up my gumption and decided to share my message of grace with them, assuming they'd disagree with it, too. Instead, to my astonishment, they lapped it up. Several said they'd already received the same insight. They'd been praying for God to send a speaker who would confirm the message for them. Eventually they even asked me to stay on as their permanent, part-time minister, despite the fact that I was untrained for such duties and had no desire whatever to become anyone's minister. Reluctantly, though—very reluctantly—I accepted. Renee and I have been part of that congregation, Grace Church, for fourteen years. Today I assume that God knew what he was talking about when he spoke through that evangelist from Texas.

A Native American Shaman Receives a Song

In his book *Native Religions of North America,* Ake Hultkrantz writes about Tudy Roberts, a member of the Wind River Shoshoni. Roberts was a well-known, twentieth-century puhagan, or medicine man. "Puha," says Hultkrantz, "is central to Shoshoni religion because the heart of this tradition is receiving power from guardian spirits, especially through visions and dreams." Roberts was especially gifted with *puha.* He healed diseases with a feather, which he used to "draw out" sickness. He foretold the weather.

Once, the Shoshoni were preparing for a momentous Sun Dance festival. Beforehand, Roberts experienced a strange dream, which he interpreted as a spiritual vision. In his dream, a woodpecker with a pink belly perched atop a tall pole at the Sun Dance gathering. The woodpecker sang a new and pleasing song that Roberts had never heard before. But the bird then spoke to the puhagan in human language. It told him to keep the song secret, because one of the young men at the forthcoming Sun Dance was meant to discover the song and sing it.

Later, during the Sun Dance ceremony, a young man among the participants experienced a dream of his own, in which Roberts gave him a song. In his sleep, the young man sang this strange new tune. When he awoke that morning he hurried to the Sun Dance camp, joined the drummers, and, as an American flag was hoisted nearby on a pole, sang his new melody. It was the same tune that Roberts had heard earlier in his own vision.

A Marian Visionary Predicts Her Own Healing

Wayne Weible is a former newspaper publisher in Myrtle Beach, South Carolina—and a Protestant—who became fascinated some years ago by the apparitions of the Virgin Mary at Medjugorje. He'd initially believed the apparition might be fodder for a column or two. But when he began researching the phenomenon, he got hooked. He eventually traveled to the former Yugoslavia and documented his experiences there. Ultimately he became a believer in the apparition's reality. He's since written such books as *Medjugorje: The Message* and *Letters from Medjugorje.*

In the former, he tells about a young woman named Vicka Ivankovic, one of the original Medjugorje visionaries. During the first seven years that the visions took place, from 1981 to 1988, Ivankovic suffered from an inoperable brain cyst. Many times, she fell so ill she nearly was comatose. Her condition was both widely known and medically documented.

During February 1988, Mary told Ivankovic that she would be miraculously healed in September of that year. There had then been, and there continue to be, many critics and doubters of the Medjugorje apparition. So in February Ivankovic wrote identical letters: one to a priest and author named Janko Bubalo and another to the pastor and a panel investigating the apparition at St. James Church in Medjugorje. The letters were sealed, with instructions not to open them until September 26, 1988.

The day before, September 25, Ivankovic's cyst was cured. On September 26 the letters were opened, revealing her prediction in February that her healing would take place in September. "It was a tremendous miracle with double grace," Weible writes in *Medjugorje: The Message.* "Vicka once again had her full health, and the commission had further proof of the authenticity of the apparitions, with records and documentation to corroborate Vicka's previous medical history."

A Mainline Pastor Receives a Prophetic Message

Steve Seamands is a United Methodist minister and a professor of Christian doctrine at Asbury Theological Seminary, a mainline Protestant school. You might recall from Chapter 3 that beginning in 1990 he became active in the miraculous Third Wave movement. His first experiences with signs and wonders didn't begin in 1990, however.

For instance, back in 1981 Seamands was serving as a pastor in Elmer, New Jersey, where he'd been involved in a successful church growth campaign in his Methodist district. He was scheduled to attend a pastors' retreat in Pennsylvania for the ministers from two New Jersey United Methodist annual conferences. On a Monday morning, exactly a week before the retreat was to start, Seamands awoke to a mental image of himself at the retreat. In his mind, he stood before the crowd of his fellow ministers, talking about the secrets of how to increase church membership. The problem was that Seamands wasn't scheduled to speak at the event. He told his wife about his vision. She was tired from their church labors and wasn't at all enthused by the idea of his assuming a leadership role at the retreat. "Oh no," she replied. "I just want to relax."

That Friday, Seamands and several other pastors from his district were to visit their area's bishop and fill him in on their church growth strategies and experiences. On the way, Seamands happened to tell his friends about his strange image of speaking at the retreat.

During the meeting, the bishop himself brought up the following week's retreat. He was scheduled to make a speech there, and he said he planned to talk about church growth. The bishop added that perhaps it would be wise to form a panel on church growth, too, which could discuss strategies after his speech ended. "Are any of you planning to go to the retreat?" the bishop asked.

"Yes," Seamands said. A woman minister replied that she would be there, too. "Good," the bishop said, "you two can serve on the discussion panel." Then he excused himself from the room. The other ministers sat there and stared at one another in awe, Seamands said.

The next week Seamands arrived at the manor in Pennsylvania

where the retreat was held, to discover that only one hour had been allotted to both his bishop's address and the panel discussion that was to
follow it. That left little time for Seamands to address such a complicated issue in the depth he'd hoped, the disappointed pastor realized.

But on the day of the bishop's address and the panel scheduled to
follow, the bishop oddly came down with a sore throat. He couldn't
talk. It was too late to reschedule his speech—so the panel of which
Seamands was a part was asked to fill the hour. "We were the whole
thing," he said. Seamands successfully delivered all his insights to the assembled ministers, just as he'd foreseen a week earlier. The preachers
were visibly enthusiastic about his presentation. "It spoke deeply to
everyone there," Seamands said. "It's like the Lord showed me what
was going to happen, before it happened."

A Hindu "Sees" Two Christian Missionaries

Richard Samuel is a native of Tamil Nadu, a state in south India.
He's an Anglican and the coordinator for Asia of Fishhook International, an international Protestant ministry. Christians are vastly outnumbered in his heavily Hindu country. Of the roughly 900 million
residents, a mere 2 to 3 percent profess the Christian faith. Of those,
Samuel said, 8 million—less than 1 percent of the population—are active believers who regularly practice their religion. Because Christians
are so greatly outnumbered, Samuel said, God tends to work especially
mightily through them at times, as if to confirm their messages to
those who otherwise wouldn't pay any attention. "The supernatural is
a big part of the gospel in my part of the world," Samuel said.

Samuel's father, who goes by the initial of his first name, P., also is
a prominent Indian Christian, who enjoys documenting stories of the
miraculous as fully as possible. One involves a man in north India who
lived in a remote village and was said to have been dying of disease
when he saw a deathbed vision. "He saw a person in white, a glorious
figure, and he was healed," Richard said. "He had not heard of the
Christian religion before." Some months later, the healed man happened to visit a village marketplace, where a traveling Christian evan-

gelist was preaching the Christian message in the open air. The evangelist used a graphics device made up of a flannel board to which he attached images of the Christian story as he talked. The villager who'd earlier been healed saw a flannel image of Jesus Christ on the board. Immediately he began to yell, "That's him! That's him!" The evangelist stopped. "That's who?" someone asked. "That's the figure I saw!" the man replied. "That's him! I saw him! I saw him! He healed me!"

When the tale eventually made its way to the Samuels in south India, the elder P. Samuel was so intrigued that he decided to travel to the village, find the man, and see whether the story was true. By this time, eighteen months had elapsed since the evangelist had preached in the man's village. But P. Samuel indeed found the healed man—and discovered that the thrilled convert had baptized eighty-three friends and relatives in a pond near his hut. They, too, had converted. "We hear of more and more instances like that," Richard said.

Another instance of a remarkable prophetic vision involves a pair of young women, Indra and Sinehalatha, who were members of a larger evangelistic team commissioned in 1989 by P. Samuel's ministry. The team had spent more than a week walking in pairs along the riverbanks of Allahabad, a sacred city in the northern India state of Uttar Pradesh, handing out Christian tracts during a festival in which millions of Hindus bathe in the Ganges in hopes of receiving forgiveness of their sins. The bodies and ashes of the dead often are released into the river, so the devout wade in among drifting corpses.

Indra and Sinehalatha had accomplished nothing during their missionary labors. They hadn't made one convert. On the evening of the eighth day, feeling blue, they asked God to prepare someone for them to help. The next morning they decided to walk through a housing area away from the crowded river, where there were few people on the streets. They couldn't explain why they did that, since it seemed contrary to their original mission.

As they walked along, they came to a large house. Somehow, again, they felt led, this time to a gate in front of the home. A gardener stood there. "What do you want?" he asked. The young Christians explained that they would like to speak with the woman of the house. Without admitting them, the gardener yelled for his employer. When she saw the two missionaries, she said, "What do you want?" One of the young women said, "The Lord told us to come here. We want to tell you some good news."

"I don't want anything to do with you," replied the middle-aged woman brusquely. "Leave. We don't want to know anything about God here."

Confused, Indra and Sinehalatha turned to leave. But then another woman's voice called from within the big house, "Don't let them go!"

The mother continued to shout at the visitors to drive them away, until her daughter, Geetha, twenty-one, rolled outside in a wheelchair. "Mum! Don't shout at them!" she said. "Last night in my dream I saw them bringing me peace."

The mother, Leela, was so taken aback that she allowed Indra and Sinehalatha into her home. Inside, Geetha asked the two Christians to sit beside her chair. Then she told them her story. She liked dance and music, she said, and she'd recently been completing her final year toward a university bachelor's degree in commerce. Her wealthy father had owned a cement factory. Recently he'd been driving to his factory when a bus hit his car. His head had been smashed. His lifeless body was carried home.

Geetha had been called home from college but not told the reason. When she entered the house, she saw a crowd of mourners there—and her father's body, his head swathed in bandages. She had shrieked and fallen on him, crying, "Daddy, where have you gone?" Hysterical, she ran to his room on the first floor, then dashed upstairs to an open terrace and flung herself from it. The jump had, among other things, broken both her legs, which is why she was confined to a wheelchair.

Her body had begun to mend, Geetha thought, but she remained depressed. One day she had called her servants to open the house's Hindu prayer room. She rolled herself inside it and shouted to the religious statues there, "Oh, you gods, to hell with you! Every day I offered many prayers before you with my daddy. But you did nothing to save my daddy." When she left the room she ordered the servants to seal it.

The night before Indra and Sinehalatha had arrived, though, Geetha had had a wonderful dream. In it, two young women had given her a tract entitled "Peace" ("*Shanthi*," in her dialect). The message on the paper had helped her. "Give me the tract," she said. Amazingly, Indra and Sinehalatha carried exactly such a tract. They handed it to Geetha, who read it straight through as the Christians sat and watched. When she had finished, the young women talked with Geetha about God's ability to save her soul and impart to her mental peace. Geetha asked many questions. Soon she prayed with her visitors, confessed her sins, and pledged her soul to Jesus Christ.

Geetha pleaded with the two young women to stay in her home and conduct their evangelism from there. "The prayer room in my house is already shut," she said. "My deities are dumb and useless. They never answered me."

Later that day, however, the two Christian evangelists left the home for a few hours to continue handing out tracts. When they were gone, Geetha ordered her servants to open the prayer room, carry out all the statues, and destroy them. Her mother objected, but Geetha said, "Jesus who forgives our sins and gives us peace lives in our hearts now."

That evening, Indra and Sinehalatha returned to Geetha's house with their street-witnessing colleagues, young women from Switzerland, Korea, and the Indian states of Manipur, Mizoram, Kerala, and Tamil Nadu. Those women, too, heard the remarkable tale of Geetha's prophetic dream. They sang some hymns. But Geetha and her mother also became frustrated. "Why didn't you come to us before my daddy's death?" Geetha asked. The other Christians admittedly held no answers to that question. At the evening's end, the street evangelists took their leave, promising to return within a few days and check on Geetha and her mother.

When the Christian team came back to visit several days later, they found Leela distraught. Two days earlier, Geetha had called her mother to her room. "Mummy! I'm going to Jesus, whom I love," Geetha said. "Tell the sisters that Jesus is with me and I love him." Saying that, the twenty-one-year-old had unexpectedly died. The Christians tried to console Leela, but she was too wounded. God seemed cruel to her, not to have sent his peace to her husband and then to have allowed Geetha to succumb from her injuries just as she seemed to be improving.

"It was as if the Lord just wanted to reach that girl," Richard Samuel told me.

But there's a footnote to this story. As said, P. Samuel likes to document such reported miracles. When he interviewed Indra for her version of Geetha's conversion, Indra said she didn't know what had ever become of Leela, the mother. So P. Samuel asked Indra to look in on the woman the next time she traveled to north India. On her next journey north, before she could visit Leela's house, Indra attended a Sunday worship service in the same neighborhood where Leela and Geetha had lived. During the service a small ensemble stood to sing a special musical number. Among them was Leela, as well as one of Geetha's older brothers. Both had become dedicated Christians.

CHAPTER ELEVEN

SPEAKING IN TONGUES

AFTER JESUS HAD RISEN from the dead and ascended to heaven, 120 of his followers gathered in an upper room in Jerusalem to pray. Among them were Jesus' mother and all the chief apostles. They'd been in that room about ten days when the Jewish festival of Pentecost arrived. Then a remarkable thing happened. Luke the physician, the author of the Acts of the Apostles, describes it like this: "And suddenly there came a sound from heaven as of a rushing mighty wind, and it filled all the house where they were sitting. And there appeared unto them cloven tongues like as of fire, and it sat upon each of them. And they were all filled with the Holy Ghost, and began to speak with other tongues, as the Spirit gave them utterance."

At the time, devout Jews from all over the world had moved to Jerusalem and others were gathered there for Pentecost. As soon as the Holy Spirit had touched them, the newly empowered Christians took to the streets, where they drew a crowd of curiosity seekers. The multinational crowd heard these disciples speaking fluently in the dialects of their own countries. Luke writes that the onlookers were dumbfounded, and said, "one to another, 'Behold, are not all these which speak Galileans? And how hear we every man in our own tongue, wherein we were born? Parthians, and Medes, and Elamites, and the dwellers in Mesopotamia, and in Judaea, and Cappadocia, in Pontus, and Asia, Phrygia, and Pamphylia, in Egypt, and in the parts of Libya about Cyrene, and strangers of Rome, Jews and proselytes, Cretes and Arabians, we do hear them speak in our tongues the wonderful works of God.'"

Luke's next sentence is particularly telling: "And they were all amazed, and were in doubt, saying to one another, 'What meaneth this?'"

Simon Peter stood among the throng that had surrounded him and his excited friends. He preached an extemporaneous sermon and three thousand were converted that morning to faith in Jesus, partly because of the miracle of dozens of people speaking in languages they hadn't studied. This legendary Pentecost marked the birth of the Christian church.

Later in Acts, Luke says that God revealed his intention to spread the message about Jesus to non-Jews as well, beginning with a Roman army officer named Cornelius. In that case, Cornelius and the members of his household spontaneously spoke in tongues, too, a verification to Peter and his fellow Christians of Jewish lineage that God had accepted the Gentiles.

Within Christianity, outbreaks of speaking in tongues have been reported in nearly every century since. Montanus's large-scale revival included tongues during the late second century. John Wesley, the founder of the Methodist faith, seemed ambivalent about reports of tongues in his own time, two hundred years ago, but endorsed the historic ministry of Montanus, Harvey Cox writes in *Fire from Heaven*. Many of the more momentous Christian renewals of our own century were inaugurated by the tongues phenomenon: the Azusa Street revival, the charismatic renewal, and the Third Wave movement.

Yet, to paraphrase Luke, wherever people speak in tongues onlookers continue to be amazed and to doubt and to ask, "What meaneth this?" No miraculous manifestation has remained as controversial or as often the subject of ridicule as this one, despite the fact that even in the Western Hemisphere speaking in tongues is surprisingly widespread.

One national poll found that 89 percent of American adults say that they pray. Of that 89 percent, 12 percent speak in tongues during prayer—a number that, if my rough calculations are correct, figures out to nearly 20 million adults in this country alone, not including teenagers or younger children. Another survey, 1995 Barna Research

Group poll, reported that 11 percent of U.S. adults say they have asked God to give them the ability to speak in tongues, and 7 percent have received the gift. Barna also finds that 27 percent of all American evangelicals have spoken in tongues. In the largest Pentecostal denomination, the Assemblies of God, 67 percent of adherents say they have spoken in tongues at some time; 40 percent continue to do so.

Why, then, is speaking in tongues so controversial even among those who believe in other kinds of miracles? Eunice Irwin, the seminary professor, offered as good an explanation as I've heard. Within Christianity, at least, there are many categories of miracles, such as healing, prophecy, and tongues, Irwin said. Christians understand all of these as emanating from the Holy Spirit. But most of these charisms prove idiosyncratic. In healing, for example, a preacher might pray for ten sick people and find that, if he's lucky, one is healed. Also, a person might be healed of migraine headaches, yet continue to suffer from gout. These miracles come and go as God pleases.

Tongues is the one gift that works differently, Irwin said. Quite often, those who speak in tongues claim to be able to do so at will, rather than periodically. Also, tongues is an immediately visible—or audible, that is—sign of God's presence *within* an individual; the Holy Spirit supposedly is speaking directly through them. Additionally, it's a miracle that easily can be distorted, intentionally or not; after all, who can tell whether a person speaking in tongues is speaking in an actual language or merely talking nonsense, unless the hearer happens to recognize the dialect?

Finally, some Pentecostals historically have categorized speaking in tongues as the only acceptable proof that a Christian has received the significant "baptism in the Holy Spirit," which for many Christians marks a powerful step upward from mere conversion. "Tongues becomes 'the' sign," Irwin said.

For all these reasons, then, speaking in tongues often has been taken as a sign that somehow endorses the person who is speaking rather than glorifies God. Sometimes it has provoked resentment and jealousy.

What Is Speaking in Tongues?

Tongues usually is called "glossolalia" in academic and professional literature. It initially was greeted with disdain by field researchers who refused even to consider that it might be supernatural in origin. "Early ethnographic reports of glossolalia treated it with contempt, calling it 'absurd nonsense, gibberish scarce worth recording,'" notes the *Encyclopedia of Religion*.

In *Fire from Heaven*, Cox devotes significant space to explaining how speaking in tongues might work—from a largely anthropological standpoint. For him, the twentieth century has suffered what he calls an "ecstasy deficit." We Westerners, particularly, have separated ourselves from our deepest feelings; we consider public displays of emotion such as weeping or shouting uncouth. That has affected our religious practices as much as any other area of our lives.

From the times of our earliest ancestors, however, we humans have badly needed some form of ecstatic release, Cox argues. For him, tongues is a means of recapturing the visceral feelings that in ancient cultures accompanied worship. Those who speak in tongues bypass the limitations of normal human speech by surrendering in an almost childlike manner to their emotions, he says. The human mind longs to express these deep-seated feelings but has no words for them, and the incoherent syllables of glossolalia can be a result. Cox calls tongues "primal speech."

Those who take a more supernatural view of tongues might find some elements of agreement with Cox and others who pose similar explanations, including the idea that glossolalia expresses thoughts or feelings too profound for day-to-day language. But generally adherents see speaking in tongues differently. For one thing, they typically report that speaking in tongues—contrary to being the ecstatic act described by secularists—generally involves little excitement or shift in consciousness. In their favor Felicitas Goodman, writing in the *Encyclopedia of Religion*, points out that on a number of psychological tests, such as the Thematic Apperception Test and the Personality Factor Test, those who speak in tongues generally possess "no inherent weaknesses in neural organization" and, in fact, appear "less subject to suggestion and better adjusted than their [anti-tongues] counterparts."

For those who practice glossolalia, it is, like other miracles, a supernatural act. In this case pro-tongues Christians believe the Holy Spirit lives inside all Christian believers. Using biblical evidence such as Chapters 12, 13, and 14 of I Corinthians, as well as Romans 8 and other texts, they argue that quite often the Holy Spirit chooses to speak through Christians in a pure and divine manner that bypasses the impure thoughts generated by the human brain. To do this, the Spirit chooses a language that the human being who is speaking doesn't understand and thus can't tamper with. Sometimes the Spirit employs the human dialects of other nations, but just as often might speak in, as St. Paul implied, "the tongues of angels"—which for some adherents explains why glossolalia may sound like gibberish to linguists who study it.

The people who practice glossolalia sometimes distinguish two uses for the gift. First, there are public manifestations, such as the one the church experienced at Pentecost more than 1,900 years ago. This gift is taken as a sign of God's presence and power, usually to non-Christians who happen to be present in the church assembly. Either the unbelievers hear an untutored Christian talk fluently in their native language—a sign which some say occurs occasionally today on Third World mission fields—or else the tongues message acts as a prophetic gift. In the latter case, one Christian speaks out a message in tongues, usually during a church service, and then she or someone else immediately receives the supernatural ability to interpret that message. At times, the interpretation relates uncannily to a private situation affecting the non-Christian whom God wants to reach.

Second, and far more common, is the gift of tongues when used as a private prayer language. People who pray in tongues usually say that the experience is a quiet one and that they remain firmly in control of all their faculties, except for the shape of the syllables flowing from their mouths. They can turn on or turn off the glossolalia at will. After they've prayed in the Spirit, though, they tend to feel refreshed, cleansed, and energized for religious service.

Not Only a Christian Phenomenon

Historically, speaking in tongues seems to have cut across many cultures. References to glossolalia are found in the Vedas, which are the three-thousand-year-old sacred writings of the Hindus, as well as in the Tibetan Tantric writings and in some litanies of Islamic Sufi mystics.

The oracle at Delphi ranked as the most important religious center of ancient, polytheistic Greece and perhaps dates as early as 750 B.C.E. Those who wanted to consult the legendary, prophetic powers of the oracle would offer sacrifices, then enter the temple of Apollo. There they submitted their questions to the Pythia, an older woman who served as the priestess of Apollo. The Pythia delivered her oracles in a voice that changed dramatically as she spoke. She seemed to enter an altered consciousness, and apparently many of her answers were so unintelligible that they had to be translated by other prophets into Greek. Some modern writers, such as Walter K. Price, understand this to have been a pagan example of glossolalia.

Cathy Luchetti's book about evangelists on the American frontier, *Under God's Spell,* includes excerpts of the writings nineteenth-century Mormon high priest Benjamin Brown. Mormons consider themselves Christians but are regarded as a quasi-cult by some more mainstream members of the Christian faith.

In one passage Brown details a prophecy in tongues he received from a small boy in Lime, New York. At the time, Brown was preparing to set out from New York State for Nova Scotia, to seek new converts for the Church of Jesus Christ of Latter-day Saints. At a farewell church meeting, the child spoke out a message in tongues, with tears running down his cheeks. Someone else, apparently, interpreted the glossolalia into English. Brown would be mobbed, beaten, and left for dead, the prophecy said. Blood would pour from his head all over his clothes. Later the interpretation was precisely fulfilled in Canada. Brown found himself surrounded by enemies of his religion, who thrashed him severely, cut his scalp, broke several of his ribs, and left him alone only after he feigned death.

An Episcopal Priest Goes Pentecostal

The massive charismatic renewal among Christians began in the late 1950s and early 1960s when Pentecostalism moved into mainstream Protestant and Roman Catholic denominations for the first time. Mainline Christianity hasn't been the same since. Many people credit—or blame—an Episcopal rector, the Reverend Dennis J. Bennett, with helping touch off that movement.

Bennett then was pastor of the 2,600-member St. Mark's Episcopal Church in Van Nuys, California. In his book, *Nine O'Clock in the Morning*, Bennett explains that his adventure began when an Anglican vicar from Northern Ireland, who had taken a church near Bennett's in California, came to see him. The Irish vicar, identified only as Frank, said he'd discovered in his congregation a young lay couple who were speaking in tongues. Puzzled, Frank asked Bennett what he should do about such a thing. The couple wasn't causing any problems, he added. As a matter of fact, they were among his church's more dedicated and enthusiastic members.

Bennett hardly knew what to tell Frank; he'd barely heard of glossolalia. A native of England, he considered himself "high church" and cerebral, almost remote emotionally—"firmly schooled never to show my feelings," he writes. He'd done graduate work in psychology and counseling at the University of Chicago. He knew about "hypnosis, hysteria, autosuggestion."

Frank asked Bennett to meet the tongues-speaking couple, but initially Bennett wanted no part of that. "You have your little problems and I have mine," Bennett told his fellow priest.

The Irish priest kept after Bennett for a solid month, until Bennett relented. One August evening in 1959, he uneasily walked up the driveway of a suburban Southern California bungalow with Frank. There he met John and Joan, the two church members in question. They explained to Bennett that they'd received the baptism in the Holy Ghost. They appeared so incredibly happy that, afterward, Bennett couldn't get them off his mind. By comparison, his own Christian faith seemed dry and impotent.

Bennett began to research the Bible, Episcopal theology, prayer books, and church history, trying to understand what John and Joan were talking about. Everywhere he looked, he said, he seemed to confirm that, yes, the baptism in the Holy Ghost and speaking in tongues were part of a vanished tradition that once had been at the heart of the Christian faith and practice.

He arranged to meet with John and Joan again.

"I was like a starving man circling a table on which a delicious-looking feast is spread, watching the people seated at the table obviously enjoying the food, while trying to make up his mind whether it is really safe," he says in *Nine O'Clock in the Morning*.

Finally, Bennett allowed John to lay his hands on Bennett's head and pray for him to receive the baptism in the Holy Spirit. "Now, remember, I want this nearness to God that you have, that's all," Bennett warned, as he writes in his book. "I'm not interested in speaking in tongues!"

After John had placed his hands on Bennett, he told the priest to pray. Bennett prayed aloud quietly for about twenty minutes. His tongue suddenly "tripped," as if he'd stumbled while performing a tongue-twister. Then he began to speak in a new language he didn't recognize. He didn't feel anything shift inside his soul, though, and soon left, still perplexed by it all.

Four days later he returned to John and Joan's house. Frank also was present. John suggested that he take Bennett to a back room and pray for him again, and Bennett agreed. John didn't attempt to pump him up emotionally. This time as they prayed, a new language flowed from Bennett.

Immediately he was struck by several realizations about tongues. It didn't seem to be a trick or a psychological compulsion. At first he didn't feel excited. He remained in control of his wits, he writes, and spoke of his own volition. He quickly learned that he could speak louder, softer, faster, or slower as he wished—just as if he were speaking in English. He could control everything except the form of the words themselves. The syllables he was speaking sounded like a real language with grammar and syntax. "This language was being given me from the central place in me where God was," Bennett writes, "far beyond the realm of my emotions."

On the other hand, the more he spoke in tongues that night, the "happier and happier" he became. When he returned to the house's front room, he said to John and Joan, "Do you mean to tell me that a Christian can feel like I do?" John and Joan said that was exactly what they'd been trying to tell him. "I'm floored!" Bennett said. "I'll be floored the rest of my life over this!"

His congregation was floored, too, on April 3, 1960, when Bennett finally stood in the pulpit at his large, staid church and announced that he'd spoken in tongues. His announcement nearly split the church. Some parishioners sided with him and sought the Pentecostal experience, too. Others were horrified. The furor drew attention from the local and national media. Bennett later departed St. Mark's under some pressure and moved to Seattle to lead a small mission church. But by that time, the debate over his experiences was slowly gearing up in churches across the country—and across the world. Unwittingly, he had helped instigate one of the most far-reaching renewal movements in Christian history.

Another Episcopal Priest Follows Suit

Moultrie McIntosh moved to Lexington, Kentucky, in 1967 from Oak Ridge, Tennessee, where he'd served as rector of St. Stephen's Episcopal Church. He'd been named rector of Lexington's immense and historic Christ Church, the largest Episcopal congregation in the eastern half of Kentucky. (It now serves as the cathedral of the Episcopal Diocese of Lexington.) Christ Church was twice the size of St. Stephen's, quite a move up in McIntosh's clerical career, but an intimidating move, too. His staff there was undersized, he discovered.

While serving in Tennessee, he'd attended a conference on the Holy Spirit that was held in Gatlinburg, a resort town in the southeast end of the state. He'd also read Bennett's book, *Nine O'Clock in the Morning*. "That was one of the things that helped me," McIntosh said. "If it can happen to an Episcopal priest, it can happen to anybody."

Soon after he'd arrived in Lexington, he met a local Presbyterian pastor who claimed he'd received the baptism in the Holy Spirit—which McIntosh now refers to as "the release of the Holy Spirit," because he believes that all baptized Christians are possessed by the third person of the Trinity; some simply haven't released the Holy Ghost to perform his mighty works.

Anyway, the Presbyterian minister visited McIntosh in his stately office at Christ Church Episcopal, and they discussed this powerful blessing. "He said, 'Would you like to?'" McIntosh recalled. "I said, 'Would I?' . . . It was just the right time in my career."

The two ministers knelt on the floor. The Presbyterian placed one of his hands on McIntosh's head and prayed. "I felt like a warm glow sort of come over me. Something really special," McIntosh said. He didn't immediately speak in tongues, as some people do when they receive the "release" of the Spirit. "I think I kind of resisted it. It seems kind of kooky to some people."

He did experience immediate results, though. McIntosh found himself filled with more power for ministry to his congregation, and with more love. He started an adult class that studied the Holy Spirit.

Months later, he said, he was returning from a day trip to a small town near Lexington. Even with the extra power he sensed in his pastoral work, he continued to feel a bit overwhelmed by his job at Christ Church. He'd been considering the issue of tongues ever since the Presbyterian prayed for him. Earlier he'd thought this gift wasn't for him, but as he'd studied and contemplated it over the previous weeks he'd changed his mind. He'd decided it was a gift available for any Christian who wanted or needed it.

As he drove along the highway that day in his blue Volkswagen, he said, "'Lord, I'm ready if you're ready.' I needed all the help I could get." Instantly a language he didn't recognize bubbled up inside him and he began speaking it aloud as he steered his VW down the road. "It just came right along," McIntosh said of the tongues.

This added dimension to his Christian experience intensified his faith in God even more. His love for people and his devotion to the scriptures multiplied. He kept his speaking in tongues to himself for a long time, but his parishioners sensed a difference in him. Spiritual power seemed to ricochet inside him. "You could really feel it," he said. "It was evidenced by things that happened around me."

For instance, a faculty member at the University of Kentucky had a daughter in her twenties who was suffering from a severe brain ailment. She was in a coma, being kept alive in the hospital on a life-support system. The professor asked McIntosh to pray for her. Not content merely to pray from his office, McIntosh drove to the hospital, walked into the young woman's room, and placed his hands on her. As he finished praying, she opened her eyes and looked straight at him, he said. Gradually, she recovered completely.

McIntosh led Christ Church Episcopal to open a ministry to college students, street people, alcoholics, and drug addicts in an old Lexington school building. "It was a real powerhouse," he said. "It was, of course, interracial." I have talked with people who attended Christ Center, as the ministry was called. They agree that, under McIntosh's leadership, Christ Center introduced them to some of the more meaningful spiritual insights of their lives.

Now retired and an amateur artist, the white-haired McIntosh in his seventies remains an impish man, with an engaging sense of humor even though he suffers from Parkinson's disease. He smiles constantly and sprinkles one-liners into his conversation. He delights in what he considers to be the constant presence of the Holy Spirit. By chance one evening I sat down next to him at Christ Church, where I had come to cover for the newspaper a speech to be given by Rabbi Harold Kushner. McIntosh greeted me, grinned broadly, and began to whisper in tongues, there in our pew near the front of the packed church. It disconcerted me but seemed to tickle him.

One sign of the depth of his faith is that he seemingly isn't troubled by his sickness. He believes God can heal him. But the disease has helped him spiritually, he insists: "I was kind of spoiled, you might say." Before, he'd always been healthy, had expected God to keep him that way, and didn't really understand the difficulties people undergo when fighting long-term illnesses. "I figure God's used these things to help me grow and understand suffering better," he said.

McIntosh also admits that it's possible God won't heal his Parkinson's, that his body will continue to deteriorate. Some people get healed, some don't, he said. He doesn't claim to know why. "We don't really understand," he said. "We'll have to find that out when we get to the other side." He appears unbothered by the prospect of withering away and dying, should that happen.

God Speaks All Languages

Like many people, I had a more difficult time accepting the legitimacy of speaking in tongues than any of the other miraculous gifts. As McIntosh said of his initial impressions, the practice struck me as kooky. Believe it or not, I am, by nature and academic training, a critical thinker. I used to take smug pleasure in that aspect of my personality. Now, I feel more uneasiness about it than anything. Often I fear that what people like me prefer to call "healthy skepticism" mostly is a euphemism for unhealthy pride.

A single event I witnessed at my father's charismatic church in the autumn of 1983 changed my mind about the gift of tongues. By 1983 my wife, Renee, and I had left Faith Church, my dad's congregation in Mount Sterling, Kentucky. We left not out of rancor but because I had, as I've mentioned, agreed to serve as the weekend pastor of the tiny Pentecostal church Renee had attended as a child, even though I didn't consider myself a Pentecostal, wasn't trained as a minister, and didn't really want to be either one. I might have been the most reluctant weekend preacher in modern Christendom. I was pleased that the little congregation had embraced my message about God's grace. Other than that, my reasons for taking the job weren't as lofty as I'd like to have you think. To put it bluntly, when the twenty-five members of the church asked me to be their leader Renee was pregnant, I had just entered graduate school—and we desperately needed the $100 a week the congregation offered me as a salary.

My only sister, Cathi, was then in her early twenties, rebellious, and not a churchgoer at all. She'd dropped out of college and moved from Kentucky to Arizona, where she worked in an office at Grand Canyon National Park.

A co-worker from Oneida, New York, became Cathi's best friend there. Barbara Ficchi was an attractive and vivacious young woman of Mediterranean lineage, with olive skin and dark hair. Her father was Italian-American and her mother Greek-American. Her dad had converted from Roman Catholicism to her mother's Greek Orthodox Church, but Barb's parents, who owned an ethnic restaurant that kept them busy, weren't avid churchgoers. During most of Barb's early life the family attended worship services a few times a year. Barb's family spoke English at home, and the little Greek she understood consisted of fragments she'd gleaned from Orthodox services. She didn't attend churches outside the Greek Orthodox denomination, she said later, because her father had warned her that other groups would lead her astray.

In Arizona, Barb found herself involved in a tumultuous romantic relationship with a man she now believes to have been disturbed. "I was living in darkness," is how she describes her life at the time. One night Barb's boyfriend beat her badly. Right in the midst of the brouhaha Cathi, my sister, banged on Barb's door. For a moment, that silenced the fight. Barb answered Cathi's knocking. "What are you doing here?" she asked. Cathi explained that she'd felt an overpowering urge to check on her friend. "I think the Lord sent me," Cathi said—which was an unusual statement for Cathi to make. Cathi could see that Barb was bruised and terrified. She left the apartment and raced to find officers from the National Park Service, who returned to Barb's place and subdued her boyfriend.

"We're getting you out of here," Cathi told Barb. They packed up their belongings and set off cross-country in Cathi's car. They decided to stop in Kentucky and visit my folks for a week or two, then continue on to Barb's home in upstate New York and see her family.

After the women arrived in Mount Sterling, my parents, my wife, and I all were taken by Barb, who was smart, witty, and outgoing. A typical preacher, Dad soon prevailed on Cathi and Barb to attend a midweek evening service at his church. Because Cathi and Barb were going, Renee and I decided to attend as well.

Cathi had forewarned Barb that she would find Faith Church much different from the ritualistic church in which Barb had been raised.

There were few rituals at Faith, no pomp, no robes, no incense. The lively music included guitars and drums. Barb never had entered such a church, because she'd remembered her father's warning that non-Orthodox groups would mislead her. But this evening she was game.

The Faith Church building, covered in brown paneling, sits atop a hill surrounded by rolling pastures. Sometimes cattle graze in an adjacent lot. The sanctuary is comparatively small. At most, 150 might be able to pack inside it, although a more typical crowd is half that size. The windowpanes are made up of small squares of glass colored red, blue, and gold. The interior walls are white. It's a modest, utilitarian place of worship. There's nothing remarkable about its appearance, or about the people who worship there.

But the night Barb Ficchi entered Faith Church, something astounding happened to her. She and Cathi walked through the double-doors that face the parking lot—and Barb saw a vision. As she stepped inside the sanctuary, she viewed a mental picture of herself surrounded by four gray prison walls. Then, the gray walls collapsed. It was as if she'd been jailed, and a supernatural power had set her free. Puzzled, she took a seat next to Cathi and waited to see what would happen next.

The service began with the congregation standing to sing choruses of various "praise songs." After a few songs, the music ended more or less spontaneously. Some worshipers started praying softly.

Then Barb heard it: a man behind her and Cathi, to their right, out of her line of sight. He was speaking Greek, bits and pieces she recognized from what little of that language she'd learned in church as a girl. The man said in Greek, as clearly as if he were an Orthodox priest, "In the name of the Father, the Son, and the Holy Spirit, amen," words the priests said as they made the sign of the cross, and "Praise the Lord." He repeated the latter phrase several times. How weird, Barb thought, to hear a guy in rural Kentucky saying these things. The man sounded so full of joy.

Barb leaned toward Cathi. "Is he Greek?" she asked.

Cathi arched an eyebrow. "No," she whispered. "He's speaking in tongues."

"What's that?" Barb said.

"It's the Holy Spirit."

Then, in a way of knowing too deep for words, Barb realized what was going on. Even if the man had been trained to speak Greek, why would he—in the middle of a worship service in the boondocks of Kentucky—spontaneously start speaking Greek now? And she only recognized a few fragments of the language herself—exactly the same phrases he was saying. "I knew the hand of God was coming to me," she said. "God was speaking to *me*."

My father, standing at the front of the sanctuary, said, "Does anyone here tonight want to receive the baptism in the Holy Spirit?"

Barb popped up from her seat and hurried to the front of the church. My dad and several others placed their hands on her and prayed. She began to pray as well. Her English became garbled, she said, and then changed into a few words of a language she didn't recognize. Now Barb also was speaking, hesitantly, in tongues: "It was there and it was coming out."

None of us who were present realized at that moment why Barb had suddenly been transformed from a curious observer into an awestruck believer rushing to the front of the church to receive the Holy Spirit.

She told us after the service. As the news raced around the sanctuary, the man who had spoken in Greek, a telephone company salesman named Kenney Edgington, was as visibly surprised as Barb had been. He hadn't had any idea what he was saying. He'd been praying privately and Barb had overheard him.

Within a couple of weeks, Barb and Cathi left Kentucky for New York State, as they'd planned. I haven't seen Barb since. Cathi returned home. The two friends have stayed in touch sporadically over the years, through occasional letters or phone calls. Kenney Edgington eventually left my father's congregation. He lives in the nearby town of Winchester, about fifteen miles west of Mount Sterling; he's since retired from the phone company.

As I researched this book I tracked down Barb and Kenney, to determine whether my memories of that night were accurate. I found

Kenney first. He recalled the incident with Barb, although not in great detail. "I didn't need any confirmation that tongues was a supernatural gift from the Lord," he said. He knew that some people would argue that glossolalia is merely gibberish. "I never did believe that, because I couldn't speak gibberish that well."

I asked Kenney about his education. I recalled that, as a young man, he'd briefly attended what was then a junior college, but dropped out. He told me he also spent a few semesters at a Bible college, but earned no degree. At one time he had served as pastor of a Baptist church in Louisville, but later left the pastoral ministry for good and never attended a seminary.

"Can you speak Greek?" I asked.

He laughed. "I flunked English. I just barely got through. . . . I hadn't studied any Greek at all." He did once eat in a Greek restaurant, he joked.

Kenney finds that he can pray in tongues most anytime he wishes. He can't describe how he feels when he does that, or how he knows it's God who's speaking. "It's just a quickening," he said. "It comes from a place you can't explain in the natural. . . . It's just there, really. The words just come out."

Barb proved more difficult to find. My sister had lost her most recent address and Barb had a new, unlisted phone number. She married years ago; her last name now is Knight. But Cathi and I found her, finally, by tracking her parents' name through a CD-ROM data base and calling their house. I left a message with Barb's mother, and a few days later Barb returned my call. She lives in Vernon, New York, near Syracuse, and works as a high school secretary.

I asked whether she remembered that experience a dozen years earlier in Kentucky. Her voice became animated. "I remember it very vividly," she said. "It was very significant to me." She filled me in on some of the details I'd never heard before, such as the episode with her boyfriend that caused her and Cathi to drive cross-country, and the vision she'd seen that night as she entered Faith Church. She corrected me about some details I'd remembered incorrectly.

Her life, she said, has undergone an 180-degree turn from what it was before she heard God speak to her in Greek. Both she and her husband are members of a charismatic church in Syracuse and share a strong faith in God. For Barb, much of the change in her began that autumn evening in Kentucky.

For me, the miracle I witnessed that evening in 1983 seems amazingly similar to the story of the first Christians on that momentous day of Pentecost long ago. The early disciples were filled with the Holy Spirit and spoke in tongues, the Bible says. Foreigners heard the Christians speaking in their native languages, recognized that actually it was God addressing them supernaturally, and were converted. In Faith Church, Kenney Edgington spoke in tongues. Barb heard him utter, over and over, the few fragments of her ancestral language that she could recognize, realized God must be miraculously talking to her, and committed her life to the Almighty.

This episode of tongues wasn't faked. The people involved had neither the opportunity nor the inclination to rig up some false miracle. In Barb's case, the results have been lasting, which is as good a test of a miracle as any. In my case the results have been lasting, too. I've never since doubted that speaking in tongues can be an act of God.

CHAPTER TWELVE

MIRACULOUS FAITH

EACH OF US POSSESSES and exercises a certain amount of faith. We work throughout a given week because we assume our employer will pay us our wages on Friday, even though we haven't actually seen the check. We assume the sun will rise tomorrow morning. We believe in God and perhaps even in the resurrection of Jesus or in certain modern-day miracles.

Still, some people innately possess more faith than others. When I was a teenager I had a friend named David who crashed his Chevrolet Nova into a tree while driving too fast. He should have died, but survived—gravely injured. His physicians agreed his recovery would take months and prove arduous. David wasn't at all religious, but he was known among his pals for his stubbornness, and he had faith in himself. He told the doctors they didn't know what they were talking about. Among his multiple injuries was a badly broken hip; David insisted he would be up within a few days, walking under his own power. And he was. By sheer willpower and faith in his own recuperative abilities, he returned to health in a fraction of the time his doctors had expected.

The Bible, however, talks about a special kind of faith that surpasses all these others, even David's faith. The Apostle Paul lists a "gift" of faith alongside such supernatural manifestations as healing or prophecy. As always, scholars disagree about just how to describe this unusual ability to believe.

Andrew G. Hadden, writing in the journal *Paraclete*, surveys definitions of this gift that have been offered by Assemblies of God general superintendents, theologians, and ministers. Even within this single denomination he finds a diversity of opinions. One Assemblies of God leader separates the gift of faith from the basic faith in God that is necessary for every Christian who hopes to receive eternal salvation. Another says the gift of faith is the same type of faith as that required for salvation, but far more intense. Others tie the gift to "the certainty of divine intervention" during disasters or illnesses. Yet another describes it as a super-faith that enables people to persevere through "'great suffering and even martyrdom.'"

Reports of such extraordinary gifts of faith are common across the world. Members of the Baha'i sect faced horrors and degradations from rival Muslims when their religion started in Persia in the 1800s. Eyewitnesses, some of whom were adherents of other religions, wrote later about the equanimity with which early Baha'is faced their tormentors. Sulayman Khan, a former army cavalier, was imprisoned with the Baha'u'llah in 1852 at the notorious Siyah-Chal prison. Sentenced to death for his religion, he first was tortured by his executioners. Using knives, they dug holes in Khan's skin and jammed lighted candles into the bloody openings. Then the executioners led the battered Khan through the streets toward his death. Witnesses said he strode to his martyrdom smiling at passersby and reciting poetry. Those escorting Khan jeered him, and said that if he was so happy he should also dance, says *The Baha'i Faith: The Emerging Global Religion*, by William S. Hatcher and J. Douglas Martin. He obliged, "twirling slowly through the stately movements of a dance created by Mawlavi mystics."

Clearly, certain humans are allotted an ability to trust their particular God that reaches far beyond the level of faith you and I typically experience. During my own journeys as both a journalist and a private Christian, I've encountered several such people, whose gifts of faith showed up during wrenching crises.

Remarkable Provision

It seems to me there's also another slightly different, but complementary, manifestation of this amazing miracle of faith. One byproduct of almost all supernatural interventions, of course, is that they tend to increase the recipients' reliance upon God. But I've met—or in some cases, read about—several people who have received miracles that seemed tailored specifically to build their faith and prepare them for some momentous ministry or difficulty that lay ahead. It is as if God is offering them small signs in the present time so they can trust him more confidently for greater help in the future.

Frequently this happens to people who are embarking upon missions work of some kind. They find themselves second-guessing their choice of vocations, usually because they're faced with an impending financial disaster. Miraculously, God delivers money or supplies to them. This otherworldly provision fulfills two purposes. First, it meets their immediate needs for food, clothing, or shelter. More important, it reassures them that God is watching over them and that he has called them to their current jobs. It's a gift of faith in the sense that it builds their spiritual confidence.

For instance, Pat Robertson has said he was the beneficiary many times of remarkable, divine provision. Robertson, of course, is a controversial figure in American religion. No matter how you look at it, though, he's accomplished many impressive feats. He's established a telecommunications empire that includes the Christian Broadcasting Network and the international talk show he co-hosts, "The 700 Club." He's a best-selling author. He's the founder and chancellor of Regent University. In 1988 he placed third, behind George Bush and Bob Dole, for the Republican presidential nomination. Afterward he created the Christian Coalition, a major force in conservative politics. That's only a partial list.

Robertson hails from a patrician family and graduated from Yale Law School. But in the late 1950s, following his Christian conversion, he found himself penniless and ministering in inner-city New York. In his autobiography, *Shout It from the Housetops*, he writes that he was fasting in Brooklyn when, he believes, God assigned him what seemed then to be a strange mission. He was to move back to his native Virginia and start a Christian television station.

According to Robertson, he traveled to Norfolk in 1959 to buy a defunct TV station with seventy dollars in his pocket. The broken-down, off-the-air station sat in a slum area in a salt-water marsh. It had been vandalized. The windows were smashed. Rats roamed around inside. Robertson didn't know where he would find financing and he didn't know much about TV. "We're going to claim it by faith," he said, according to his book. He opened a commercial bank account with three dollars. Amazing things happened. The owner agreed to sell him the station, although Robertson had no money. The station's lapsed license was renewed.

Meanwhile, Robertson and his impoverished family existed on a diet of little but soybeans. Small amounts of money, five and ten dollars, began showing up in the mail before the Christian station even went on the air.

But everything about starting the TV station cost money. And at times donations dried up. Once, Robertson and his family were broke and low on food. Their rent would be due in a few days and they had no way to pay it. Robertson grew despondent. He wondered whether he'd somehow misunderstood God's direction. Maybe he wasn't supposed to be in a television ministry.

"Lord, if I have been wrong, if this isn't of you, then I want you to show me that I should stop," Robertson prayed. He told his wife, Dede, that if God didn't pay their rent on time, he was quitting outright.

Two days before the Robertsons' rent was due, Pat received a call from the Reverend Paul Morris, a Presbyterian pastor and an old friend from Jamaica, New York, whom the Robertsons hadn't seen in months. God had been prodding him for three weeks to come visit them, Morris said. At 7:30 P.M. the next night, only hours before the Robertsons' rent was due, Morris arrived. He brought with him an unexpected check and said it was to help cover their personal needs. Pat looked at the slip of paper and thought it said $80, far short of the $250 he needed. He looked again. It was for $8,000.

Similarly John Smith, a founder of Jesus Movement in Australia and a minister to bikers and other members of the counterculture Down Under, told me of an unusual provision he received in 1972, as his nontraditional work was just coming into bloom. When his ministry among drug-addled hippies and violent motorcycle gangs began, Smith was employed as a youth evangelist by a mainstream evangelical organization, Campaigners for Christ. During this period Smith also started an alternative Christian newspaper called *Truth*, whose five thousand initial copies he distributed free of charge.

Smith's wife, Glena, was pregnant with their third child when Smith decided to lead a missions jaunt to the outdoor Sunbury pop festival. There he, Glena, and some friends hoped to tell the rock fans about their Christian faith and hand out free copies of the first issue of *Truth*. But Smith's supervisors in Campaigners for Christ questioned his plan. Media reports had predicted the Sunbury festival would be rife with drugs and nudity. The supervisors didn't think a minister ought to be seen in such a milieu. Smith argued that Sunbury was exactly where a preacher needed to be. In the end, Smith defied his superiors and attended Sunbury anyway. He returned elated. He'd talked with many troubled youths who seemed remarkably open to the Christian message of love, redemption, and inner peace. The church could reach those folks, he'd decided, if it would simply venture out among them.

Unfortunately, when Smith arrived back at the office of Campaigners for Christ, he was greeted with devastating news: in his absence, he had been sacked by the executives there. He returned home to Glena that day wounded. He wondered how he would support her and their two small children, much less the new baby that was on its way. When John broke the news to his pregnant wife, they clutched each other, stood in their kitchen, and cried.

The Smiths already had pasted up a second edition of *Truth*, which was ready to be sent to the printer. John had received three months' salary as severance from Campaigners for Christ, but he needed that to pay his household bills until he could find another job. He and Glena discussed their options. Glena told him that, in her estimation, God definitely was behind the publishing of this newspaper. John should send the materials to the printer, she said. She wouldn't budge and finally John agreed, although he had no idea how he would pay the $450 printing bill when it came due a month later.

John delivered the pasteups to the printer. Later the same day, two checks arrived unexpectedly in the Smiths' mail. Both were from students at Adelaide University. Neither knew anything of John's situation. The amount of the two checks together? Exactly $450.

The second issue of *Truth* appeared on time, under the new name of *Truth and Liberation*. Those two checks helped give John the faith to press ahead. Eventually *Truth and Liberation* grew to a circulation of more than thirty-five thousand, distributed among Australia's outcasts, including prisoners and gang members.

Jackie Pullinger is yet another religious worker for whom God has miraculously provided. She's a woman from Great Britain who attended the Royal College of Music and some years ago felt herself "called" by God to a missionary work perhaps even more unusual than John Smith's. She entered the infamous Walled City of Hong Kong, hoping to live there and spread God's love to criminal gangs, addicts, and streetwalkers. Her efforts have achieved notable results, including hundreds of reported conversions and many stories of addicts who have been freed from drugs and gangsters who have been restored to respectable, nonviolent lifestyles.

In her autobiography, *Chasing the Dragon,* Pullinger tells how she opened a home on Lung Kong Road where she cared for displaced boys trying to escape lives of crime. She had no idea how God would meet the financial burdens of her operation, but everything she needed showed up, day by day. "Sometimes a cheque would arrive in the post," Pullinger writes. "Sometimes a friend would give exactly the same amount as I had been praying for." Pullinger needed a rubber boat to use on a swimming trip she had planned for the boys. "[A] friend sent the right sum from England without knowing the need," she writes.

Another time, on a Sunday after the morning church service, Pullinger invited guests to her house for lunch, some of whom badly needed the meal. But there was no money for extra food. She told her resident boys to boil what rice they had, and then they prayed together for more food to put on top of it. "Ten minutes before lunch a panting and sweating visitor arrived carrying tins of food and fresh bean sprouts," Pullinger writes. The man's Bible class had held an impromptu food drive that morning and the other members of the class had sent him to Pullinger's house with the wares they'd collected.

Here's one more example of this faith-building kind of gift. You will recall that John Rohrer of Columbus, Ohio, is the former basketball coach turned preacher who exorcised a demon from a young intellectual in Florida. The church Rohrer leads now is small, and he and his wife have five children, but Rohrer devotes his full time to his ministry.

He learned early, as a new Christian, that God could provide for his needs, he said. He then was single and living in Gainesville, Florida, where he was preparing to enter the ministry. In the meantime he painted houses for income. But he and his partner were between painting jobs. Rohrer owed a past-due note on which the bank had demanded full and immediate payment; otherwise the bank intended to sue him. He'd managed to save about $1,200 to pay the bill, but as he started to write the check one Saturday night, he felt as if God wanted him to give the money to his church instead. So he didn't do anything.

The very next morning during his church's Sunday morning worship service, the minister, David Houston, rather apologetically spoke a supernatural "word of knowledge." He said God had told him that somebody there was to give away all the money he had in the bank— and learn to trust God for his income rather than the institutions of this world.

John knew the word was for him. He wrote a check for the amount he had saved toward his bank note, $1,200, and dropped it in the collection plate. But on the drive home he experienced a change of heart. He pulled his truck to the side of the road and yelled at God for allowing him to suffer financial problems, then demanding even more money from him. Now he still had a past-due bill and a bank threatening to sue him, but he had no money and no painting jobs lined up. Even if he and his partner did land a new job, they wouldn't be paid until it was finished.

As he walked through the door of his apartment, the phone was ringing. He hurried to answer it. On the other end of the line was his painting partner, Bob. "How was your day?" Bob asked jovially. John was in no mood for pleasantries, so Bob got right to the point. He said he'd just hung up the phone from a conversation with a woman who needed her house painted. She wanted to pay Bob and John $5,000. She'd agreed to give them half in advance—$1,250 each. That provided Rohrer enough to pay his bank note, and left him an extra $50, with which he bought himself a steak dinner to celebrate. Ever since, he's trusted the Lord to act as his paymaster. "God somehow always comes through," he said.

Faith Under the Surgeon's Knife

Kathi Wyatt of Flint, Michigan, experienced the more traditional manifestation of the gift of faith—a calming assurance of God's presence during a medical crisis. Wyatt suffered menstrual periods so brutal that they left her seriously anemic. She'd had the problem since puberty and no medical treatment ever seemed to help. Finally, when she was thirty-four, her physician told Wyatt she must undergo a hysterectomy.

Wyatt was heartbroken. She desperately wanted children but had been unable to get pregnant. She and her husband, Richard, had tried twice to adopt. They'd started the process both times with high hopes, only to have the proceedings fall through—once because the birth grandmother decided she wanted the child and once because, far into the adoption process, a church adoption agency learned that the Wyatts had changed denominations and were ineligible. After a hysterectomy, all chances of Kathi's giving birth herself would be gone, too.

She also grew more terrified by the day. This was in the mid-1980s, and AIDS had just burst upon the national consciousness. Because she was anemic, Kathi's doctor said, she likely would lose more blood during surgery than most patients and would require a transfusion. The doctor assured her that she wouldn't contract the virus that causes AIDS from the transfusion, because the blood would be screened for HIV. Kathi wasn't nearly as certain as the physician. There also was a possibility that Kathi's menstrual problems were the result of a cancerous tumor festering inside her. It was an awful, harrowing time for her. She literally trembled with anxiety.

"I was very unhappy, very scared," said Kathi, an ex-IBM employee who now works in the computer laboratory at the University of Michigan at Flint and teaches part-time at a community college. "I was pretty well distraught."

Kathi had been raised as a Roman Catholic and has since returned to that denomination. But at the time she and Richard were attending Trinity Assembly of God Church in Flint. During a service there shortly before Kathi's surgery, the minister gave an altar call open to anyone who needed healing.

Kathi rose from her pew and walked toward the front of the church. Before she reached the podium area where the pastor and his assistants had begun praying for the sick, Kathi realized her trembling had stopped. The terror that had haunted her for days had vanished, too. She continued on to the podium. Someone anointed her with holy oil, laid hands on her, and prayed.

Two days later, she returned to her physician for a presurgery consultation. The doctor appeared confused, she said. His previously frantic patient was so calm that he thought something was wrong. He carefully explained to Kathi again the implications of the surgery she faced, that she wouldn't be able to have children afterward, that she almost certainly would need a blood transfusion. "He says, 'You understand that?'" Kathi recalled. The physician spoke to her slowly and carefully, as if she were a child. He asked her to repeat back to him the surgery's implications. By this time Kathi was grinning. Yes, she understood, she assured him. But she now was at peace.

Kathi entered a hospital in Flint for surgery. Her doctor already had arranged for blood to be held in reserve for her transfusion. But when she awoke from the anesthesia, she found that she felt amazingly good. Nurses asked whether she needed a shot for her pain. She declined. The nurses told her she was brave. Kathi replied that she wasn't brave; she just wasn't hurting.

Her physician came in to see her. He stood by her bed and held her hand. "Your surgery went very, very well," he said. Indeed, it had proved to be one case out of thousands, he told her, a "dry surgery" in which Kathi barely had lost any blood. She'd needed no transfusion after all. There was no cancer.

Kathi told the doctor that what she really wanted was a good hot shower. The surgeon replied that she wouldn't be able to get out of bed at all until the next day, and added that she would be hospitalized for at least three or four days. But Kathi felt so good that, after he left, she got up anyway and gave herself a sponge bath. The next day, she was cleared to check out of the hospital and she went home, ahead of schedule.

True, Kathi hadn't been miraculously healed when she walked forward in church and asked for prayer. Still, a marvelous change happened to her after she stood up to go receive prayer at Trinity Assembly of God. Her terror vanished and she found herself uncharacteristically filled with serenity. She faced surgery with a giddy assurance that all would be fine, that her fate was secure in God's gentle hands. And it was. She'd suffered no pain. She'd needed no transfusion. She'd developed no malignancies. She'd returned home in record time. Forty days later, she walked eighteen holes with Richard in a golf tournament. "My healing was very complete," she said.

Even her sadness over her inability to bear or adopt children has been muted, she said. Her youngest half-sister, eighteen years Kathi's junior, lives nearby in Flint and has three kids. Kathi is so close to them geographically and emotionally that she feels as if, in a way, God gave her children after all.

"I count all of that as a miracle," she said.

A Tough-Minded Lawyer Gets His Perspective Broadened

Tim Philpot is the kind of guy who seems born to rub against the grain of any establishment he confronts. He's witty and friendly, but he's made a career of doing things his own way. He's well known in Kentucky as a very conservative Republican state senator who has publicly battled the legislature's Democratic majority. He also opposes abortion and specific legal protections for gays. He's been lampooned as a bigot by opponents.

On the other hand, he earns much of his income as an attorney whose forte is civil rights cases in which he defends members of minority groups, such as African-Americans, who have been wronged by their employers. Philpot appreciates the incongruity of an archconservative conducting a legal practice that, on the surface, would seem more naturally the domain of the American Civil Liberties Union. He appears to delight in the contradiction.

But to his mind all his views are based on his understanding of Christianity and the Bible. Philpot is the son of a widely known Methodist preacher, the late Reverend Ford Philpot, and takes his faith seriously. He spends much of his spare time as a lay speaker at Christian meetings, particularly those that build moral awareness among men. He helps sponsor overseas missions work through Fishhook International, an organization he heads.

Philpot's Christianity is, like his politics and his law practice, a no-nonsense one. He doesn't enjoy it when people become too emotional. He's married to Sue Philpot, who says she was healed of bone cancer when she was a girl, but Tim never has cared a great deal about tales of miracles. He'd rather raise money for a hospital than lay hands on sick people.

In 1993, though, Philpot took a missions trip to south India. He wasn't prepared for what he saw, heard, and smelled. The poverty and the stench in some areas were unimaginable. He found that in small villages, particularly, Christians resorted to prayers for God's intervention because there were no medical professionals available to them.

While he was there, Philpot and an American friend helped an Indian evangelist conduct an outdoor camp meeting in a village called Mount Zion. People kept coming forward for prayer, and in one service Philpot and his American friend prayed for sick, disturbed, and unhappy people for two solid hours, something he wasn't used to in his home country.

The next morning, the Indian preacher leading the camp meeting asked those who had been touched by God to stand and give public testimonies. Many did so. But the Christian residents of the village seemed particularly excited about a little boy in the crowd, Raji. They'd been praying for him to give his heart to God, and he'd done so. When it came Raji's turn to speak, he didn't stand. Curious, Philpot looked more closely. Raji was nine or ten years old—and pitifully crippled. The Indian evangelist interpreted Raji's testimony for Philpot as the child spoke. "I sure would like to walk," Raji said. Philpot learned that Raji had been stricken with polio, and that he had to drag himself around the village with his arms because his wasted legs remained useless.

That night, Philpot was scheduled to speak in the evening service at the camp meeting. When he'd finished his message, an unusual feeling struck him. "I just felt this tremendous compulsion," he said—a compulsion to call Raji to the podium for prayer. Philpot obeyed this inner direction.

Raji was lifted onto the stage with Philpot. It was, the lawyer said, the most frightened he'd ever been. There was no "plan B" in this village. Either God would heal Raji or the child would never walk normally. "I wasn't scared he *wouldn't* walk off the stage," Philpot admitted. "I was scared he *would*." That is, if God used Philpot to heal Raji, Philpot didn't know what the implications might be for his own beliefs, his career, and his lay ministry. He picked up Raji and held the skinny boy in his arms. Philpot offered an uncharacteristic prayer. He asked God to let Raji walk away in a normal gait, under his own power.

Nothing visible happened. Raji wasn't healed, and Philpot still isn't sure why. Later, Philpot even tried to arrange for Raji to be flown to the United States for medical treatment, but that didn't work out, either. A doctor said no medicine or surgery would help the child.

Philpot believes that God did perform one extraordinary act that night, though. Here Philpot was—a mainstream Methodist, a rationalist, a hard-nosed lawyer, a bad-boy politician—laying hands on a crippled child for supernatural healing, with a strong faith that God might just cure Raji before his eyes. "The miracle probably was me, not the kid," he said.

Faith in the Valley of Death

Dennis Deppisch was dying. The pain that had started under his sternum, pain that his physician suspected was an ulcer, had turned out to be inoperable cancer instead. Cancer of the stomach. And the esophagus. And the liver. With luck, Deppisch might have a year left, he thought when I first interviewed him in October 1994. Or he might have much less.

Deppisch was a stocky man who lived in a middle-class house in a manicured subdivision. At forty-five, with a wife and three stepsons, he couldn't have run into death at a worse time. Yet he was facing his bleak future with a quiet assurance and an uncommon faith that had left his friends awed. I know because a couple of them had called me at the *Lexington Herald-Leader* and told me I needed to meet him. You won't believe this guy's story, they said.

Thing was, Deppisch didn't think his future was bleak, he told me after I invited myself to his house. He simply thought he was dying. He was a Christian, he said, and so death wasn't terrible news. It meant an eternity in God's presence.

Until then, there would indeed be difficulty ahead. The stuff the doctors were giving him for his pain had irritated his digestive tract. He required more medicine for nausea. He'd undergone a bit of chemotherapy and it was awful. Further along his liver would fail, he said. He would lapse into a coma. "I know what the end's going to be like, and it's not going to be pretty."

But he wasn't afraid. "God will provide for me enough comfort," he assured me. He'd explained that to his wife. They'd already talked with her two teenaged sons. They were waiting to share the worst parts of the news with her youngest son, who was eight.

Someone had told Deppisch he was supposed to be angry at the injustice. "Hey, people die all the time," he'd answered. Many of those who died happened to be older than he was, but others died in childhood. Deppisch said he'd come to believe that God truly was in control. If Christians claimed to live by faith, then they ought to depart by faith, he said. Besides, if they lived meaningfully during the time they were here, they didn't need any extra years.

Deppisch hadn't always known such things. He'd started attending a good church seven years before his illness was discovered. There he'd found something he'd lacked without even realizing he lacked it. He'd discovered the power of the scriptures. "I can open to any page and show you a truth I never knew before I started studying the Bible," he said. "They're all amazing to me." Those truths were sustaining him under the shadow of death.

Other people had insisted that he should be praying for a miraculous cure. That would be fine, he said. But mainly he just wanted to bear witness that even though his time appeared to be short, he was at peace. If he could touch a few people with that message, he said, "then I've done my job here on earth." At times when he talked his eyes brimmed with tears. Tears that appeared, from his facial expressions, to be tears of joy.

At the time, he remained active. He continued to sing bass baritone in his church choir. As a layman, he sometimes led worship services for the aged at a retirement community. He was plugging along in his marketing job. He worked out at the YMCA. "I've got a lot of friends down at the Y that I joke around with," he said.

When his pals there had learned of his illness, one had asked what they could do to make him happy. Could they take him on an outing to a racetrack? If you really want to do something for me, Deppisch had said, come to my church. Twenty-five showed up for a Sunday-morning service in which Deppisch sang a solo and spoke about his life. At the end of his presentation, the entire congregation, more than six hundred strong, stood and applauded.

As word of Deppisch's equanimity had leaked out, he'd begun getting invited to speak to churches and civic groups about living in the face of death. Ultimately, he visited dozens of them. There's no telling how many people he encouraged. "I'm really excited about the opportunity," he said. "I'm happy to be doing God's work for my last days."

I called him several months later to see how he was. As it turned out, he was down to his last few days of life in this world. He was in pain. But his attitude hadn't changed, he said. He remained at peace. He still was happy that through his illness he had been allowed to reassure others. I didn't stay on the line with him for very long. He was weak and finding it difficult to speak. Dennis passed away on June 23, 1995, a man of awesome faith.

A Faith Tried by Fire

It was a sunny afternoon, April 6, 1983, and the students of the Montgomery County, Kentucky, public schools were on their spring break. Jane Martin had seized an opportunity to urge her two older boys, Mark, sixteen, and Rodney, seventeen, to do some household chores. Rodney was in the den washing its paneling. Mark, a husky, good-natured boy who grinned constantly as if he knew a mischievous secret, was cutting firewood in the backyard. Jane's younger daughter and son, Missy and Shannon, were playing with neighbors.

Outside, Mark's chainsaw sputtered to a halt, out of gas. Jane watched through a window as he walked across the yard and disappeared into the basement, carrying the chainsaw. The phone in the den rang. Jane answered it. A friend of hers had called just to chat.

Boom! An explosion from the basement rattled the house. "Oh my God!" Jane screamed, dropping the phone. Just then Missy, her daughter, walked into the house with a playmate.

A second boom shook the brick home. Jane shouted at Missy and her friend to run, then rushed down the basement stairs to look for Mark. As she descended, black smoke rolled up toward her. She flipped on the light switch and discovered that she still couldn't see for the thick smoke. Jane felt her way through the room, searching for her son. The other end of the basement contained a cistern. As she approached it, she saw a blaze lapping. "Mark!" she cried. "Mark!" She pushed herself toward the fire and realized that it was a rope that Mark used to start the chainsaw, burning on the floor. Jane stomped on the rope and, as she did, stumbled over Mark lying on the concrete, semiconscious. Now she screamed for her oldest son. "Rodney, call an ambulance! Call the fire department!"

Jane knelt beside Mark's smoking body to help him. The soles of his shoes still were afire. As she struck at the flames with her hands, she began to pray. Strangely, a sense of serenity welled up inside her. She and her husband, Dean, had become Christians a few years earlier, and their faith had grown until it was the most important part of their lives. Mark had given his life to God, too, and played drums in their church's praise band.

Rodney appeared at the bottom of the basement steps, having placed his emergency phone calls. "Get a water hose!" Jane ordered him. "We've got to put out the fire on Mark!" A neighbor rushed in, ripped down a curtain and smothered the flames on Mark's feet. "Instantly, Mark raised up and said, 'Mom, you're in worse shape than I am,'" Jane recalled later. That was so much like him, always joking. He managed to climb to his feet. Jane saw that all his clothes had been burned off, except for a wallet he wore attached to a chain around his waist. Mark walked outside through the outside door he'd used minutes earlier to enter the basement, and sat down on a low wall made of concrete blocks. Sometime during all this, Mark had momentarily grabbed Jane's wrist—and his touch had painfully charred her skin, she discovered.

Soon, an ambulance arrived, its siren wailing. Jane jumped into the vehicle with Mark and rode beside him to the local hospital. "Mark," she said on the way, "talk to the Lord." "Mom, God said I was his child," Mark replied. That sense of serenity rippled through Jane again.

At Mary Chiles Hospital in Mount Sterling, medical workers said Mark needed to be airlifted to Lexington, where another ambulance would meet the helicopter and transfer Mark to a burn center at the University of Kentucky Hospital.

A neighbor had called Jane's husband, Dean. He'd been at work at a local factory. By the time Dean arrived at the hospital, Mark's helicopter had departed. Jane, Dean, and Dean's sister-in-law drove to Lexington, thirty five miles away, as fast as they could. They beat Mark to UK.

Soon, though, Mark was wheeled into the emergency room. Until he saw his son with his own eyes, Dean didn't realize how horrendously Mark had been injured. Third-degree burns covered 99 percent of the boy's body. He was seared everywhere except the bottoms of his feet, which had been protected by the soles of his burning shoes, and the back of his head, which had lain on the basement floor. Nobody would ever know how it had happened, but the can from which he'd been pouring gasoline into the chainsaw somehow had ignited.

In the emergency room, Dean found a physician. Will Mark need skin grafts? he asked. Sadly, the physician replied that, yes, burns as severe as Mark's normally would require grafts. But Mark was burned so extensively that he had no remaining skin to which doctors could hope to attach any grafts. Reality hit Dean like a runaway Mack truck careening down an Appalachian mountain. Dean threw his arms around the physician and clutched him in a bear hug. "Take my flesh!" he sobbed. "Here, take my flesh!" The doctor hugged Dean, too. The men—both helpless to save Mark—grieved together.

Then, instantly, Dean felt as if God touched his heart. His sobs stopped.

As she watched all this, the skin scorched from her own wrist by Mark's grasp, Jane longed to scream and cry and kick the emergency room's walls. But she couldn't. Unaccountably, peace had taken root inside her, a peace beyond her own ability to understand it. "The Spirit of the Lord was so strong within me," she said later.

Hospital workers moved Mark to the burn ward, where they labored to clean his massive injuries and bandage him. Dozens of the Martins' friends and relatives gathered in an upstairs waiting room nearby. Dean and Jane joined them; they wouldn't be allowed in to sit with Mark until the doctors and nurses had finished their preliminary work.

Dean continued to find a tremendous sense of comfort welling up in him, too, despite his earlier breakdown. He and Jane talked with each other. They grew steadily more convinced that God intended to heal Mark. Their church believed in divine healing. Dean, whose father was a Pentecostal preacher, had seen people cured by God many times.

Hours later, Dean and Jane were outfitted with sterile surgical masks and gowns. No one could have prepared them for what they saw when they finally were led into the burn ward, though. The skin from Mark's face had melted like hot plastic; the handsome, jolly boy looked like a creature from a science fiction movie. Mark's arms and legs, now swollen three times their normal size, were swathed in bandages and one arm had been suspended in traction. A respirator tube had been inserted into his mouth. He writhed in the bed, trying to talk but unable.

Jane and Dean assured their son how much they loved him. Jane asked him whether he was talking with Jesus. A tear rolled from the corner of Mark's eye. The doctor and nurses in the burn ward started to weep.

Eventually, Dean stepped outside the burn ward to speak with a friend, while Jane remained beside Mark's bed. In the midst of this awful mess, she heard a strong internal voice that she took to be the Holy Spirit: "He's going to be like Lazarus," it said. "I'm going to raise him up."

Within a few hours Mark's arms and legs swelled so badly that the swelling cut off the blood to his extremities. A doctor slashed his limbs with a scalpel to release the bodily liquids strangling his veins.

But none of this could shake Jane and Dean's inexplicable sense of calm. They knew the Lord could raise Mark up no matter how badly he was hurt. At one point, as the night wore on, Dean even lay down on a table in a conference room and napped.

Eighteen hours after he'd reached the University of Kentucky hospital, Mark Martin died.

Jane was with him when he stopped breathing. She was as much perplexed as heartbroken. She'd felt so certain that God intended to heal Mark. Now, after agonizing hours and terrible sights beyond anyone's imagination, Mark had passed away. Jane knew her other children might be destroyed by Mark's loss. Still, that serene assurance wouldn't leave. "The thought of losing him hurt, but the peace was so peaceful in me," she said. She knew that Mark now was standing joyfully in the presence of Jesus.

As Dean and Jane walked from the hospital toward the car that would take them back to Mount Sterling, they talked about spiritual truths they'd learned from the Bible and from their church, not about their loss. "The pain wouldn't come," Dean said. "God wouldn't allow pain."

Over the next days people poured into the Martins' house: co-workers from Dean's factory, members of the Martins' church, relatives. Jane felt as if she needed to grieve, if for no other reason than that all these folks rightly expected her to be destroyed. But she couldn't. Peace filled every cell of her mind. Her visitors didn't understand. "They thought I was on drugs."

Dean experienced exactly the same sensation. "It was a peace that surpasses all understanding," he said. "It's beyond me to tell you—it's not my nature to act that way. It's my nature to holler and cry and weep and stand in remorse. But it's God's nature to do what the [Bible] says, to shout and be happy at death, and to cry at birth."

At the funeral home, just before public visitation hours began, Dean saw Mark's disfigured body in a private viewing; for the public there would be a closed casket. Minutes later he watched as hundreds of mourners, including many of Mark's high school classmates, thronged outside the funeral home waiting to enter. Dean stood looking through a glass doorway at them when God spoke to him. "The Lord said, 'I want you to minister to these people as if it was their child and not yours,'" Dean recalled.

For the first time since Mark's death, Dean bristled. He'd been strong long enough and now he intended to mourn fully. "I said, 'No, I'm not going to do that.'" The internal voice, which he attributed to the Holy Spirit, spoke to him a second time. Again he refused. The voice spoke a third time. "The third time, I said, 'If it happens, you're going to have to do it.'"

And God did. During the visitation and at the funeral itself—among the largest in the town's recent history—Dean and Jane both moved through the crowd, smiling, hugging people, comforting them, assuring them that Mark had gone to a far better place. Dean remembered: "I felt the peace of God so strong, so strong, that I didn't want people to cry or mourn. I wanted them to rejoice." Particularly he and Jane tried to help Mark's school friends.

Again, there who those who whispered that Dean and Jane must be medicated or in shock. If it had been drugs or shock, Dean said recently, the peace soon would have worn off, once Mark was buried and the crowds had gone home. "God has never allowed me to feel the pain of that loss," he said. "I haven't lost him. As far as I'm concerned, he's still very much alive."

Today, Jane feels confident that was the meaning of the message she received in the burn ward, when she heard God say he would resurrect Mark like Lazarus. "I know what it means now," she said. In the biblical story of Lazarus, Jesus hears that his friend is sick, but delays visiting him until Lazarus already has passed away. Then he raises his friend from the tomb. As far as Jane and Dean are concerned, Mark's flesh might have died, but his spirit ascended into the presence of a loving savior. For them, Mark already is resurrected, in one sense. They expect to see him again someday.

"Faith is a gift," Jane said, "and it's not there all the time. It's not manifest all the time. But then something like this happens and God raises that assurance up in you. It's just something he brings alive within you."

CHAPTER THIRTEEN

WHY NOW?

I
T'S HARD TO SAY FOR CERTAIN whether more supernatural acts occur today than among our ancestors one hundred, two hundred, or three hundred years ago. We can't know with authority how many miracles our forebears witnessed that might have been lost to history. We can't guess how many of the acts that our contemporaries report as miracles truly constitute divine interventions and how many are fakes, exaggerations, or coincidences.

Evidence from a variety of sources—clergy, scholars, pollsters, the media, skeptics, and true believers—certainly suggests that *reports* of modern-day miracles, at least, have risen sharply in recent years. Coinciding with that has been a growing willingness among many ministers, health industry professionals, and the general public to accept such reports.

I've cited the growth of various branches of Pentecostalism as examples of this increasing acceptance of miracles here and abroad. But consider just two more tidbits. At the Korean War's end, Christians made up roughly 4 percent of the Korean population. Now, 40 percent of Koreans are Christians, nearly all of them Pentecostals. One Korean Pentecostal congregation, the Yoido Full Gospel Church, started in 1958 with 5 members; it now has 800,000. Then there's the Assemblies of God, a Pentecostal denomination based in Springfield, Missouri. It expanded more than tenfold in twenty-eight years, from 2.2 million adherents worldwide in 1965 to 25.4 million in 1993. It grew more than 40 percent between 1987 and 1993.

So you can argue pretty convincingly that many people are more accepting of the miraculous, more willing to embrace it publicly. That doesn't necessarily mean that more miracles are taking place, however. We might just be living in an era in which it's easier to talk about them.

Still, over the past several years in my work as a reporter, I've interviewed scores of people who claim to have experienced supernatural interventions and I've talked with numerous experts about such phenomena. In my more personal journey as a Christian, I've witnessed remarkable acts, experienced a few myself, and met numerous men and women who say they've been healed of ruptured disks in their backs, have spoken in tongues, or have been rescued by angels.

The opinion among most observers with whom I've spoken—an opinion I share—is that the latter few decades of the twentieth century indeed have brought with them a dramatic increase in genuinely supernatural manifestations.

But why are some people more willing today to report supposed miracles—and still others more willing to believe those reports? If miracles truly are increasing in frequency, why do the powers from beyond seem more willing to distribute those acts?

There are a number of theories. The most common answer to the first question, one I've heard again and again until it's almost a mantra, is that we Westerners, particularly, are becoming more open about the possibility of divine intervention today because the Enlightenment paradigm on which we so long depended has failed us miserably. Proponents of the Enlightenment always have taught that human nature is innately good and that, if educated properly, almost all people will become honest, productive citizens. The Enlightenment view says that governments, if freed from religious dogma, will produce fair, impartial, and consistent laws that honor everyone's rights. The Enlightenment view argues that individual self-expression in areas ranging from sexual behavior to artistic creation is far more important than promoting self-restraint in favor of the common good. The Enlightenment view claims that given sufficient funding and academic freedom for research, science eventually can prevent or at least control most illnesses, as well as many other problems.

For quite a while then, the leading academic and legislative minds in America and Europe have extolled secular education and secular government, individualism, and science. Then we find that in America, at least, we have more college-educated citizens than at any previous time in the nation's history—and the highest rates of psychopathy in our history, too. With the fall of the Iron Curtain we have seen plainly that the least religious governments of our century, such as Stalin's Soviet Union, proved to be even more barbaric than the Spanish Inquisition. Runaway self-expression in areas such as sex and art have left us with a 50-percent divorce rate, a spiraling out-of-wedlock birthrate, 1.6 million abortions a year, and a level of graphic violence on television and in films that would have made us faint even a generation ago. In medical circles, we hear more these days about the many ills that scientists can't cure than those they can: AIDS, a plethora of drug-resistant viruses such as Ebola, many strains of cancer, nuclear contamination. In short, our planet remains in turmoil.

At the same time, certain breakthroughs in the theoretical sciences such as physics have suggested that our cosmos is not the closed, precise, predictable universe that Newtonian scientists assumed, but rather that it contains quirky, unpredictable agents and events.

All in all, we have increasingly found ourselves moving past the Enlightenment paradigm into a postmodern period that has for artists, physicists, and just plain folks reopened the cosmos to the possibility of the transcendent. We have begun to look elsewhere for answers. "There's a hunger to believe that the universe is in the control of benevolent forces, because the world doesn't look like that," said Robert J. Miller of the Jesus Seminar, which mostly is quite skeptical of the supernatural.

Besides, others say, the cerebral, systematic Enlightenment worldview simply overlooked two potent ingredients for a meaningful human life: emotional release and spiritual experience. Even within much of Christianity and Judaism, experiential religion was for a long time abandoned in favor of a more refined, intellectual system of doctrines. Religious leaders, influenced by the Enlightenment, taught us to look down our noses at those whose faith was "too emotional," as if emotions somehow were sinful.

That, too, has proved to be a trap, said Eunice Irwin, the seminary professor. For many people, particularly lay people, a purely intellectual faith is unfulfilling. On the street level, she said, "people believe because they have experienced something. That's the arena of everyday life: what I can see and know and touch and feel. . . . I'm not saying that's right." But that's the way it is, she said. "They believe something that's happened to them." Today, many are turning to faiths that offer the promise—or at least the possibility—of a direct encounter with God. "It may be that people already are in a time of turmoil and are finding a true solution," Irwin said.

Similarly Charles Kraft, the Third Wave anthropologist, said that people inside and outside the religious world were taught to seek solace in the ministrations of psychologists and psychiatrists. That, too, has proved to be a problem, he said: "There's no power in psychological techniques. People are basically buying a friend."

Spiritual power of the supernatural variety, however, is absolutely real, he said. That's why some secular counselors have recently tapped into the far more potent techniques of New Age practitioners, who teach that God is an inner force lying within each of us and that we must learn to activate that force. For Kraft, a Christian who worked among animistic Third World peoples, that's an even worse problem, however. He believes this "inner god" power is dangerous. "Basically it's demonization," Kraft said. "Unfortunately, Satan reels them in later on. Satan heals to deceive and, later on, gets them." Kraft thinks the only truly beneficial way to receive supernatural spiritual power is through faith in, and obedience to, the person of Jesus Christ.

The "End-Times" Theory and Other Ideas

There are other theories for why the earth might be experiencing an explosion of genuinely supernatural works. Several people over the years—including several mainline Protestant seminary professors, a Catholic priest, and the author of a famous book about the supernatural—have suggested to me that our increased willingness to accept divine intervention plays a key role in and of itself. Our new openness to the supernatural, they speculate, has helped motivate the spiritual powers to reveal themselves to a greater extent.

For a newspaper article, I once interviewed John Killinger, a respected liberal Protestant scholar who used to teach at Vanderbilt Divinity School in Nashville. Over the years, you'll recall from an earlier chapter, he has become a believer in many stories of supernatural intervention. I asked him about the spectacular kinds of miracles reported in the Bible, where Moses parts a sea, Jesus walks on water, fish and loaves are multiplied. Didn't he think those accounts might have been exaggerated in the retelling by people who lived in an age more gullible than ours?

Possibly, Killinger said. But by the same token, ancient people were no more accustomed to seeing a man walk on water than we are—and while they didn't understand twentieth-century science there's no reason to suspect they were inherently more easily duped. There's another possibility, Killinger said. It might be that because their minds were untainted by modern skepticism, the ancients possessed a far greater ability to receive mighty help from God. Doubt is much more our stock-in-trade than faith, Killinger said. And that doubt could limit God's ability, or God's willingness, to work among us.

Charles Kraft, speaking from a more theologically conservative point of view, suggested much the same. "I believe there is a 'science' in the spirit realm," he said. Part of that "science" is the fact that people normally must cooperate with spirits to receive their help. Kraft, as I've said, divides the spirit world into two distinct kingdoms: the principalities of God and those of Satan. He says that the more fully people obey God and the more strongly they believe in God's power, the more mightily God will act in their lives. The same principle works for those who choose to obey Satan, Kraft said. The more fully they submit to the devil, the more powerfully demonic forces can operate.

Kraft cited a chapter from the Hebrew Bible, II Kings 3, as a prime example. In this account Jehoram, the King of Israel, Jehoshaphat, the King of Judah, and an unidentified King of Edom set out to wage war against Mesha, King of Moab. Along the way, they run short of water in the desert and Jehoram becomes terrified they've journeyed out only to die ignominiously.

Jehoshaphat, the righteous King of Judah, insists that he and Jehoram must consult with Elisha, a famous prophet of their Hebrew

God. They do, and Elisha secures God's supernatural blessing for the invading kings, who receive a refreshing rain that saves them and their soldiers. With God's endorsement the kings and their armies continue on to Moab and nearly destroy their enemy's country, conquering city after city.

Just as it appears that Mesha, the King of Moab, will himself be overrun, he likewise appeals for supernatural help. Mesha offers his oldest son as a human sacrifice to demonic entities. The result is implied rather than explicit, but apparently these counter-spiritual forces rise up in "great indignation against Israel," as the Bible says. Now the three invading kings are driven back to their homes and Mesha survives. What this biblical passage shows, Kraft said, is that supernatural help did not appear to be forthcoming for either the invading kings or Mesha until they actively sought it and cooperated with it.

If people today are in larger and larger numbers opening their minds to the possibility of supernatural help and in many cases actively seeking that aid, then it stands to reason—according to this theory—that the number of miracles happening in the world would rapidly increase.

Certain Christian thinkers also believe that God has his own preordained plans in all this. We live in an auspicious time: the brink of the year 2000, which marks not only the beginning of a new century but also of a new millennium. In the past, as such landmarks approached on the calendar, reports of supernatural phenomena increased. The year 1000, for instance, was heralded with heightened expectations that Jesus Christ would return to earth—and consequently with renewed religious zeal in the Christian world and claims of all sorts of divine acts and omens. The transition periods between certain centuries since then have seen similar outbreaks, such as the Second Great Awakening at the cusp of the nineteenth century and the birth of Pentecostalism at the dawn of the twentieth century. For some, the approach of the third millennium is more significant than any of those previous dates.

In 1890 Pope Leo XIII reportedly saw a vision in which Christ appeared to him and said he planned to allow Satan to run amok in the world for one hundred years. In his 1991 book, *The Hiding Places of God,*

British journalist John Cornwell quotes Archbishop Emanuel Milingo as saying that in recent years he has witnessed an unprecedented activity by demonic spirits, which are thrashing desperately among the human race because they know their time is nearly up, just as Pope Leo predicted. By Cornwell's account, Milingo might not be the most credible of authorities. Yet one would assume that if Pope Leo and Archbishop Milingo are correct at all, the last gasps of Satan's minions would be counterbalanced during the period of their overthrow by unprecedented activity from God's forces, too.

More ominously, some Christians have long speculated that the return of Jesus to earth would take place roughly two thousand years after his birth and death in the ancient Middle East. Almost all of them have agreed that the Second Coming will be preceded by explosive activity in the spiritual domain.

"Since 1900, God has been trying to give back to the church the gifts of the Holy Spirit," said Steve Seamands, the Methodist professor. Seamands, like most reputable Christians, wants it made clear that he sets no dates, but he speculates that God possibly is empowering the church for an even greater revival than the one that attended the birth of Pentecostalism ninety years ago. This revival might even usher in Jesus' return. "The supernatural is going to be a very important part of this," he said.

Throughout the centuries, countless others inside and outside the church have expressed similar thoughts. The prophecies of Nostradamus are nearly indecipherable, but his students say he predicted that Christ would return about the year 2000.

If nothing else, it's interesting that students of these divergent sources—the modern Holy Spirit movement, Pope Leo XIII, Nostradamus—all predict the closing days of our century to be an ominous period for supernatural events.

Someone else pointed me to the Hebrew book of Joel, in which that prophet, speaking for God, predicts the world's final days: "And it shall come to pass afterward, that I will pour out my spirit upon all flesh; and your sons and your daughters shall prophesy, your old men shall dream dreams, your young men shall see visions: and also upon the servants and upon the handmaids in those days will I pour out my spirit. . . . And it shall come to pass, that whosoever shall call upon the name of the Lord shall be delivered."

Could it be that we're living in these last days? I don't know, of course, and neither does anyone else. But it makes for interesting office-party conversations.

CHAPTER FOURTEEN

WHAT THESE ACCOUNTS HAVE IN COMMON

To an extent, every miracle is as unique as the individual people it touches. We often miss opportunities for divine intervention, I think, because we "put God in a box," as a preacher once said. That is, we formulate rules and regulations about how the Almighty must act: he quit performing signs and wonders in 100 C.E., or he only works miracles for members of our denomination, or a person who needs a miracle must first meet certain religious criteria such as baptism. When we invent such regulations, we forget that God is God. He makes the rules and can do pretty much as he pleases. When we close our minds to possibilities, we risk by passing blessings.

I've said that through an odd series of circumstances I ended up, more or less against my will, leading a little Pentecostal congregation. To my mind at the time, Grace Church was everything I wouldn't have wanted in a congregation even if I had felt called to become a pastor somewhere. Its theology was a fundamentalist legalism and I was neither a fundamentalist nor a legalist. It had a contentious history, with numerous splits; it had suffered another breakup just before the congregation asked me to become its pastor. The building was poorly constructed. Most of the people were working-class folks who were older than I was. I felt the job was beneath my considerable dignity. However, my dignity notwithstanding, I was broke, so I accepted the offer, expecting to stay a few months until something better turned up. I'm still waiting.

That was in 1982. Fourteen years later, the congregation has grown and been transformed—but more to the point, so have I. For the first decade of my part-time pastorate I felt as if God might shut the doors on the place at any moment, that he would be justified in doing so. But in the meantime, I grew to love and respect the people there, and to learn a great deal from them. One valuable lesson I learned was that my self-appointed dignity needed to be whittled down before I could begin to apprehend God.

From the beginning, I was uncomfortable with much of what I saw in Pentecostalism. I found it too emotional and not intellectual enough. But I've witnessed far too many inexplicable and even miraculous moments to ignore them, in a variety of settings and through a variety of manifestations. As I sometimes tell fellow skeptics, one such episode is a coincidence. Five episodes is coincidence. Fifty? A hundred? That's not coincidence.

Here I offer one example: the healing practice of "leg lengthening." In this practice, you'll recall from Chapter 5, people suffering from back or leg problems sometimes are asked by those offering prayers to sit in a chair or a pew. The person ministering kneels before the ill person, lifts his or her legs, and compares the length at the heels. Frequently the legs appear uneven (arguably because the sick person is sitting off-center or is tense). The minister prays for the ill person while still holding his or her legs. One legs seems to "grow" until the heels are an even length. Often, the pain evaporates.

James Randi has contended that the practice is a trick of charlatans. My opinion always has differed, as I said: I assumed the stunt was sincere but misguided, that any cure likely was psychological and probably short-lived. My wife, Renee, by the way, who was raised as a Pentecostal, has never had a problem believing in the reality of this cure.

Then, some time ago, a Christian friend of ours came forward during a portion of a Sunday church service that we set aside for prayer requests. He asked me to pray with him that God would heal his back. He's in his mid-fifties and works in a demanding blue-collar job. He said that for thirty years he'd suffered pain in his lower back, hip, and leg. The pain had grown progressively worse, he said, until it had become nearly unbearable. It hurt with every step he took and was threatening to render him unable to work at all. He couldn't afford to quit his job.

For some reason I can't explain fully—it felt like a hunch or an impression or a thought—I asked our friend to sit down so that I could adjust his legs. Renee, who directs the church's music, was standing near the piano at the front of the sanctuary, and I asked her to step over and pray with me. Maybe I saw it as an experiment, I really don't know. But I didn't have much faith in this type of practice, even though I'd suggested it. I was perplexed at my own actions.

Our friend sat on the church's front pew, and I knelt and lifted his feet in my hands. The heels of his shoes looked uneven by three-quarters of an inch. I pushed his shoes firmly against his feet to make certain the difference in lengths wasn't due to one shoe or the other having slid forward. Renee walked behind him and placed her hands lightly on his back. We all closed our eyes and I offered a quiet prayer. The whole time, I was thinking about how little sense this leg-lengthening exercise made. After the prayer I opened my eyes. Our friend's heels were even. He stood up and returned to his own pew. It struck me as curious, but I didn't think any more of it. The service continued.

Weeks later, our friend came back to me privately. "Paul, I want to tell you something," he said, grinning. "Ever since you all prayed for me I've been completely pain free. I was so used to compensating for the pain that I just expected it and tried to block it out of my mind. One day I was on my job and went to step up on a ladder. I braced for the pain—and it was gone. I realized it had been gone ever since you and Renee prayed."

Needless to say, I found that surprising, if not amusing. My first thought was that his ailment must have been psychosomatic and that his faith in the leg-lengthening cure had eased his mind to such a degree that the pain had departed. So I was taken aback by what he said next.

"You know," he said, "I hate to admit this, but I've never believed in praying for people's legs like that. I've seen it done, but I always thought it was a bunch of junk. When you told me to sit down and stretch out my legs, all I could think was, 'Boy, this is a waste of time.' But you know what? It worked."

My friend, who had received the healing, hadn't believed the prayer would be effective, so it's hard to argue that the cure was purely psychological. Neither had I believed in the leg-moving exercise. However, he'd been delivered from a possibly debilitating ailment. I began to think that someone else must have been involved in that moment beyond my friend, me, and even my wife, who'd had no doubt God could heal a person's back by adjusting his legs. Maybe God was trying to teach me something as well as heal my friend.

Others might still argue that there was a psychosomatic element to my pal's healing, as there is with many "miracles." So what if there was? Increasingly, even medical science has acknowledged that the human body works holistically, that the flesh and the mind are interrelated and influence each other's well-being. For me, it's not too great a leap to believe that the spirit also is connected to all this. As Charles Kraft has suggested, some healings, for example, might take place on multiple levels: a spiritual touch from God affects our emotional state, which then releases the tension from our pain-wracked bodies. To say that a healing isn't a miracle because the illness was partly psychological seems to beg the point. To paraphrase Kraft, if your head's aching and aspirin pills don't relieve it, if you then ask for prayer at church and your headache disappears instantly, then you probably received a touch from God—whether your headache's cause was mere job stress or a brain tumor.

Thus, I've tried to divest myself of holding too many rules about how God works and how he doesn't. He's God and he does what he wants, when he wants, to whom and through whom he wants. The best thing we can do is cooperate with him.

Nevertheless, Some Generalizations

That said, I think miracles do follow discernible patterns from which we can make a few generalizations.

First, God seems to have what scholar Eunice Irwin called *an economy of miracles*. "He doesn't do too many and he doesn't do too few," she said, and others have expressed similar thoughts. The idea is that miracles often arrive in refreshing clusters after decades or centuries of spiritual drought. Frequently they tend to precede, or coincide with, epochs of enormous social upheaval or massive church revivals. They empower people who face great obstacles.

The Fátima apparition of Mary, which is officially recognized by the Catholic Church, occurred in 1917 during the horrible devastation of World War I. The Medjugorje apparition in the former Yugoslavia served as a precursor to the genocidal civil war that later ravaged that land. The great outpouring of the Holy Spirit on Timor in 1965 struck four nights before an attempted government coup by Communists.

Another of the great miraculous outpourings of our time—although one less-reported—erupted in December 1971, at a Bible school at Nha Trang, South Vietnam, during the dark days of the Vietnam War. Spontaneously, students began to confess their sins and to minister to each other with a tremendous sense of joy. They decided to go out witnessing about their newly charged faith. Wherever they went, miracles shot out from the Nha Trang Biblical and Theological Institute into the countryside like Roman candles. Sensational healings and exorcisms became particularly common, but there also were reports of dead bodies that were resurrected through prayer. The students helped convert a number of U.S. servicemen. Less than four years later, South Vietnam fell to the Communists. Many of these same students were exiled to harsh reeducation camps. "Their faith was preserved because of those miracles," Irwin said.

A generation ago, C.S. Lewis observed that most miracles take place "at the great ganglions of history—not of political or social history, but of that spiritual history that cannot be fully known by men." The majority of humans, because they don't live at the junctures of such auspicious eras or near the spiritual seers who lead world-changing religious movements, likely won't ever witness wholesale outbreaks of miracles, he said. Nor would they desire to if they understood why such miracles happen: "'Nothing almost sees miracles but misery,'" Lewis writes. "Miracles and martyrdoms tend to bunch about the same areas of history—areas we have naturally no wish to frequent." If our present generation is experiencing an explosion of signs and wonders, as many argue, it once again leads me to wonder what trials lie ahead for us.

A second generalization is that, even if large numbers of miracles do cluster around certain periods, and even if we today are living in such a miraculous era, the *individual miracles that make up those clusters appear a bit unpredictable.* We have seen many examples of that in this book.

Dr. Jud Chalkley was, you'll recall, debilitated by sarcoidosis, an inflammatory lung disease that had left him unable to walk up a flight of stairs without losing his breath. In 1980, after Chalkley had been sick for eighteen months, a voice spoke to him as he stood on a track preparing to walk off a heavy meal. "It's okay," the voice said. Chalkley knew he was cured—and he was, instantly, although he'd never met anyone who'd been divinely healed. Later, though, Chalkley's sarcoidosis returned. Later still, Chalkley's wife, Robin, was diagnosed with a serious throat infection and chronic fatigue syndrome. She's never recovered. Why would God instantly heal Chalkley, a man who didn't expect a miracle, and then allow his disease to return for a time? If God healed Chalkley, why wouldn't he cure Chalkley's wife, who believes very strongly in divine healing and has traveled to large healing services seeking a total recovery? There are no clear answers.

Or take the case of Frank Morgan's family. We met them, too, in the chapter on healing. As a boy in Ohio, Frank received a divine cure from tuberculosis in both lungs and eventually became the outstanding male athlete in his high school class. After he'd married, his wife, Wyvonna, contracted crippling arthritis that ravaged her body and left her barely able to care for their four children. In the mid-1950s, during a healing service at a Church of God in Marion, Ohio, Wyvonna was instantly cured.

But one of Frank and Wyvonna's daughters, Diana, apparently inherited her mother's arthritis. She's in her forties now, has never been healed, and doesn't expect to be. In 1986, Wyvonna herself died of lymphoma, from which she obviously wasn't healed. Her other daughter, Barbara, also suffered from a lymphoma nearly identical to Wyvonna's. Barbara recovered after receiving a prayer for healing at her church.

Still another generalization we might make about miracles is that *they're always temporary.* The physical results of some miracles, such as Dr. Chalkley's reprieve from sarcoidosis, clearly don't last long. Donn

Hollingsworth, the American businessman who worked in China, received helpful ministrations from Madame Moe, a Buddhist healer. Yet his angina invariably returned and he finally died from heart disease in February 1996. He had lived years longer than anyone expected, but he didn't live forever.

The Bab, an early leader of the Baha'i faith, escaped the bullets of a huge firing squad. The bullets cut the ropes that bound him but left him unscathed. The result? His persecutors formed a second firing squad, which successfully executed him.

Remember, too, Margaret Hillenmeyer Bohan, who found herself in God's presence one day during a period of intense despair after her husband had died. Jesus apparently touched her shoulder and then somehow spoke to her. She was washed in a divine peace she'd never experienced before. Despite her many problems—grief, financial hardship, the rigors of trying to get two children through college—Margaret remained steadfastly at peace for ten years. Eventually, though, unavoidably perhaps, the peace wore off.

All miracles then, have their limitations. In the final estimation, we live in finite bodies. We all must die, and even before death suffering is an unavoidable part of our world. Even if we are so fortunate as to be healed permanently of cancer today, we might just as easily be run over by a bus next year.

The early Christians knew this well. "Because of the relatively constant threat of persecution, Christians in the first three centuries who believed in God's miraculous intervention could not possibly have believed that he would alleviate their every affliction," writes scholar James E. Bradley in an issue of the academic journal *Pneuma*. Bradley says that in the early Church "suffering and martyrdom were ranked . . . as important as divine miraculous interventions for the 'proof' of the gospel."

A related generalization about miracles is that they aren't ends in themselves: *They happen for a purpose beyond the miracle.*

Quite often, people who receive miracles believe they know exactly why they were touched by God. Frank Morgan told me that after he was healed of tuberculosis he went on to teach Sunday school for fifty years, a volunteer duty he took very seriously. He never became a professional teacher or a member of the clergy, but he's certain that God spared him from TB because God had placed a calling upon his life as a teacher.

The Sikorsky helicopter carrying Governor Brereton Jones of Kentucky lost power, crashed into the Kentucky countryside, and disintegrated upon impact, but astoundingly Jones and everyone aboard survived. At the time, Jones said he believed God had spared him so he could pass a vital health-care reform package for his state. Several years later, in November 1995, I talked with him about the accident in a small private room near his office in the state capitol building at Frankfort. Did he still feel the same way? I asked.

To a large extent, he did, he replied. He was able to negotiate a health-care reform package through the legislature, although not in the form he'd hoped. Universal coverage didn't pass, but he did make certain that insurers couldn't discriminate against customers on the basis of their preexisting conditions. "That's helped thousands and thousands of Kentuckians," he said. He also helped establish a fund for health care for the indigent.

Looking back, though, he'd decided there was another meaningful by-product of his survival. It helped him define what really mattered in life and politics. "I was so sensitive to what the media said prior to that, it was making it extremely difficult for me to function as a chief executive," he said. "I was too ego-involved." Afterward, the opinions of the *Lexington Herald-Leader* and the Louisville *Courier-Journal* just didn't seem as important. "I literally got to the point where I could laugh at the very negative editorials," he said. He was able to focus on doing what he thought was right, without regard to his professional naysayers.

Dr. Patrick Schneider is the family physician who in 1992 began attending Marian apparition sites. He takes along his video camera, with which he has documented strange manifestations such as a pulsating sun during daytime apparitions and spontaneous flashes of light in the sky at midnight.

There's a common theme to what Mary tells visionaries at the various sites, he said. "It's basically prayer, penance, fasting—traditional calls to holiness. There's an incredible consistency. . . . It's just the same message." He thinks the apparitions are harbingers of some even more amazing supernatural event that will occur by the year 2000.

The appearances by Mary have deepened his personal devotion to his Roman Catholic faith. "I say the rosary every day," Schneider said. "I do things I didn't do in the past. I work in Salvation Army homeless clinics." He's taken an active leadership role at his large hospital and stops at its chapel to pray before every staff meeting. Schneider has even begun tithing 10 percent of his income to charity, a "Baptist" trait that the Lord urged upon him, he said, smiling. He prays regularly with his family, too.

Miracles are truly significant only inasmuch as they lead us to a closer spiritual relationship with our Creator. The human body that is healed of tuberculosis will soon die of something. The spirit that doomed body contains will live forever—one hopes in the presence of the ultimate healer.

A final generalization is this: *Miracles affect the lives of bystanders as profoundly as they affect those touched directly by God.*

Surprisingly, sometimes these reactions are for the good and sometimes they aren't. On the surface, it would appear that friends, family members, and fellow churchgoers could only rejoice when a loved one receives miraculous help. The truth is more complex. Their immediate reaction generally is joy. Afterward, their elation can turn into anger, jealousy, disbelief, or dismay.

That's because bystanders are left with the residual effects of a miracle, but without having experienced the infusion of supernatural power themselves. A delightfully profane best friend who receives a divine vision from God might suddenly become less earthy and begin attending Mass every day; those who liked her the way she was will inevitably find her shift in personality distressing. A wife who is healed of breast cancer might, like Schneider the physician, want to give away 10 percent of the family income to the church, while her husband prefers to invest the money in a vacation fund. A minister who performs an exorcism in a congregation that frowns on such "power encounters" might find himself derided by his parishioners; his loss of credibility, not to mention the possible loss of his job, will unavoidably distress his wife and children.

In a way, miracles serve as a divinely administered ink-blot test for those who merely observe them. Our reaction to the works that God performs in others' lives reveals more about us and our relationship with the Lord than we'd like to think.

Perhaps I've already cited the Bible too much, but a wonderful story illustrating this principle can be found in the Gospel of John. Jesus is ministering in Jerusalem when he happens across a beggar who was born blind. Before continuing on his way, Jesus makes a paste of spittle and clay, rubs it in the man's sightless eyes, and tells him to go wash off the mixture in the pool of Siloam. The beggar returns from the pool seeing.

Immediately his neighbors become divided. One group says, in effect, "This is the guy who used to be blind. This fellow Jesus cured him." Another group says, "No, it can't be that blind beggar. But it's a guy who certainly looks like him." To this second group, it's all a strange coincidence.

Then an organization of legalistic religious leaders, the Pharisees, gets into the argument. They demand to know how Jesus restored the man's eyes, so the beggar tells them. One faction among the Pharisees is upset because this is the Sabbath and according to their theology no one but a sinner would do any work on the Sabbath, including supernatural work. Another faction argues that, while Jesus might not have acted according to their rules, it's clear that a miracle has taken place— and how could Jesus perform such a wonder unless God helped him? Unable to reconcile their dispute, they turn to the beggar again.

"What do you say about this miracle worker?" they ask.

You can almost see the beggar shrug. "I'd say he must be a prophet," he answers.

Some of those present, however, continue to insist that this beggar isn't the same man who previously was blind, but merely one who bears an uncanny resemblance to him. The Pharisees summon the beggar's parents. "Is this your son?" they ask. "And if so, how do you explain that he can see?"

The parents have been forewarned that if they admit Jesus has healed their son on the Sabbath, they might be barred from the synagogue. The miracle is threatening to cause them unwanted difficulties, even though they apparently weren't present when their son was healed. So they hedge: "Well, we know that's our son. He was born blind. But we don't know how he can see now. He's of legal age, you'll have to ask him."

The beggar is called in once more. The Pharisees caution him, "We're certain the man who helped you is a sinner."

"Sinner or not, I can't say," the beggar replies rather sarcastically. "The only thing I know is this: I used to be blind, and now I can see quite well."

"All right," the exasperated officials respond. "Tell us again how he healed you. Exactly how did he perform this work?"

"I told you once and you didn't listen," the beggar says. "Why do you want to hear it again? Do you want to become his disciples?"

The Pharisees and the healed man go on like this at some length, comically, until finally the sublimely composed beggar is expelled for his impertinence.

This story, in a nutshell, portrays the whole range of human responses to a miracle. The beggar has absolutely no doubt what's happened to him: he has been healed by God. He's utterly at peace. Some observers, although they weren't touched directly by Jesus themselves, agree with him. Others say, "No, it's not a miracle, just a coincidence." Oddly, it's the religious leaders who argue most vocally against the wonder, using their dogmas to explain why God wouldn't have done what God obviously just did. And then there are the parents, who one would assume should be weeping with elation that their sightless son has been cured. Instead, they're frightened by the controversy and quickly dump all the responsibility for it onto their child. Fortunately, he's up to the challenge.

Not much has changed in the nearly two thousand years since then. In his book *Medjugorje: The Message,* journalist Wayne Weible recounts the various reactions after the Virgin Mary allegedly began appearing to six youths in the former Yugoslavia. By the fourth day of apparitions, as the word leaked out, Communist officials grew alarmed and called the six visionaries to a police station for interrogation and examination by a physician. State officials then demanded to see Father Jozo Zovko, the pastor of Medjugorje's St. James Church. They commanded him to put a stop to the religious gatherings taking place on a hillside near the little village.

Zovko already had talked with the youths; his opinion was that they might be taking hallucinogenic drugs. His assistant pastor, Father Zrinko Cuvalo, feared an outright hoax and soon began questioning the visionaries endlessly, trying to catch them in an inconsistent answer. A third priest arrived. He suggested that the six youths must submit to an exorcism, but Zovko and Cuvalo thought that would be going too far.

Throughout the ordeal, the six young visionaries maintained their insistence that it was Mary who was appearing to them. No one, no threat, could shake them. Within a week of the first apparition, police decided to arrest the teenagers. After several narrow escapes, they fled on foot toward St. James Church. Father Zovko was inside, praying at the front of the church alone when a voice told him, audibly, "Go out now and protect the children." He ran for the church's back door and reached it in time to see the teenagers rushing toward him, the police pursuing them. The teens called for his help. Impetuously, Zovko hid them in the rectory until the police left the area.

Later that same day, Zovko called his parishioners to the church. Mary appeared there to the visionaries—and to Zovko, who saw her himself and became a fervent believer. He soon was arrested on a trumped-up charge of sedition that stemmed largely from his support for the visionaries. His church was ransacked by the police. Zovko later was released from jail, but was forbidden from his bishop from celebrating mass again in Medjugorge.

Miracles, then, tend to grant those who experience them directly an otherworldly assurance. Many of us struggle through life alternating between blind trust that God exists and nagging nighttime doubts that he doesn't. For the fortunate folks who have received miracles, doubts and double-mindedness are replaced by a nearly absolute faith. They know the Almighty is real, because they've felt his power. I heard one preacher express that kind of belief like this: "I know that I know that I *know*," he said. Moreover, such fortunate people know not only that God exists but that he has recognized them as individuals and that he cares for them personally. For a time, at least, they live in an enviable state of peace and grace. Turmoil may surround them, but it doesn't touch their serenity.

As I've pointed out, that serenity nearly always produces dramatic changes in their lives. Kathy Bland, whom we met in the chapter on deliverance, awoke from her near-death experience a different person. Before nearly dying, she'd been a wastrel partier who gave hardly a thought to God or an eternal reckoning. Now that she'd been redeemed from the pits of hell, she didn't want to return there. She was grateful for the life she'd nearly destroyed. She gave up her old ways, began praying daily, and devoted herself to her young child.

My father had dedicated his career to the Southern Baptist faith, which is by and large a good one. He'd been a Baptist pastor for about a quarter-century and an administrator at a Baptist college. He'd held offices in various Baptist associations. But after he was healed of cancer and began exploring the possibility that God was commonly performing other signs and wonders today, he found himself the object of intense criticism from many of his longtime colleagues and from some among his own congregation.

Like the critics of the blind man in the New Testament, otherwise fine and churchgoing people appeared quite determined to demonstrate to my father the myriad reasons why God couldn't possibly do what God clearly was doing.

In that troubled time, Dad's assurance that God had healed him and that God was leading him like a gentle shepherd provided him with the courage to break with his old denomination when breaking away seemed necessary. Under normal circumstances such a fissure would have been devastating to him. Instead, he said God would take care of us all, and God has for twenty years now.

I've seen similar patterns of changed lifestyles and empowered faith again and again with others who have received miracles.

My mother and I also knew that God had healed my father. His cure was so dramatic and inexplicable that you could hardly arrive at any other conclusion if you were front-line witnesses, as we were. Even one of his physicians had said there was no other explanation. But neither my mother nor I had actually received the miracle. Neither of us had heard the Almighty tell us that he was going to touch us, as Dad had felt God promise to heal him.

So when we left the Baptist denomination and moved with my father to a charismatic church, my mother and I were far more reluctant pilgrims. My father now accepted the miraculous easily. Mom and I looked askance at every new manifestation we saw. We stared like calves at a new gate when anyone prophesied or fell under the Spirit's presence. While I never doubted Dad's healing, I wavered constantly on such other supposed "signs and wonders." I stepped many times back and forth across the line between belief and disbelief, between embracing miracles and criticizing them, between participating in prayers for divine help and cringing at them.

For me, it was only a vast accumulation of hundreds of inexplicable events over a period of years that forced me to finally take my stand on the side of the miraculous. I just couldn't deny it any longer.

Even so, in a sense the healing that changed my father's life and career twenty years ago had ultimately changed mine, too—not as quickly nor as dramatically, but just as surely. Miracles always have such ripple effects. The mystery of how they affect those who observe them is just that, a mystery, one as complex as personality or intelligence or marital fidelity. Some eyewitnesses latch on to others' miracles as joyfully as the recipients themselves and share in their peace. Some dismiss the acts as coincidences. Others are infuriated and threatened.

If I have one regret on this subject, it's that it took me so long to surrender myself fully to the truth that God cares enough about his creation to interject himself powerfully into the lives of ordinary humans like you and me. When I at last surrendered to that beautiful fact, it filled me with the kind of assurance I had witnessed in so many people. It was a kind of miracle in itself.

CHAPTER FIFTEEN

HOW YOU CAN RECEIVE
A MIRACLE

S ECULAR SKEPTICS AND MOST reputable folks who believe in miracles agree about one thing: nobody can promise you supernatural
intervention. Even advocates of signs and wonders say their hackles
are raised by the kinds of evangelists who offer miracles to sick or distraught people in exchange for financial donations—or who claim that
God is obligated to provide miracles for anyone who follows a series of
steps defined by the ministers, such as praying in steadfast faith, studying the Bible, and speaking only positive statements.

Darrell Whiteman, the anthropologist who worked among Pacific
islanders, says that such claims smack of the "magic" of animistic
shamans, some of whom operate by trickery or even under demonic
powers. "The Melanesians *demand* that the supernatural provide an answer," said Whiteman, a Christian. "That's when my red flags go up."

The God of Christianity, Judaism, and Islam is not so easily ma-
nipulated. Christianity—the faith to which 84 percent of Americans
subscribe, at least nominally—generally assumes that miracles constitute a case of "man proposes, but God disposes," as the old saying goes.
That is, we humans are encouraged to ask for miracles, but there is no
incantation or formula by which we can force God to act against his
will, his wisdom, or his plan for a specific situation.

That creates a certain tension. We are taught to pray and to rest
assured that God can provide supernatural answers. At the same time,
we're warned not to petulantly attempt to manipulate God, but instead

to assume that he knows best. A Missouri pastor named Steve D. Eustler has written in the journal *Paraclete*—perceptively, I think—that "Christians live in the 'already, not yet' stage. Healings do occur; but they cannot be counted on like the electric bill," he writes. Ultimate, final healing comes to believers only in the Second Coming of Christ, he says.

Anyway, if a person is, say, seriously ill, the most crucial issue isn't whether she will be physically healed, said Charles Kraft, the professor at Fuller Theological Seminary. "It's how do I feed my relationship with God?"

But Kraft added: "With that in mind, he loves to heal."

Increasing Your Chances

That, I think, is a crucial point. There's a delicate balance that we must carefully maintain when we're talking about miracles; it's easy to fall out of the canoe on either side. It's wrong to say that God always will work a miracle when we want one, if we can just discover the proper incantations. It's equally wrong to say that God never works miracles or, for that matter, that there's nothing we can do to better our chances of receiving one.

My impression is like Kraft's: God and his supernatural agents absolutely love to work wonders. God primarily has revealed himself as a God of love, and there's plenty of evidence that he regularly provides money for the poor, healing for the sick, deliverance for the downtrodden, comfort for the grieved, and revelation for the confused. It happens every single day, in every state in this nation and in every nation on this planet.

And there are things we can do to profoundly increase our chances of receiving supernatural aid. Let's look at some of those:

1. *Pray.* Almost everybody I've met who has received a miracle reports that he or she had first prayed about the matter. Many are people who prayed habitually long before serious difficulties arose in their lives. Others prayed desperately as their world fell apart. But nearly all of them prayed.

Governor Brereton Jones beseeched God as his helicopter plummeted from the sky—and was saved from almost certain death. But he said he'd established the faith that led to his deliverance long before his crash. He'd been a lifelong churchgoer, had earlier considered entering the ministry, and knew that God still was in the miracle business. He was "prayed up" before his chopper went down. No one can develop that kind of relationship with God for you, Jones said. That's something you must do for yourself.

Still, it's always good to ask other people to pray for you, too. It never hurts to have as many prayers as possible ascending on your behalf.

2. *Expand your worldview.* Many of us have been trained to be overly suspicious of the supernatural. Skepticism helps us avoid charlatans and kooks. But it can become unhealthy if we reject the idea that miracles are at least possible, if not commonplace.

Many of us in the West need to relax our intellectualism a bit in favor of a stronger belief in the spiritual—an arena whose rules sometimes don't make sense to the secularly educated mind. John Rohrer, the Columbus, Ohio, ex-coach who has worked successfully in supernatural arenas such as exorcism and prophecy, said half-seriously that one reason God has been able to use him is that he's not very smart. The human mind not only finds it difficult to understand God's principles but frequently wars against them, he said. God operates on the basis of faith and obedience, not IQ or university degrees.

Kraft's book *Christianity with Power* includes a number of tips for changing our traditional ways of thinking about the supernatural. Among them is this: "Accept the possibility that God may be doing things in other contexts that he's not doing in yours. Don't adopt the attitude of a preacher who said something like, 'If these gifts were for today, they would have come to us first.'" Kraft also suggests that we read the biblical accounts of miracles with an eye open to the fact that God still possesses the ability to do such things now.

3. *Associate with people who openly believe in miracles.* Perhaps you won't find many of these folks at faculty-club dinners or physicians' staff meetings. You might not find them at your church. Because a public belief in the supernatural power of God often has been greeted with raised eyebrows among society's more "respectable" folks, you might

have to seek the company of people who at first strike you as odd. That certainly was my own experience when I first found myself among charismatics and, even more so, Pentecostals. Some murdered the king's English. Some wore pompadours. Some seemed way too uncritical. Some were too emotional. I was put off—until I realized that a few of them possessed a spectacular power and an intimate knowledge of God I hadn't witnessed anywhere else.

Dr. Jud Chalkley pointed out that the faith healer Kathryn Kuhlman was a terribly eccentric person who sometimes appeared to focus more on showmanship than on God. Yet she believed God would use her to heal the sick, and many times God did.

When you associate with people who believe in miracles and have experienced them, you inevitably learn to see the world in new ways, which again enlarges your worldview and opens your eyes to new possibilities. By the same token, if you spend most of your time with people—even ministers—who are spiritually impotent and who don't believe in God's direct intervention, you will find your worldview narrowed and your faith weakened.

It's also good to read books and other materials that build your faith and open your mind.

4. *Examine yourself to see whether you really want a miracle.* I used to puzzle over a particular passage in the New Testament. Jesus walks up to a lame man who is lying beside a pool believed to contain curative powers. The local legend has it that periodically an angel swoops down and swirls the waters; the first one in gets healed. This poor man, crippled thirty-eight years, keeps getting shoved aside before he can crawl into the pool.

Yet the first question Jesus asks him is, "Do you want to be healed?" The first few times I read that I thought to myself, "Well, why else would the guy be there?" Jesus' question could be merely rhetorical, but it appears not to be. Instead, it seems keenly directed at this particular man.

Eventually, I realized that Jesus' question is truly perceptive. There are people, even among those lined up at healing services, who really don't want to experience a miracle. Some sick people, for instance, secretly glory in their illnesses. Sicknesses or tragedies or financial problems can be attention-getting devices that some folks don't want to relinquish.

Even more to the point, fear and pride can make us leery of embracing the miraculous. We're sometimes afraid to reach out for a miracle, afraid it won't be real—and perhaps even more afraid that it will be real, like Tim Philpot, the lawyer and state senator in the chapter on miraculous faith. It's somehow better to linger on the periphery, doubting and speculating, than to cast our faith desperately in favor of the supernatural.

We've been let down by people so often that we can't deal with being let down by God, too. At the same time, we're afraid of looking foolish. That, of course, is a form of pride, the original sin and probably the besetting one of the twentieth century. I'm talking about pride in the sense of spiritual and intellectual arrogance that makes us want to believe that we are wiser than God. One way of doing that is to minimize his power and maximize ours. We exercise our power over God by explaining away his acts. If we surrender and accept a miracle, we also surrender our power. Miracles, after all, create demands upon us. If God touches our lives so directly, he may want us to change our behavior afterward, or our friends, or our church. That could embarrass us.

But if God truly is God, if he is real, if he is present here and now, then what choice do we have? If the God of the universe loves us enough to care about and cure our arthritis, doesn't it stand to reason that he loves us enough to look out for our best interests in other realms of our daily lives? If he does cause certain of our friends to make unkind jokes about how flaky we've become, might he not replace them with wiser, more perceptive friends?

5. *Learn to obey God.* Charles Kraft believes this is one of the most important elements in receiving a miracle, for Christians, at least. "Obedience is the gut-level thing in Christianity," he said. None of us is perfect, obviously. But many, many religious leaders have warned that blatant, willful sin can push us away from the flow of God's power.

Moultrie McIntosh, the retired Episcopal priest who has walked in the miraculous power of the Holy Spirit for several decades, said that to receive a miracle it's also important that we be faithful to the things

God already has given us, such as our church and the Eucharist. God isn't very likely to trust us with new blessings until we obediently use the ones we already have.

6. *Accept that God wants the best for you.* "God is love," St. John said. Many people have been raised with hellfire-and-brimstone images of a God who delights in making people suffer. That image makes for dramatic preaching, but it hardly does justice to the God of, say, the New Testament, who sacrificed his own son to impart blessings to wrongheaded men and women like us. "If God be for us, who can be against us?" St. Paul wrote. "He that spared not his own Son, but delivered him up for us all, how shall he not with him also freely give us all things?" God wants to bless us so much that when we leave matters to his discretion, often we find that they turn out even better than we'd hoped.

7. *Take spiritual authority over your situation.* This sounds paradoxical, given that we are to submit obediently to God's will, but some experts insist that we humans also have been entrusted by God with a surprising amount of supernatural authority over demonic and physical forces. "Jesus never prayed for healing," said Kraft. "He commanded it." Jesus' prayers were a means of discerning God's plans. Once Jesus had heard from the Almighty, though, he no longer bothered God about a bad situation. He simply commanded it to straighten out. "It was a matter of authority," Kraft said.

None of us is Jesus. Nevertheless, Christ did in many ways serve as a model for all of us as we seek God's will and then endeavor to walk in it. There comes a time—once we feel we've genuinely heard from God and our hearts are aligned with his—when we can order any hindering forces to depart.

8. *Thank God in advance.* When we begin to believe that God always wants the best for us, we find it easy to thank him in advance for the work he is doing on our particular problem. We might not know exactly the course that divine intervention will take, but we can feel certain that God is doing something good just for us. And so we praise him for that, even before we see the results. That in itself lifts our spirits and builds our faith. As we praise, we remove the barriers of negativity and self-pity from our minds that can hinder the flow of divine

blessings. "Without faith it is impossible to please him," said the writer of Hebrews. Praise and thanksgiving are great faith-builders.

Wrapping It Up

Nothing, as I've said, will guarantee that we receive a supernatural miracle. Many good people do not. In 1991 another reporter for the newspaper where I work covered the story of the Reverend Bert Benz, forty-seven, who had come to Lexington from another state to receive a bone-marrow transplant in hopes of defeating cancer. It was a poignant story. The marrow donor for Benz, a Baptist minister, was his daughter, Lauren, twelve. She was roughly the age my sister had been when our father, then also a Baptist minister, was diagnosed with cancer in 1976. My sister wasn't called upon for marrow and neither was I. Our father was miraculously, instantaneously healed. Bert Benz died. I never met him, but I thought a lot about him after reading of his painful struggles.

Miracles, I decided, can create as many problems as they solve. How do you explain God's choices? If God works wonders, why doesn't he work them for everyone? My father is a good man, but I don't know that he's any better than Bert Benz was. I love my father, but no more, I imagine, than Benz's daughter loved her father when she gave him her own marrow.

A few years ago, my wife's nine-year-old nephew, Jason, passed away after a long illness. Why would God spare my father and not heal Jason? The questions multiply. How do you proclaim a miracle in your own family, when all around you people are dying? Your good fortune must be a bitter rebuke to their loved ones. For that matter, my father's healing didn't spare him from the grief of this world. During the twenty years since his miraculous cure, he has watched his father, three sisters; and mother-in-law all die lingering deaths.

I am forever grateful for his healing miracle. I don't have a complete answer for it. There are both wonderful and troubling mysteries concealed in the mind of God. Even those of us who trust God have to reconcile ourselves to that. When Bert Benz died, his wife was quoted as saying, "It was just God's will. . . . It's true, even though it hurts." That's pretty much the truth, I suspect.

One challenge we all face is to maintain our trust in God even when supernatural intervention doesn't seem forthcoming. Doubting Thomas believed in the resurrected Jesus because he saw a miracle: the man whom he knew to be dead suddenly stood before him, alive. But Jesus rebuked Thomas like this: "Thomas, because thou hast seen me, thou hast believed: blessed are they that have not seen, and yet have believed." The annals of religious history are full of those who continued to stand firm in their faith, and grow in their relationship with God, even though no miracles rescued them.

A bishop in the predominately black Christian Methodist Episcopal denomination once told me that for centuries African-American slaves prayed desperately for the miracle of freedom. For the great majority of them no freedom ever arrived except for the final freedom of the grave. Still, Christian faith persevered among the slaves, and even triumphed. Today, statistically, the African-American descendants of those slaves maintain a deeper religious commitment than their comparatively more "blessed" white counterparts. The faith that was forged through centuries of harsh servitude without miracles has proved inordinately strong, the bishop said.

Hebrews 11—the Christian Bible's "faith chapter"—details the many wonderful signs granted those who stood steadfast in their relationship with God: Abel, Enoch, Noah, Abraham, Isaac, Jacob, Joseph, Moses, Rahab, Gideon, and others, who "subdued kingdoms, wrought righteousness, obtained promises, stopped the mouths of lions, quenched the violence of fire, escaped the edge of the sword, out of weakness were made strong, waxed valiant in fight, turned to flight the armies of the aliens." The chapter ends, however, by extolling those who weren't delivered, who were laughed at, persecuted, and even tortured to death.

In the final estimation, then, we should seek and serve a God who is quite capable—and regularly willing—to serve up miracles for people great and small. But we also should know that sometimes God has a purpose in not performing miracles. He might indeed allow a difficult situation of ours to run its course, as a way of arousing compassion among those who witness our travails, or of deepening our dependence upon him, or even as a means of disciplining us for our flagrant sins.

I think that God desires to forge gold from every crucible. British journalist John Cornwell cites Sister Briege McKenna, the Roman Catholic healer, as saying that "there's always something to be 'learned' through *praying* for miracles, whether the results [are] 'successful' or not. . . ." If we allow it, God uses our troubles to lead us into a more abiding knowledge of him. At times we glimpse God in the flashing light of a miracle. Other times, we grope and find him in dark disillusionment when no miracle occurs. That latter faith, formed among the shackles of a slavery that never ends or the agonies of a cancer that does not recede, might just be the most powerful wonder of all.

Yet I would be remiss if I didn't end this book by pointing out, again, a glorious fact: miracles occur daily, far more often than many of us have been led to suppose. Quite literally hundreds of millions of people—from every race, every tribe, and every religious sect—report that God has powerfully intervened on their behalf and delivered them from all manner of evil, against overwhelming odds.

True, we can't demand miracles. Perhaps we can't predict exactly if, when, or how they'll strike. But we desperately need to open our eyes to the possibilities God has spread before us. As we've seen in these pages, God straightens crippled bodies and mends shattered hearts. He's performing miracles all around us all the time. We should watch for his hand of mercy everywhere. We should anticipate his powerful presence as we sit in our offices each day, as we drive home to our families, as we nervously visit our doctors for tests, as we kneel to pray in our churches. You just never know where God is going to show up next. Maybe smack dab in the middle of your life.

SELECTED BIBLIOGRAPHY

Books

Ahlstrom, Sydney E., *A Religious History of the American People* (New Haven and London: Yale University Press, 1972).

Ariel, David S., *What Do Jews Believe?: The Spiritual Foundations of Judaism* (New York: Shocken Books, 1995).

Barrett, C.K., *The New Testament Background: Selected Documents* (San Francisco: Harper and Row, 1989, revised and updated edition of a book first published in 1956).

Beaver, R. Pierce et al., editors, *Eerdman's Handbook to the World's Religions* (Grand Rapids, Mich.: Wm. B. Eerdman's, 1982).

Bennett, Dennis J., *Nine O'Clock in the Morning* (South Plainfield, N.J.: Bridge Publishing, 1970).

The Book of Mormon (Salt Lake City: The Church of Jesus Christ of Latter-day Saints, 1977).

Burnham, Sophy, *A Book of Angels* (New York: Ballantine Books, 1990).

Catechism of the Catholic Church (San Francisco: Ignatius Press, 1993).

Chevreau, Guy, *Catch the Fire* (Toronto: HarperCollins, 1994).

Clarke, Peter B., consulting editor, *The World's Religions: Understanding the Living Faiths* (Pleasantville, N.Y., and Montreal: Reader's Digest Association, 1993).

Colson, Charles W., *Born Again* (Old Tappan, N.J.: Chosen Books, 1976).

———, with Ellen Santilli Vaughn, *Kingdoms in Conflict* (William Morrow/Zondervan Publishing, 1989 paperback edition of a book first published in 1987).

Cornwell, John, *The Hiding Places of God* (New York: Warner Books, 1991).

Cox, Harvey, *Fire from Heaven* (Reading, Mass., etc.: Addison-Wesley Publishing, 1995).

Deal, William, *John Newton* (Westchester, Ill.: Good News Publishers, 1974).

Dossey, Larry, *Healing Words: The Power of Prayer and the Practice of Medicine* (San Francisco: HarperSanFrancisco, 1993).

Dunnavant, Anthony, editor, *Cane Ridge in Context: Perspectives on Barton W. Stone and the Revival* (Nashville, Tenn.: Disciples of Christ Historical Society, 1992).

Eddy, Mary Baker, *Science and Health with Key to the Scriptures* (Boston: First Church of Christ, Scientist, 1994 paperback edition of a book first published in 1875).

Eerdman's Handbook to the History of Christianity (Grand Rapids, Mich.: Wm. B. Eerdman's, 1977).

Eliada, Mircea, editor, *Encyclopedia of Religion* (New York: Macmillan Publishing, 1987).

Epstein, Daniel Mark, *Sister Aimee: The Life of Aimee Semple McPherson* (San Diego, New York, and London: Harcourt Brace, 1993).

Finney, Charles Grandison, *Memoirs of Rev. Charles G. Finney* (New York: Fleming H. Revell, 1911).

Goldston, Robert, *The Sword of the Prophet* (New York: Fawcett Crest, 1979).

Greig, Gary S., and Kevin N. Springer, editors, *The Kingdom and the Power: Are the Healings and Spiritual Gifts Used by Jesus and the Early Church Meant for the Church Today?* (Ventura, Calif.: Regal Books, 1993).

Harrell, David Edwin Jr., *Oral Roberts: An American Life* (San Francisco: Harper and Row, 1987, first published by Indiana University Press in 1985).

Hatcher, William S., and J. Douglas Martin, *The Baha'i Faith: The Emerging Global Religion* (San Francisco: Harper and Row, 1985).

Hultkrantz, Ake, *Native Religions of North America: The Power of Visions and Fertility* (San Francisco: Harper and Row, 1987).

Judd, Naomi, with Bud Schaetzle, *Love Can Build a Bridge* (New York: Villard Books, 1993).

Kraft, Charles H., *Christianity with Power: Your Worldview and Your Experience of the Supernatural* (Ann Arbor, Mich.: Vine Books, 1989).

Lewis, C.S., *Miracles: A Preliminary Study* (New York: Macmillan Paperbacks Edition, 1978, first published in 1947).

Luchetti, Cathy, *Under God's Spell: Frontier Evangelists 1772–1915* (San Diego, New York, and London: Harcourt Brace Jovanovich, 1989).

Ludlow, Daniel H., editor, *Encyclopedia of Mormonism* (New York: Macmillan, 1992).

Magruder, Jeb Stuart, *An American Life: One Man's Road to Watergate* (New York: Atheneum, 1974).

————, *From Power to Peace* (Waco, Tex.: Word Books, 1978).

McDonald, Kilian, and George T. Montague, editors, *Fanning the Flame* (Collegeville, Minn.: Liturgical Press, 1991).

McKenzie, Peter, *The Christians: Their Beliefs and Practices* (Nashville, Tenn.: Abingdon Press, 1988).

Miller, Robert J., editor, *The Complete Gospels: Annotated Scholars Version* (Sonoma, Calif.: Polebridge Press, 1991).

Moody, D.L., *Secret Power: Or, The Secret of Success in Christian Life and Christian Work* (Chicago: F.H. Revell, 1881).

Neame, Alan, *The Happening at Lourdes: The Sociology of the Grotto* (New York: Simon and Schuster, 1967).

Neiman, Carol, *Miracles: The Extraordinary, the Impossible, and the Divine* (New York: Viking Studio Books, 1995).

New Catholic Encyclopedia (Palatine, Ill.: J. Heraty, 1989).

Nickell, Joe, *Looking for a Miracle: Weeping Icons, Relics, Stigmata, Visions & Healing Cures* (Buffalo, N.Y.: Prometheus Books, 1993).

————, *Inquest on the Shroud of Turin,* updated edition (Buffalo, N.Y.: Prometheus Books, 1987).

Parsons, A.W., *Great Churchmen, Number Five: John Newton* (London: Church Book Room Press, n.d.).

Peters, George W., *Indonesia Revival: Focus on Timor* (Grand Rapids, Mich.: Zondervan Publishing, 1973).

Pimlott, John, consulting editor, *The Middle East Conflicts: From 1945 to the Present* (New York: Crescent Books, 1983).

Pollock, John, *Amazing Grace: John Newton's Story* (London, etc.: Hodder and Stoughton, 1981).

Pullinger, Jackie, with Andrew Quicke, *Chasing the Dragon* (Ann Arbor, Mich.: Servant Books, 1982).

Rahner, Karl, editor, *Encyclopedia of Theology: The Concise Sacramentum Mundi* (New York: Crossroad N.Y., 1975).

Randi, James, *The Faith Healers* (Buffalo, N.Y.: Prometheus Books, 1987).

————, *Flim-Flam: The Truth About Unicorns, Parapsychology and Other Delusions* (New York: Lippincott and Crowell, 1980).

Robertson, Pat, with Jamie Buckingham, *Shout It from the Housetops* (Plainfield, N.J.: Logos International, 1972).

Roper, William, *The Life of Syr Thomas More,* as reprinted in *English Recusant Literature 1558–1640,* Volume 4, selected and edited by D.M. Rogers

(Menston, Yorkshire, England: Scolar Press, 1970. Roper's narrative was first published in 1626).

Siegel, Bernie S., *Love, Medicine and Miracles* (New York: HarperPerennial paperback edition, 1990, first published by Harper and Row in 1986).

Smith, John, and Malcolm Doney, *On the Side of the Angels* (Oxford, England: Lion Publishing, 1987).

Steinkamp, Orrel N., *The Holy Spirit in Vietnam* (Carol Stream, Ill.: Creation House, 1973).

Tari, Mel, with Cliff Dudley, *Like a Mighty Wind* (Green Forest, Ark.: New Leaf Press, 1971).

Weible, Wayne, *Medjugorje: The Message* (Orleans, Mass.: Paraclete Press, 1989).

Yogananda, Paramahansa, *Autobiography of a Yogi* (Los Angeles: Self-Realization Fellowship, 1993, twelfth edition of a book first published in 1946).

Zakaria, Rafig, *Muhammad and the Quran* (London: Penguin Books, 1981).

Periodicals

"Apparitions of Mary Throughout the World," *Our Lady Queen of Peace*, Winter 1992, p. 1.

Barber, Laurence J., "How I Was Blessed," *Christianity Today*, September 11, 1995, p. 26.

Beverly, James A., "Toronto's Mixed Blessing," *Christianity Today*, September 11, 1995, pp. 23–27.

Bradley, James E., "Miracles and Martyrdom in the Early Church: Some Theological and Ethical Implications," *Pneuma: The Journal of the Society for Pentecostal Studies*, Vol. 13, No. 1, Spring 1991, pp. 65–81.

Burke, Greg, "Modern Miracles Have Strict Rules," *Time*, April 10, 1995, p. 72.

Cartledge, Mark J., "Charismatic Prophecy," *Journal of Pentecostal Theology*, Issue 5, October 1994, pp. 79–120.

Davies, Stevan, "Whom Jesus Healed and How," paper presented to the Jesus Seminar, Sonoma, California, March 5–6, 1993.

Dossey, Larry, "Does Prayer Heal?" *Reader's Digest*, March 1996, pp. 116–19.

Eutsler, Steve D., "Why Are Not All Christians Healed?" *Paraclete*, Spring 1993, pp. 15–23.

Galli, Mark, "Revival at Cane Ridge," *Christian History*, Issue 45, pp. 9–14.

Gelpi, Donald L., "The Theological Challenge of Charismatic Spirituality," *Pneuma: The Journal of the Society for Pentecostal Studies*, Vol. 14, No. 2, Fall 1992, pp. 185–97.

Gibbs, Nancy, "The Message of Miracles," *Time*, April 10, 1995, pp. 64–73.

Gill, James G., "Miracles by the Millions," *Human Development*, Vol. 16, No. 3, Fall 1995, pp. 3–4.

Girolimon, Michael T., " 'The Charismatic Wiggle': United Methodism's Twentieth-Century Neo-Pentecostal Impulses," *Pneuma: The Journal of the Society for Pentecostal Studies*, Vol. 17, No. 1, Spring 1995, pp. 89–103.

Hadden, Andrew G., "Gifts of the Spirit in Assemblies of God Writings," *Paraclete*, Winter 1990, pp. 20–32.

Harris, Virginia S., "Harvard Symposium: Spirituality & Healing in Medicine; Christian Science Spiritual Healing Practices," *The Christian Science Journal*, February 1996, Vol. 114, No. 2, pp. 33–38.

"The Holy Spirit: God at Work," *Christianity Today*, March 19, 1990, pp. 27–35.

Hughes, Paul A., "Speaking God's Message: The Holy Spirit and the Human Mind," *Paraclete*, Spring 1992, pp. 17–22.

Hunt, Stephen, "The Anglican Wimberites," *Pneuma: The Journal of the Society for Pentecostal Studies*, Vol. 17, No. 1, Spring 1995, pp. 105–18.

Koch, George Byron, "Pumped and Scooped?" *Christianity Today*, September 11, 1995, p. 25.

Lovelace, Richard F., "The Surprising Works of God," *Christianity Today*, September 11, 1995, pp. 28–32.

MacDonald, William Graham, "Biblical Glossolalia," *Paraclete*, Spring 1993, p. 7.

Piwowarski, Linda, "Heaven Helped Them," *Catholic Digest*, April 1994, pp. 11–13 (from a story that originally appeared in *Crossroads*, January 31, 1993).

Prather, Paul, "Belief in the Modern Miracle," *Lexington Herald-Leader*, December 19, 1993, Today section, p. 1.

———, "Did God Save Jones? The Answer Isn't Easy," *Lexington Herald-Leader*, August 15, 1992, Topics section, p. 1.

———, "The Gospel According to Billy Ray," *Lexington Herald-Leader*, February 14, 1993, p. A1.

———, "The Great Prayer Revival," *Lexington Herald- Leader*, April 16, 1995, Today section, p. 1.

————, "Man with Terminal Illness Spreading Message of Peace, Faith," *Lexington Herald-Leader,* October 15, 1994, Lifestyle section, p. 2.

————, "Near-Death Experience Took One Woman on Visit to Hell," *Lexington Herald-Leader*, April 16, 1994, Lifestyle section, p. 2.

————, "Religion Plays a Big Part in the Life of Naomi Judd," *Lexington Herald-Leader*, November 27, 1993, Today section, p. 2.

————, "A Spirit-Filled Revival," *Lexington Herald-Leader,* December 6, 1992, Topics section, p. 1.

Rousseau, John J., "Background Information on Traditional Healing in the Time of Jesus: Investigating Ancient Healing Practices of the Bedouins," paper presented to the Jesus Seminar, Sonoma, California, March 5–6, 1993.

Seamands, Steve, "The Healing Power of the Risen Christ," *Pillar of Fire,* April 1995, pp. 5–8.

Stone, Barton, "Piercing Screams and Heavenly Smiles," an excerpt from Stone's autobiography, republished in *Christian History,* Issue 45, p. 15.

Warner, Wayne E., "The Miracle of Azusa Street," *Charisma,* April 1996, pp. 37–41.

"What Are the Approved Marian Apparitions?" *Catholic Update*, a publication of the Archdiocese of Cincinnati, March 14, 1994, p. 2.

Wigger, John H., "Taking Heaven by Storm: Enthusiasm and Early American Methodism, 1770–1820," *Journal of the Early Republic,* Volume 14, Summer 1994, pp. 167–94.